What Governments Can Do

Seventh Annual Report on the State of World Hunger

Hunger 1997

BREAD FOR THE WORLD
INSTITUTE

1100 Wayne Avenue, Suite 1000
Silver Spring, MD 20910
USA

Printed on recycled paper.

Bread for the World Institute

President
David Beckmann

President Emeritus
Arthur Simon

Director
Richard A. Hoehn

Editor
Marc J. Cohen

© 1996 by Bread for the World Institute
1100 Wayne Avenue, Suite 1000, Silver Spring, MD 20910, USA
Telephone: (301) 608-2400 Fax: (301) 608-2401
E-mail: bread@igc.apc.org WWW: http://www.bread.org

Design: Dennis and Sackett Design

Printer: HBP, Hagerstown, MD

Cover photo: Harvey Finkle/Impact Visuals

Manufactured in the United States of America
First edition published October 1996
ISBN 1-884361-05-6

Table of Contents

Chapter 6 – Development Aid and International Institutions

Chapter 7 – Call to Action

Appendix

Tables

ACKNOWLEDGMENTS

We are deeply grateful for the valuable insights provided by sponsors, cosponsors and colleagues at a consultation related to this report and in response to earlier drafts. Those who provided comments include:

Carol Capps, Church World Service/Lutheran World Relief; Jindra Čekan, Catholic Relief Services; Kimberly Miller, office of Congressman Tony Hall; Ginena Dulley Wills and Kelly Jones, United Methodist Committee on Relief; Ellen Messer, Alan Shawn Feinstein World Hunger Program, Brown University; Joanne Csete, United Nations Children's Fund; Andy Pugh and Marianne Leach, CARE; Marisa Nightingale, Share Our Strength; Robin Shell and Sally Digges, Food for the Hungry International; John Halvorson, Karen Bloomquist and John Stumme, Evangelical Lutheran Church in America; Mark Brown, Lutheran Office on Government Affairs; Martin McLaughlin, Center of Concern; Howard Hjort, Charles Riemenschneider, H. de Haen, John Lupien, Simon Chevassus-Agnès, Jean-Pierre Cotier, L.N.R. Naiken, Jorge Mernies and Nikos Alexandratos, Food and Agriculture Organization of the United Nations; J. Larry Brown and John T. Cook, Center on Hunger, Poverty and Nutrition Policy, Tufts University; Rob Fersh, Food Research and Action Center; Sam Harris and Kim Posich, RESULTS; Elaine Richter, Lutheran Church – Missouri Synod World Relief; Barbara McCuen, Community Nutrition Institute; Paul Montacute, Baptist World Alliance; Ben Harrison, Appropriate Technology International; Jan Pate, YMCA of the USA; Andy Ryskamp, Christian Reformed World Relief Committee; Bill Sornborger, North Star Co. Inc.; and Robert Greenstein and Sharon Parott, Center on Budget and Policy Priorities.

We appreciate assistance from the following people in obtaining data: Sami Zerqua, Food and Agriculture Organization of the United Nations; Simon Scott, Organisation for Economic Co-operation and Development; Sakiko Fukuda-Parr and Selim Jahan, U.N. Development Programme; Carl Haub, Population Reference Bureau; James L. Garrett and Gaurav Datt, International Food Policy Research Institute; Kris Martin, The World Bank; David Smith, U.S. Department of Labor; Jean Tash, U.S. Bureau of the Census; Eve Weisberg, Saba Beyene and Jason Hawkins, Office of the U.N. High Commissioner for Refugees; Professor Graham Riches, University of Northern British Columbia; Professor Janet Poppendieck, Hunter College; Michael Lipsey, Michigan State University; and Willie L. Brown and Robert Williams, University of Maryland.

The following Bread for the World members and Bread for the World/Bread for the World Institute board members and staff provided comments and assistance: Marie Bledsoe, Robert Cahill, Kay Furlani, Paul Gloeckner, Michael Linder, David Miner, Maria Otero, Jim Shields, Arthur Simon, Michelle Tooley, Sr. Christine Vladimiroff, Donna Wenstrup, Bill Whitaker, Nancy Anderson, Arlen Erdahl, Chuck Lutz, Sheena Pappalardo, Nancy Alexander, Marcos Ballestero, Winnie Chapman, Tinna Damaso, Lynette Engelhardt, Michael Harning, Donna Hodge, Barbara Howell, Ellen Jennings, Christine Matthews, Dorota Muñoz, Elisa Munthali, Susan Kay Park, Shohreh Kermani Peterson, Dorothy Pilkington, Kathy Pomroy, Michael Rubinstein, Hari Scordo, Kathy Selvaggio, Katherine Simmons, Katherine Smith, David Suley, Michele Tapp, Joel Underwood, Gretel Van Wieren, Tammy Walhof, Mizanekristos Yohannes and Dolly Youssef.

Jashinta D'Costa prepared the statistical tables. Copy editors were Lynora Williams and David Fouse.

Introduction

by Richard A. Hoehn

An estimated 34,000 children under age 5 die daily from hunger and preventable diseases – 24 children every minute, the equivalent of more than three 747 airliners, each holding 430 children, crashing every hour, every day, year-round and leaving no survivors. In the United States, more than one child in four is hungry or at risk of hunger.

*What Governments **Can** Do* argues that despite widespread skepticism and criticism, governments have crucial roles to play in reducing hunger and poverty. Governments at all levels – local, subnational, national and international – must establish a framework in which people can secure their own livelihoods, ensure that basic needs are met for people who cannot secure their own livelihoods and enhance the quality of our lives together. National governments must ensure national standards and meet global responsibilities.

Individual and private voluntary activities make important and creative contributions to ending hunger and poverty in the United States and developing countries, but cannot accomplish a task of this magnitude on their own.

The active political participation of citizens – including hungry and poor people themselves – is needed to ensure that government activities are effective. Many existing programs have worked well to alleviate hunger and poverty, and an engaged public can help make further improvements.

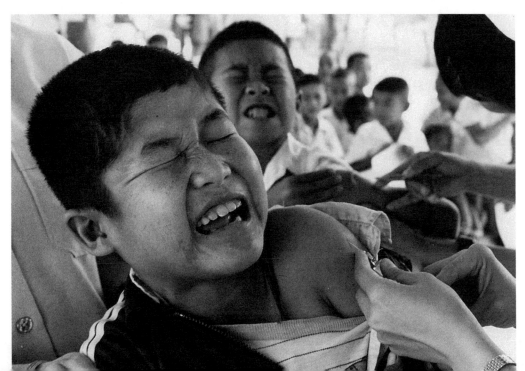

Low-cost immunizations and preventive health measures – also known as child survival programs – save millions of children's lives annually.

UNICEF/1915/Sprague

Chapter 1, "Overview of World Hunger," says there are fewer hungry people in the world than 25 years ago. However, hunger persists in the industrial countries, especially the United States. An increased number of people are hungry or at risk of hunger in countries in transition from communist rule, too. Hunger is endemic and on the increase in Africa. The largest number of hungry people live in South Asia, but there and in most of the rest of the developing world, hunger has declined.

Malnutrition and misery among children pierce our hearts. In the United States, Colbert I. King describes a boy "who climbed into a garbage can [because] he said he felt he was worthless – and wanted to be thrown away."[1] Words like "scandal" and "shame" leap to mind. Decent people of all races, creeds, ages and nations have responded through history by feeding people who are hungry, housing those who are homeless, caring for those who are sick, waging preventive peace and seeking even-handed justice.

Over time, people, often through religious organizations, founded schools, hospitals, charitable programs and agencies, as well as governments, to respond to human needs. The 20th century brought massive population growth and changes, gruesome violence, and complex technological innovations that increased the scale of problems and the separation of peoples. These changes led people to believe that governments should play a larger role in resolving social problems. Chapter 2 reviews how and why

government's role in food assistance programs has grown during much of this century, the history of programs currently under attack and the debates of the 1980s.

Today, many people question the ability of governments – especially national and multinational institutions such as the United Nations – to solve hunger or reduce poverty in an efficient and effective manner. Critics ask whether this is even the role or responsibility of governments. An extremist fringe needing an enemy now that the Cold War is over thinks of government as the new "evil empire." Chapter 2 describes the recent onslaught against welfare in the United States.

Mainstream conservatives say that government should, for the most part, keep out of the way of the free expression of individual interests and should only do those things that people cannot do alone or through private organizations. Progressives and liberals say government is a major avenue through which societies pursue the common good.

The 104th Congress has leaned toward the conservative view. It cut deeply into federal anti-poverty programs and, with the president's concurrence, did away with the long-standing guarantee of cash assistance to poor families with children. It also slashed the little that the U.S. government was spending to help reduce hunger in poorer countries.

The third chapter joins the debate now raging in the United States about the government's role in reducing domestic poverty. It weighs the dominant arguments, and then analyzes them in the light of the leading federal poverty programs.

Most people on the sliding scale of differences agree that governments have limits, that a large bureaucracy is a blunt instrument, but also that governments do have a role in structuring our common life. Each of us can drive carefully, but, individually cannot build a highway. We can be careful about what we eat, but, alone cannot be sure about the fat, parasite or pesticide content of the food. We can fight to defend our

The civil government's distinctive calling by God is to maintain peace, to establish justice, to protect and advance human rights and to promote the general welfare of all persons.

LUTHERAN COUNCIL U.S.A.

country, but alone, cannot win a war or keep the peace. And few people, no matter what their political point of view, turn down government cash or credit when they are struck by a natural disaster; or think the governments should not promote safety regulations that prevent airplanes from plummeting into watery graves.

When governments monopolize social services, they tend to become authoritarian. When they ignore human need, they lose their moral legitimacy. The answer lies somewhere in the middle. "The Mixed Economy," in Chapter 2, says that modern economies are, and should be, a mix between the free market and government responsibility.

Societies should prevent needless tragedies through individual deeds, private charities and public programs. They should encourage individual initiative, compassion and moral courage. They should also guarantee that those who are most vulnerable do not pay the price when other people are unable or unwilling to provide adequate help.

There is no question about the need for governments; only about where to draw the line as to what they should and should not do. People at all income levels have become increasingly dependent on governments for the security of their families and to address problems beyond their immediate capacities. Social problems are huge. Not everyone does all they can, and not everything can be solved by individuals.

Judgments about actual policies and programs are complex. Many people are confused, uncertain or sometimes more certain than they have a right to be, given their limited knowledge of how programs really work. Stereotypes and demagoguery prevail in public debate.

My grandparents had a stereoscope, an optical instrument like a pair of large eyeglasses with two lenses that combined two images on a card, making the picture look three-dimensional. This annual series of reports on the state of world hunger replaces stereotypes with timely, accurate, stereopti-

cal information that helps bring depth to the flat public debate about what governments – locally, nationally and internationally – can and should do about hunger and poverty.

It is scary, but true, that in democracies, adults get the governments they deserve because that's the government they choose. Forty percent of the U.S. public cannot name the vice president; about 50 percent cannot name the speaker of the U.S. House of Representatives; only one-third know the name of the representative from their congressional district; only one in four can name both of their senators; and 58 percent think more of the federal budget is spent on foreign aid than on Medicare.[2] Foreign aid is less than 1 percent of the federal budget; Aid to Families with Dependent Children (AFDC), just over 1 percent; Medicare, more than 10 percent.

The public debate consists of sound bites. It is difficult to get a sense of how well programs do or do not work, relative costs or just what it takes to get a big job, such as a United Nations peacekeeping effort, done.

For example, many people who are concerned about the federal deficit would be surprised to learn that the total U.S. household mortgage debt is about the same size. Though our public choices are castigated, we innocently make similar choices in our private lives. The federal deficit is a serious issue but should be seen in the context of our full range of social choices.

Social programs also should be seen relative to other choices we make. U.S. citizens spend twice as much on videotape rentals as the federal government spends on the Special Supplemental Nutrition Program for Women, Infants and Children (WIC); one and-a-half times as much eating and drinking at places outside homes as on Medicare.

Those who say we cannot afford federal programs to help hungry and poor people may not know that U.S. citizens bet three

The alleviation of hunger and poverty in environmentally sustainable ways should be the leading purpose of Canadian foreign aid. Food security, understood as "sustainable freedom from hunger" and defined as "access, at all times, by all people to enough food to live active, healthy lives," is a key component of equitable global security and sustainable human development, and as such, should be a key component of Canada's foreign policy.

CANADIAN FOODGRAINS BANK

times as much on legal gambling ($482 billion) as we gave to charity, including to churches and synagogues ($146 billion).

In 1993, U.S. citizens spent about the same amount on cruise ships and theme parks together as the federal government spent on AFDC. The information the public hears is more often a slice rather than a loaf of bread, a few grains rather than a bowl of rice. We need to know the relative nature of both our private and our public choices and then be responsible for them.

The problem, in fact, is not lack of money, but a series of decisions about how money gets spent. Enough money is available to end worst-case poverty in a few years and enough food to provide everyone in the world with a minimally nutritious diet right now.

Pundits assert that churches and private charities should pick up more of the social load (see Chapter 3). Maybe so. But not everyone is aware that, for example, in 1994 about two-thirds of Catholic Charities' (domestic) and of Catholic Relief Services' (international) human needs budgets were federal dollars. Private charities may often be

more innovative and provide more personal care than government programs, but many depend on major infusions of government funds to carry out their programs; and with fewer government dollars they will do less, not more. The distinction between private and public – who's doing what – is not as neat as it first seems.

None of the above argues for or against particular programs. Programs can be improved, changed or abolished. New public-private initiatives should be started. We argue in *Hunger 1997* for stereoptical rather than stereotypical information and an honest examination of the real values and priorities that drive public life.

The ability of governments, both local and national, to shape social policy is being limited by an increasingly global economy. Competitive pressures drive government decisions as well as those of firms, affecting both domestic and international policies. Global markets, if they are to succeed and to contribute to secure livelihoods, will require global rules. But policy-making remains fragmented among nations and states.

Chapter 4, "Employment, Governments and the Global Economy," analyzes some of the reasons that global employment does not measure up to the bright promise of the global economy, and suggests that nations must work cooperatively to improve the way markets work.

Developing countries are also caught up in the global trend to rely less on governments and more on markets. Chapter 5, "Governments and Hunger in Developing Countries," focuses on the experience of liberalization in India, Mexico and Ghana, and concludes that governments have important roles to play in shaping development in ways that benefit poor and hungry people.

The United Sates and some other industrial countries are cutting those parts of foreign aid that help poor people and support international institutions. "Development Aid and International Institutions" (see Chapter 6) documents the cuts in aid and challenges the argument that aid only supports counterproductive government interventions in the economy. It argues that aid can work and should be reformed rather than cut. Finally, this chapter discusses useful roles and needed reforms in intergovernmental institutions.

The final chapter summarizes how our conclusions emerge from the analysis and issues a "Call to Action" for everyone to do her or his part in overcoming hunger. A transformed politics of hunger would feed a hungry world.

The analysis in this report is predicated on moral principles. We do not identify with those who think that morality is relative or irrelevant, nor with those who withdraw in cynicism, selfishness or apathy. But neither do we agree with those who wear their morality on their sleeves but propose programs that are harmful to hungry and poor people. Bread for the World Institute seeks justice for hungry people by engaging in research and education on policies related to hunger and development. We work closely with Bread for the World, a nationwide Christian movement that seeks justice for the world's hungry people by lobbying our nation's decision makers.

We seek justice – economic justice, social justice, political justice – because hunger results from injustice. Everyone has the right to fair treatment, not only by individuals but in the economy, society and political life. Justice is predicated on "the dignity of the human person, realized in community with others."

The preamble to the U.S. Constitution prescribes the type of society that should be guaranteed by governments:

> ...to form a more perfect Union, *establish justice*, insure domestic tranquility, provide for the common defense, promote the general welfare, and secure the blessings of liberty to our selves and our posterity.... [emphasis added]

Economic justice implies a fair or equitable opportunity to a sustainable livelihood, including food, education, jobs, shelter, clean water, sanitation and health care. Distributive justice examines the way in which a society, and in particular governments, distribute benefits. We take a particular tack on distributive justice and believe that public policies should be judged first and foremost by how they affect hungry and poor people. While affirming well-being for everyone, we measure that well-being first in terms of the way societies respond to their most vulnerable citizens. In some circles this is called "the preferential option for the poor."

Social justice implies organizing a society in ways that seek the common good; paying particular attention to class, race and ethnicity, gender and age, since these factors influence who is more likely to be hungry and poor. In the U.S. context, social justice means that a group that happens to be poor should not have fewer basic services than those who are rich. A person's geographic location should not make the difference between success and failure, health and illness, life and death. Standards should cross state lines.

Political justice implies citizen participation – in politics and policy as well as in charity and service. Governments at every level should be representative, engage in open decision-making processes and be based upon consent of the governed. Poor people need to be involved in the design, implementation and evaluation of anti-hunger programs and projects. An open, public process and strong organizations of civil society empower citizens, encourage them to keep better informed about decisions that affect their lives and help governments to respond to problems. Public discourse should be civil – not simply zapping adversaries, but rather moving the community's conversation forward.

We believe that policy decisions should be made and carried out at the lowest possible level – by individuals, households,

I recently heard a story on the radio. It happened in Bosnia, but I think it has meaning for all of us. A reporter was covering that tragic conflict in the middle of Sarajevo, and he saw a little girl shot by a sniper. The back of her head had been torn away by the bullet. The reporter threw down his pad and pencil, and stopped being a reporter for a few minutes. He rushed to the man who was holding the child, and helped them both into his car.

As the reporter stepped on the accelerator, racing to the hospital, the man holding the bleeding child said, "Hurry, my friend, my child is still alive." A moment or two later, "Hurry, my friend, my child is still breathing." A moment later, "Hurry, my friend, my child is still warm." Finally, "Hurry. Oh my God, my child is getting cold."

When they got to the hospital, the little girl had died. As the two men were in the lavatory, washing the blood off their hands and their clothes, the man turned to the reporter and said, "This is a terrible task for me. I must go tell her father that his child is dead. He will be heartbroken."

The reporter was amazed. He looked at the grieving man and said, "I thought she was your child." The man looked back and said, "No, but aren't they all our children?"

Aren't they all our children?

Yes they are all our children. They are also God's children as well, and he has entrusted us with their care in Sarajevo, in Somalia, in New York City, in Los Angeles, in my hometown of Perry, GA, and here in Washington, DC.

SENATOR SAM NUNN (D-GA),
THE NATIONAL PRAYER BREAKFAST,
WASHINGTON, DC, FEBRUARY 1, 1996.

Forced from their home by fighting, refugee children in Bosnia gather firewood. Billie Rafaeli/Panos Pictures

communities or sub-national political units before national-level or international action is undertaken. This principle is sometimes called "subsidiarity." This suggests that individuals bear serious responsibility for self-reliance. Government should remove barriers that prevent individual, household and community self-determination; meanwhile assuring national standards for achieving the common good. Chapter 3 explores the policy tension between subsidiarity – making decisions at the state level – and social justice, which argues for national standards.

Injustice is a larger cause of hunger than inadequate food supplies. The elimination of the injustice of hunger is more important than whether the policy that achieves this is decided at the municipal or national level, or whether it is the market or civil society that actually carries out the policy. But it is the role of governments to see that justice does prevail.

National governments and international organizations also have the duty to uphold the principles embodied in such agreements as the Universal Declaration of Human Rights, the Charter of the United Nations, the International Covenants on Civil and Political Rights and on Economic, Social and Cultural Rights, and the 1974 Universal Declaration on the Eradication of Hunger and Malnutrition, which states:

> Every man, woman, and child has the inalienable right to be free from hunger and malnutrition in order to develop fully and maintain their physical and mental faculties….
> It is a fundamental responsibility of governments to work together for higher food production and a more equitable and efficient distribution of food within countries and between countries.

Finally, we are deeply rooted in religious values and vision. People of many different religious beliefs agree that the Creator intends Garden-of-Eden-goodness for both nature and the human community; that deprivations such as hunger and poverty should be abolished; that those who love their neighbors as themselves should be active in making that happen. All people are God's children, and ours. They are our children, mothers and fathers, sisters and brothers whether they are child prostitutes on the streets of Bogotá, hard-working bookkeepers in Bangalore or hungry children in Birmingham.

There is a poem in which the earth sings about the people who claim to own her, who own the land. Earth says: "They survey me, stake out territories, claim ownership, till the soil and pass me on to their children. But how can they say they hold me, when, in the end, I hold them?"

We claim to own goods and property. But at the beginning they all come as gifts to us and in the end all pass on to someone else. We only get the middle game – not to own, but to use for a while.

You did not invent the language you speak, the culture you express in food, clothing, work and home life. Our rich heritage in the arts and sciences come as gifts from other people, though indeed we all contribute to passing them along even through such small acts as buying a ticket to a performance. Intelligence and talents come as gifts, though to be sure we are accountable for the ways we develop and use them.

When I was a child, our family often sat in the balcony of our high-steepled, small-town church. After the offering every Sunday, we sang "We give Thee but Thine own, whatever the gift may be; all that we have is Thine alone…." Or was it "Thine a loan," or maybe "Thine on loan?" I listened closely Sunday after Sunday but was never sure. Every gift we receive is on loan to us.

Stewardship is an old-fashioned word – older than stereoscopes, older than the U.S. Constitution. Hunger and poverty are bad stewardship. We cannot afford to lose human lives, talents and energies due to malnutrition and starvation. Whether called sustainable development, ending hunger, contributing to the arts or enhancing public life, being good stewards is our first calling in life – stewards of all God's children (including ourselves) and all God's good earth.

President John F. Kennedy said shortly before his death:

> I do not want it said of us what T.S. Eliot said of others some years ago: "These were a decent people. Their only monument: the asphalt road and a thousand lost golf balls."[3]

The world has enough food. The world has enough wealth. At bottom, the guiding question is "what sort of people do we want to be?" When we become clear that the answer is "good stewards," we will do private deeds and support public policies that end hunger, reduce poverty; that nurture us physically, ennoble us morally and enrich us spiritually; not only ourselves, but all the world.

DR. RICHARD A. HOEHN *is director of Bread for the World Institute.*

Hunger in the 1996 U.S. Elections

During 1996, Bread for the World, with whom Bread for the World Institute works closely, conducted an *Elect to End Childhood Hunger* campaign to make hunger among U.S. children a significant issue in the 1996 congressional elections. About 13 million children under age 12 in the United States are hungry or at risk of hunger – more than one in four. A greater proportion of children live in poverty in the United States than in any other industrial country. While the gap between rich and poor widens, low-income families are struggling to survive.

Yet the 1995-1996 Congress began dismantling the national safety net, slashing programs targeted to hungry children. Anti-poverty programs can certainly be reformed to make them more effective, but dismantling or slashing anti-poverty programs exacerbates the problem of hunger. Without a strong bipartisan majority in Congress that supports anti-hunger legislation, hungry children will continue to shoulder an unfair share of budget cuts.

Bread for the World members and supporters nationwide contacted all candidates for Congress, asking them to sign a pledge to vote for legislation and support federal programs that will help overcome childhood hunger in the United States.

Thousands of churches and other community organizations held letter-writing meetings before their local primaries or the November elections to urge candidates to sign the commitment. More than 200 organizations, ranging from the American Public Health Association and the Children's Defense Fund to the U.S. Catholic Conference, have endorsed Bread for the World's campaign.

Elect to End Childhood Hunger educated congressional candidates, the church community and others about the extent of hunger among U.S. children. By making childhood hunger a significant issue in congressional campaigns, Bread for the World members assured that the 105th Congress will know that many constituents care deeply about how their decisions will affect hungry children.

Hundreds of candidates from across the country signed the Candidate Commitment to End Childhood Hunger. Signers included Republicans, Democrats, independents and third party candidates. Citizen activists intend to hold candidates accountable for their promises during the next cycle of debate. A society should be judged by how it treats its most vulnerable members. It is not too late to help the children of the 21st century.

Candidate Commitment To End Childhood Hunger

Recognizing that:

- Childhood hunger in the United States is preventable and unacceptable;

- More than one in four U.S. children under age 12 is hungry or at risk of hunger;

- Good nutrition in childhood saves money by preventing nutrition-related medical, education and future welfare costs;

- The nation's nutrition programs, including the Special Supplemental Nutrition Program for Women, Infants and Children (WIC), school lunch and breakfast, summer and child care meals and food stamps, have significantly improved children's nutrition, have bipartisan support and will continue to undergo change to make them more effective;

- Churches and charities have responded generously to growing hunger, but do not have the capacity to replace public programs; and

- While all sectors must do their part to overcome widespread childhood hunger in our richly blessed nation, the federal government has a legitimate and necessary role in setting nutrition standards and providing resources to assure that all children in the United States have access to a nutritionally adequate diet.

If elected to Congress in 1996, I promise to vote for legislation and support federal programs that will help overcome childhood hunger in the United States.

CHAPTER 1

Overview of World Hunger

by Marc J. Cohen and Jashinta D'Costa

There are fewer, and a smaller proportion of, hungry people in the world than 25 years ago.[1] The world has enough food to provide every human being with a minimally adequate diet. In November 1996, heads of state gathered in Rome at the World Food Summit to recommit themselves to the principle of "food for all."

But over 800 million people are still too poor to afford the food they need for active, healthy lives. Widespread hunger is on the rise in Africa. Government downsizing has increased hunger in other parts of the world, even in rich nations – and hunger persists among children in the United States.

Hunger in Industrial Countries

Hunger is much less widespread and severe in the industrial countries than in Somalia or Bangladesh. But even in industrial countries, millions of people do not have an adequate diet. Children in low-income and single-parent households, homeless people and members of ethnic minorities are especially vulnerable. Widespread hunger among children in the United States is clearly unnecessary and especially shocking.

In 1985, 20 million people were hungry in the United States. By 1995 that number had increased to 30 million.[2] The Food Stamp

Extreme poverty forces many children in Brazil and other developing countries to live and work in the streets.

UNICEF/Claudio Edinger

Childhood Hunger in the United States

- Children make up almost half of the population in poverty.

- More than 21 percent of U.S. children under age 18, and 25 percent of children under age 6, are poor. Sixty-four percent of children under 6 who live in female-headed, single-parent families are poor.

- In the early 1990s, approximately 4 million children under age 12 were hungry and an additional 9.6 million were at risk of hunger. This means that 29 percent of U.S. children – more than one in four – were hungry or at risk of hunger.

- The infant mortality rate is closely linked to inadequate nutrition among pregnant women. The United States ranks 23rd among industrial nations in infant mortality. African American infants die at nearly twice the rate of white infants.

- Low-income children depend on the National School Lunch Program for one-third to one-half of their daily nutrition.

- Over 80 percent of food stamp benefits go to households with children.

- A child living in a wealthy U.S. family is, on average, better-off financially than the typical wealthy child in any other country. At the same time, the average child in a low-income U.S. family is worse off than the average poor child in 15 other industrial countries.

Program, the main federal government food assistance channel, currently serves 26 million people (about 10 percent of the U.S. population) per month. A similar number of people relies on private charitable food assistance, provided by a national network of 150,000 agencies. A 1995 survey of 29 major U.S. cities by the U.S. Conference of Mayors found that requests for emergency food increased by an average of 9 percent over the previous year. Emergency programs were, on average, unable to meet 18 percent of those requests.

In 1994, 38 million people (14.5 percent of the population) lived in poverty. The U.S. government's measure of poverty is based on the income needed to purchase a minimally adequate diet. The poverty rate was 9 percent for non-Hispanic whites and 31 percent for both African Americans and persons of Hispanic origin. People who are poor are those who are likely to be hungry, so it is

no surprise that a recent government survey found that food insecurity is also higher among African Americans and Hispanics than whites.[3]

Canadian hunger is paradoxical.[4] Canada ranks first in the world among 174 countries in the United Nations Development Programme's (UNDP) 1996 Human Development Index, based on education, wealth and health. Yet as of 1994, 2.5 million people (9 percent of the populace) relied on private charitable food assistance from a network of 456 food banks. In 1992 there were 2 million people using food banks. The largest province, Ontario, had the largest number of food bank users, while Québec, the second largest province, had the fastest rate of increase. Emergency food demand also exploded in Regina, the heart of the wheat belt, and Edmonton, capital of the oil-rich province of Alberta.

Those particularly vulnerable to hunger include people on public assistance, working poor people, families with children (especially female-headed, single-parent families with young children), single men, disabled people, Black Canadians, those of First Nations (i.e., indigenous) and Latin American ancestry, and refugees.

Countries in Western Europe are experiencing economic hardship. In France, 200,000 to 600,000 people are homeless, including 30,000 in Paris. Four million French people live in substandard housing and more than 3 million (12 percent of the work force) are looking for jobs.[5] Unemployment in Germany, once Europe's "economic engine," has reached 11 percent, about the same level as for the European Union as a whole.[6] In the United Kingdom, 1.5 million families receiving government welfare payments were too poor to provide their children with an adequate diet in 1994. Poor children are susceptible to illness and even death as a result. Emergency food assistance agencies are spreading rapidly in Western Europe. But despite indicators of vulnerability to hunger, there are no systematic studies of the extent of food insecurity in the region.

WORLD REGIONS

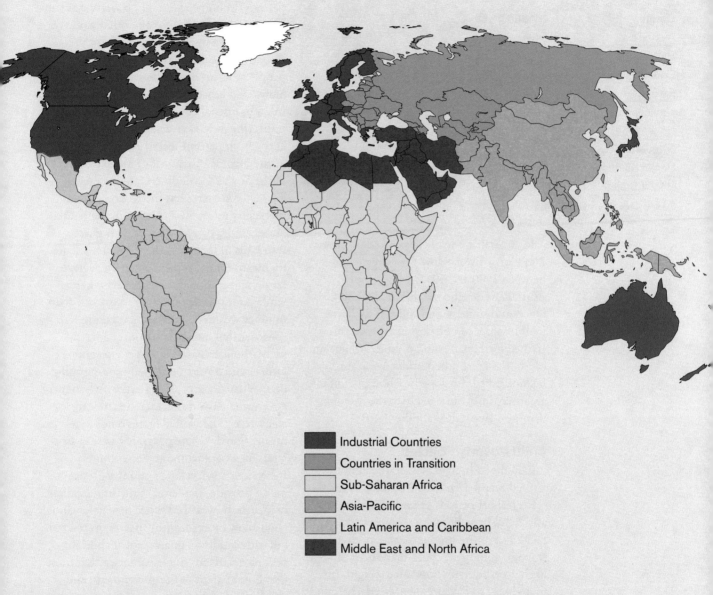

Industrial Countries

Countries in Transition

Sub-Saharan Africa

Asia-Pacific

Latin America and Caribbean

Middle East and North Africa

TABLE 1.1

Child Poverty in Selected Industrial Countries
(percent of children who are poor)

Country	1986-1988	1990-1991
Australia	n/a	14.1
Belgium	3.1	n/a
Canada	13.7	13.5
Finland	2.9	2.5
Netherlands	4.1	n/a
Norway	3.8	4.6
Sweden	3.9	2.7
United Kingdom	9.9	n/a
United States	22.9	21.5

Source: Luxembourg Income Study.

In Australia, one of eight people – about 2 million – lived below the poverty line between 1990 and 1992. Many poor Australians depend on charitable food assistance, and some periodically go without food in order to obtain shelter or clothing. In the Northern Territory, up to 20 percent of Aboriginal children under age 2 are malnourished. Nationally, Aborigine infants are three times more likely to die in infancy than non-Aboriginal children.

Child Poverty Policies

Childhood hunger is widespread in the United States despite enormous affluence.

Even short periods of undernutrition can affect children's behavior, cognitive development and future productivity. Children who are hungry are more than three times as likely to experience unwanted weight loss, more likely to have frequent headaches, and are four times more likely to suffer from fatigue and have difficulty concentrating. Children who are hungry have a hard time learning, are more often sick and absent from school and have a much harder time paying attention in class.

The Urban Institute estimates that the 1996 welfare act will push another 1.1 million children below the poverty line. Congress refused to include funds to monitor the effects of the act on hunger and poverty.

The United States already has the highest child poverty rate of any industrial country. Table 1.1 compares U.S. child poverty rates with those in eight wealthy nations in two periods. In both, U.S. child poverty was substantially higher than in any other country.

There are a number of reasons for the disparity. The gap between rich and poor people tends to be greater in the United States. A study of income inequality in 1995 in 25 industrial countries found inequality ratios (the ratio between incomes of people at the 90th percentile and 10th percentile of the income distribution) range from 2.25 in the Slovak Republic to 6.84 in Russia. The United States has the second highest inequality ratio, 5.67. Although the United States enjoys one of the world's highest standards of living, its sharp income inequality means that rich people are, on average, far better off than rich people elsewhere, while poor people tend to be worse off than in other wealthy countries (see Figure 1.1).[7]

Most other industrial-country governments' policies have a stronger effect on hunger and poverty, especially among children. Virtually every other industrial-country government assures access to health care for all citizens. The United States tends to rely on means-tested welfare programs, basing assistance on strict income and asset limits. Instead, other developed-country governments provide "universal" benefits regardless of income or wealth. Typical benefits include child allowances (monthly payments to families with children); guarantees of child support payments for single parents, either from the absent parent or the government; and child care. In addition, tax policies of most industrial nations help reduce poverty more significantly than do U.S. policies.

In France, every mother receives $2,400 upon the birth of a child, a monthly allowance of $120 following the birth of a second child, and free hospital and medical care before and after each birth. Working mothers are entitled to a six-month paid maternity leave and up to three years of unpaid leave without losing their jobs.[8]

The United Kingdom continues to provide generous universal child allowances and national health care after 17 years of political rule by anti-welfare state forces.

The combination of relatively low benefit levels and over-reliance on means-tested programs contribute to poverty among single-mother families in the United States; they are poorest among nine Western countries. In the mid-1980s, the United States had the lowest levels of support for both single- and two-parent poor families among 36 wealthy countries.

Tax and government benefit programs in the United States have a weaker impact on single-parent family poverty than those of other countries. In the 1990s, these programs lifted at least 75 percent of all single-parent families out of poverty in the Netherlands, Sweden and the United Kingdom, compared to 50 percent in France, a third in Germany, 20 percent in Canada and just 4.6 percent in the United States (see Figure 1.2).[9]

Government can do much to reduce child poverty:

> The contrast between the long-run trends in the United States and Canada, which have experienced similar economic and demographic changes, suggests the important role of government. The Canadian child poverty rate was 2 percentage points above the United States rate in 1970, but 8 points below it by 1991 due in large part to activist social policy.[10]

All industrial countries face a growing number of economically vulnerable single-parent families, changes in the labor market resulting from economic globalization and an aging population. The costs of the welfare state, especially for old-age assistance and for education to meet demand for technologically skilled workers, have escalated dramatically.

In many countries, there is considerable pressure to reduce spending. Most wealthy

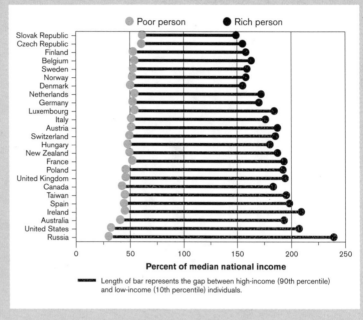

FIGURE 1.1

Income Gap in Industrial Countries
1982-1992

Source: Luxembourg Income Study.

nations place a higher priority on programs for elderly people than on those for children. Child care in Italy and the United Kingdom, once free, now requires user fees. Germany, France and Belgium have expanded their reliance on means-testing. The governments of France, Sweden and Germany have all sought to scale back the extensive array of social programs their citizens have long enjoyed. This has led to political protests in France and Germany. Italy is considering raising the retirement age. The Netherlands may tighten eligibility for disability benefits, while many countries are debating more modest unemployment benefits. Japan, which has not provided an extensive safety net, now faces slower economic growth, increased joblessness and substantial budget deficits.

In Canada and the United Kingdom, as in the United States, there are demands that single parents work instead of relying on welfare programs. In Scandinavia and France, where single parents regularly

FIGURE 1.2

Impact of Government Intervention on Child Poverty in Industrial Countries
1982-1992

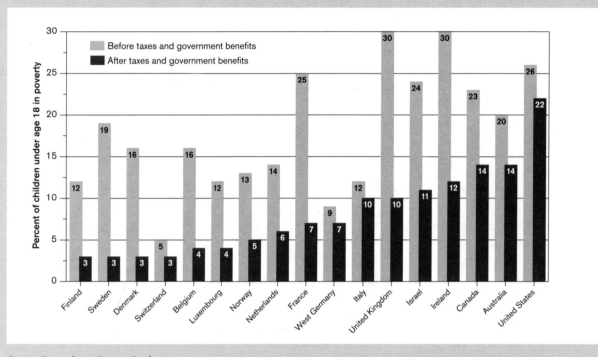

Source: Luxembourg Income Study.

combine work and public assistance, benefit programs enjoy much stronger political support.

But while all the industrial countries are curtailing social programs somewhat, the United States has higher rates of childhood hunger and has cut back more drastically than any other industrial nation on programs that help children.

Countries in Transition

The transition from planned to market economies in Central and Eastern Europe and the newly independent states (NIS) of the former Soviet Union has dislocated and created hardships for many people. Poverty and inequality have increased. Food prices have generally increased more rapidly than incomes, which has especially affected unemployed persons, pensioners and others on fixed incomes. The sudden dismantling

of government social programs, coupled with the slow development of markets and private sector jobs, have contributed to food insecurity. In parts of the former Yugoslavia and some NIS countries, violent conflict has uprooted hundreds of thousands of people, leaving them at serious risk of hunger and disease.

Between 1979-1981 and 1990-1992, daily per capita calorie supplies fell from 3,400 to 3,230 in the NIS and Eastern Europe.[11]

Problems are especially severe in the Central Asian areas of the NIS, where absolute poverty has increased and nutritional deficiencies are widespread. Poverty rates are 70 percent in Russian Central Asia, compared to 10 percent in Moscow and St. Petersburg.

In Russia, 4 percent of children under age 2 were underweight in 1993 and 21 percent stunted (only 10 percent were stunted in 1992).[12]

Hunger in Developing Countries

Abdul Karim and his wife, Ayesha, and three children live in Puthimari village of Chilmari Thana, one of the most distressed areas of Bangladesh. The family's one-room house, with a straw roof and walls made of bamboo and wild grass, is too small. Their skeleton-like features disclose their extreme malnutrition and poverty.

Recently, a neighbor gave Abdul five taka (about 12 cents) and a meal of rice and lentils for a whole day's work weeding a radish field. The next day the neighbor only offered Abdul three taka and a meal, probably because Abdul was so weak. But Abdul accepted and worked from morning until evening.

Abdul spends his eight taka buying a kilogram of wheat. Ayesha soaks the wheat in salt water and fries it in an earthen pot. The wheat becomes hard and brittle, almost inedible. It is all the family has for two days' meals. If, instead, Ayesha made flour from the wheat, it would only yield a few pieces of bread. The children are so hungry that they would consume the easy-to-eat bread too fast and soon cry for more, which she does not have. Instead, she makes the meal from uncrushed wheat so her children will chew it for a long time.

Last month, Ayesha sold her gold nose pin to a neighbor for one-fourth the price her husband paid for it. With that money, the family bought some rice and wheat.[13]

In the developing world, millions of families face the same gut-wrenching choices as Abdul and Ayesha. Few families in the industrial world or countries in transition suffer such severe or persistent hunger.

But there is good news in the developing countries. The number of hungry people (those who have inadequate access to food, and so consume fewer calories than required for an active and healthy life) fell from 918 million during the 1969-1971 period to 906 million in 1979-1981 and further to 841 million in 1990-1992. The proportion of the population of the developing world that goes hungry also dropped, from 35 percent in 1969-1971 to 28 percent in 1979-1981, to 20 percent in 1990-1992 (see Figure 1.3).

Progress against hunger varied widely among countries and regions. The Food and Agriculture Organization of the United Nations (FAO) reports that among 98 developing countries surveyed, the prevalence of hunger increased in 39 countries, 23 of them in Africa (see Figure 1.4).

Africa

In sub-Saharan Africa, the proportion and absolute number of hungry people has increased between 1969-1971 and 1990-1992. The proportion rose from 38 percent to 43 percent, while the hungry population doubled, from 103 million to 215 million. In Ethiopia and Somalia, the proportion of hungry people increased to more than 55 percent.[14] Per capita food consumption among hungry people in Africa declined from 1,490 to 1,470 calories per day, far

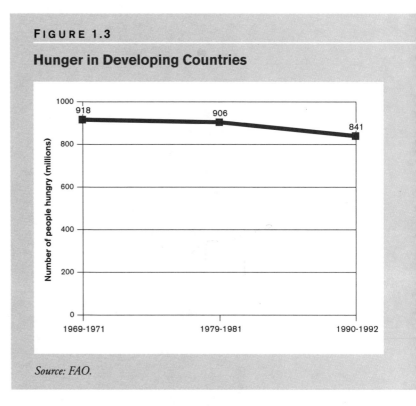

FIGURE 1.3

Hunger in Developing Countries

Source: FAO.

When their remote village in the northern lowlands of Ethiopia experienced a severe drought on the heels of two years of dry weather, Tesfaye Getachew and his wife, Senait Gebre-Selassie, had to sell the last of their belongings to buy food. But their assets were meager, and the money was not enough to see them through more than a month or two. When what little food they had ran out, Tesfaye was forced to beg.

As the famine dragged on, conditions worsened for everyone in the region. Desperation cut a violent swath through the couple's peaceful village. Neighbors who had helped each other build homes and work the land now fought over a handful of roots left in the parched fields. Meanwhile, the water supply became contaminated with cholera.

At the peak of the famine, cholera swept through the village. Twenty-five of the 100 families living there were wiped out. Senait was among the victims.*

* According to the International Food Policy Research Institute's Initiative, *A 2020 Vision for Food, Agriculture, and the Environment.*

FIGURE 1.4

Number of Hungry People in Developing Regions

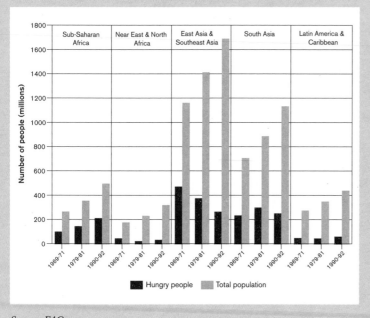

Source: FAO.

below minimum requirements of 2,350 calories. Eleven of the 14 countries where relative food inadequacy (the gap between actual food supplies and needs for people with inadequate access to food) is higher than 15 percent are located in sub-Saharan Africa. On the other hand, in Burkina Faso and Tanzania, the proportion of hungry people decreased substantially over the two decade period. The Iringa District in Tanzania has established a model child health program, with a strong emphasis on community participation, that has achieved remarkable reductions in child undernutrition.

These dismal overall regional trends resulted, in part, from high population growth (2.9 percent for Africa as a whole) and harsh external realities (low export prices, unpayable debts and declining aid). Internal problems have plagued Africa as well, notably governments in many countries that have failed to put a high priority on meeting people's needs. Numerous governments on the continent have been both incompetent and corrupt. In recent years, foreign aid donors and the international financial institutions have pushed for sudden and dramatic shifts toward a reduced government role in African economies. But the international financial institutions themselves now admit that their policy prescriptions have not worked well in Africa (see Chapters 5 and 6). Civil conflict and drought have further undermined food security and good governance on the continent.

The food outlook remains grim. FAO projects that the number of undernourished Africans could rise to 265 million (30 percent of the region's population) by 2010. The International Food Policy Research Institute similarly predicts that growth in food production by the year 2020 is unlikely to outpace population growth in sub-Saharan Africa. Increased exports are unlikely to generate enough foreign exchange to import adequate food, and African countries cannot count on sufficient aid from abroad.[15]

Asia-Pacific[16]

Most of the world's hungry people live in Asia (62 percent). Nevertheless, between 1969-1971 and 1990-1992, the number of hungry people in Southeast Asia fell from 476 million to 269 million, and the proportion declined from 41 percent to 16 percent. In South Asia, the proportion declined from 33 percent to 22 percent. Because of rapid population growth, the absolute number increased from 238 million people in 1969-1971 to 303 million in 1979-1981, but then dropped back to 255 million in 1990-1992. The proportion of hungry people increased in Afghanistan, Bangladesh, Mongolia, Sri Lanka and Vietnam between 1969-1971 and 1990-1992. In some countries of the region, the undernutrition rate among adults and adolescents is substantial: 49 percent in India and 13 percent in China, for example.[17]

Government policies such as investment in agricultural research, rural development and public health have spurred progress against hunger in Asia and the Pacific. During the 1970s, national public policies, supported by aid donors, along with the hard work of the region's farmers and agricultural scientists, achieved a 33 percent increase in cereal output. India, Indonesia and Thailand have extended basic health and nutrition services to hundreds of thousands of villages, with the active participation of local communities playing an essential role. In each country, this has led to substantial gains in the well-being of children, in particular.

Even very poor countries in the region have carried out effective anti-hunger policies. India has not experienced famine since independence in 1947. According to Indian hunger scholar Amartya Sen, this is due to

> an administrative system which compensates the loss of entitlement as a result of such calamities as droughts and floods by providing employment – often at cash wages – giving the affected population renewed ability to command food in the market.[18]

It was hard for the farmers from the small, highland village of La Lima, Honduras, to transport their produce to markets outside of their village before 1985. The capital city of Tegucigalpa was less than 30 kilometers away as the crow flies, but the trip often took six hours or more. Farmers trucked their vegetables to market when they could, but the dirt road was impassable when it rained. The village of about 500 people mainly sustained itself by growing subsistence crops and a few vegetables for sale.

In 1985, an all-weather road was built between Tegucigalpa and a nearby town, reducing the trip from La Lima to the capital to only 40 minutes and dramatically lowering the costs of transporting produce to the city. This made it feasible for the farmers to grow more perishable vegetables like tomatoes, zucchini, squash and green beans. These vegetables were much more profitable than potatoes, particularly when grown off-season, and soon a thriving commercial vegetable industry grew. Because the farmers had more money, they could invest more in their farms, constructing small-scale irrigation and taking measures to improve the soil such as leveling the land, clearing rocks and adding manure and fertilizers on small plots. Most farmers gradually stopped growing corn on the steep hillsides and concentrated on growing staple foods and vegetables on higher-quality, smaller pieces of land. This change in farming practice decreased hillside erosion and reduced the pressure to clear forest land.*

* According to the International Food Policy Research Institute's Initiative, *A 2020 Vision for Food, Agriculture, and the Environment.*

More recently, Sri Lanka has managed to maintain food security for most citizens despite a debilitating 13-year civil war.[19]

Latin America and the Caribbean

In Latin America and the Caribbean, the proportion of hungry people was constant between 1979-1981 and 1990-1992. But the absolute number increased from 48 million to 64 million due to population growth.

Poverty is still widespread. Most governments have attempted to make their economies more market- and export-oriented, but their efforts have not generated enough job opportunities, and disparity in wages between low- and high-skilled jobs has widened.[20]

Middle East and North Africa

In this region, the proportion of hungry people has remained fairly stable, but the absolute number increased – from 27 million in 1979-1981 to 37 million in 1990-1992. Algeria, Saudi Arabia, Tunisia, Lebanon and Syria experienced high growth in per capita food availability. Kuwait experienced about a 15 percent increase in the number of people with inadequate access to food. Economic sanctions are reported to have caused substantial food and nutrition problems in Iraq, including a dramatic increase in child undernutrition.

The Faces of Hunger

The word "hunger" conjures up images of famine and starvation, but most hunger does not result from such emergencies. Instead, hungry people typically live lives of grinding poverty that make it impossible for them to meet their food needs. Hunger statistics represent quiet human suffering and injustice on a scale inconceivable to most of us. The numbers represent flesh-and-blood people who are struggling to survive against extraordinary odds: a Filipino woman, forced to temporarily abandon her two young children so she can find work in the city to pay for food; a Peruvian boy who is forced to leave school to help supplement the meager family income; a new mother in Senegal who walks for six hours, house to house, begging for the equivalent of 10 cents so her sick baby may be seen by a nurse.[21]

Poverty

Poverty is a main cause of hunger. Poor people often lack access to land to grow food or adequate income to buy it. According to the World Bank, the number of poor people in developing countries and countries in transition who live on the equivalent of less than a dollar a day (in 1985 prices) increased from 1.2 billion to 1.3 billion between 1987 and 1993. However, the proportion of such people declined 0.7 percent (see Table 1.2).[22] Seventy percent of these absolutely poor people are women. Inequality in labor markets, ill treatment in social welfare systems,

---

TABLE 1.2

Number and Proportion of People Living Below $1 (U.S.) Per Day
Developing Countries and Countries in Transition, 1987-1993

Regions	Number of poor people (millions)				Percent of population			
	1987	1990	1993	Change (1987 to 1993)	1987	1990	1993	Change (1987 to 1993)
East Asia and the Pacific (excluding China)	464.0 (109.2)	468.2 (89.3)	445.8 (73.5)	-18.2 (-35.7)	28.2 (23.2)	28.5 (17.6)	26.0 (13.7)	-2.2 (-9.5)
Eastern Europe and Central Asia	2.2	n/a	14.5	12.3	0.6	n/a	3.5	2.9
Latin America and the Caribbean	91.2	101.0	109.6	18.4	22.0	23.0	23.5	1.5
Middle East and North Africa	10.3	10.4	10.7	0.4	4.7	4.3	4.1	-0.6
South Asia	479.9	480.4	514.7	34.8	45.4	43.0	43.1	-2.3
Sub-Saharan Africa	179.6	201.2	218.6	39.0	38.5	39.3	39.1	0.6
Total	1,227.1	n/a	1,313.9	86.8	30.1	n/a	29.4	-0.7
Total (excluding Europe and Central Asia)	1,224.9	1,261.2	1,299.3	74.4	33.3	32.9	31.8	-1.5

Source: The World Bank.

and lower status and power in the family are some of the reasons for women's poverty.[23]

According to UNDP, 3 billion people – a majority of humanity – live on less than $2 per day, while the world's 358 billionaires have assets exceeding the combined annual incomes of countries with 45 percent of the world's people.[24]

As the world's population grows at least 40 percent, from nearly 6 billion people today to 8.5 billion or more by the year 2025, the global labor force will grow even faster, by 60 percent, increasing from 2.5 billion to 4 billion workers. Add today's several hundred million unemployed or underemployed workers, and the pressing need is to create 2 billion new economic opportunities over the next 30 years.

Child Undernutrition

Hunger hits young children especially hard. Poor nutrition during the first few years of life can result in permanent physical and mental damage, and often death.

In 1990, 179 million of the developing world's children under the age of 5 – one out of three – were undernourished, as measured by being underweight.

Seventy-five percent of the underweight children lived in the Asia-Pacific region (see Table 1.3). South Asia's child undernutrition rate was much higher than that of any other region (58 percent, compared to 30 percent in sub-Saharan Africa).

The possible reasons for high levels of child undernutrition in South Asia include the large population size, high population density and the rainy climate, which spreads diseases such as intestinal disorders that cause malnutrition.

Two hundred fifteen million children under age 5 in the developing world (40 percent), are stunted (i.e., have low heights for their age, indicating chronic undernutrition). The rates, again, are highest in South Asia.

An estimated 95 million children under age 15 in developing countries work to help their poverty-plagued families. An equal number are homeless, destitute "street children," vulnerable to hunger.

TABLE 1.3

Number and Percentage of Undernourished Children Under Age 5 by Region, 1990

Regions	Undernourished children (underweight)	
	Percent	Number (millions)
Sub-Saharan Africa	30	26.2
Near East-North Africa	25	12.5
South Asia	58	90.7
Southeast Asia	24	42.5
Latin America	12	6.7
Total	34	178.8

Source: WHO; FAO.

Micronutrient Malnutrition

Even when people are able to obtain the calories and protein they need, they may still suffer from life-threatening malnutrition. Micronutrient malnutrition, especially iodine deficiency disorders, vitamin A deficiency and iron deficiency anemia, seriously undermines the health and productivity of poor people. Over 2 billion people worldwide are vulnerable to this "hidden hunger" (see Table 1.4), which has deep consequences. Lack of vitamin A can cause blindness and death from infectious disease. Iron deficiency is a cause of anemia, which lowers productivity by reducing work and school performance and increasing susceptibility to disease. In 1990, anemia afflicted more than half the pregnant women in the developing world, putting them at heightened risk of death in childbirth or bearing low birth-weight babies, who in turn are vulnerable to disease and impaired development.

Iodine deficiency can lead to goiter (an enlargement of the thyroid gland) and mental retardation. There are significant iodine deficiency problems in some European countries as well as in the developing world. The Chinese Ministry of Public Health recently reported that iodine shortages during infant brain development have left 10 million people mentally retarded, including hundreds of

TABLE 1.4

Number of People Affected by Micronutrient Malnutrition by Region (in millions), 1995

Region	Iodine deficiency		Vitamin A deficiency		Iron deficiency
	At risk	Affected (Goiter)	At risk	Affected (Xerophthalmia)	Affected (Anemia)
Africa	181	89	52	1.0	206
Americas	167	63	16	0.1	94
Southeast Asia	486	175	125	1.5	149
Europe	141	97	n/a	n/a	27
Eastern Mediterranean	173	93	16	0.1	616
Western Pacific	423	139	42	0.1	1,058
Total	1,571	656	251	2.8	2,150

Source: WHO.

thousands of cretins (people with severe mental and physical impairment).[25]

Ironically, although the costs of micronutrient malnutrition can be enormous – up to 5 percent of a country's gross domestic product in disability and lost lives and productivity – relatively inexpensive public health interventions can prevent micronutrient deficiency disorders. Iodizing salt supplies cost about 5 cents per person per year. Consumption of small amounts of green, leafy vegetables provides adequate vitamin A. For 6 cents per child per year, children over 6 months of age can also receive three doses of vitamin A capsules. It is likewise inexpensive to fortify sugar and cooking oil with vitamin A. Pregnant women can increase their iron intake with a daily tablet of iron sulfate that costs one-fifth of a cent.

It would not be difficult to overcome this widespread "hidden hunger." But it requires a sustained government commitment. Active community involvement – education, advocacy and carrying out of programs – is critical, too. The good news is that many governments are committed to tackling the problem. In 1995, the United Nations Children's Fund (UNICEF) reported that 58 of 94 countries with iodine deficiency problems were on track to iodize 95 percent of their salt supplies by the end of the year. China is making a major effort to fully iodize its salt supply by the year 2000. Bangladesh, Brazil, India, Malawi and the Philippines provide children with vitamin A capsules in conjunction with immunization efforts.[26]

Urbanization of Hunger

For half her life, 10-year-old Bilkish has lived in a hut of black plastic on a sidewalk in central Bombay. It's a small space, about three by four meters, too low for an adult to stand in. Nine people live there: Bilkish and her five brothers and sisters, her parents and her father's brother. The hut's only opening is the "door," a dirty quilt draped over a rope. There is no other ventilation or source of light, and even in the breezy Bombay winters black plastic makes a hot, dark and airless home.

Every morning at 5 a.m., Bilkish and her sisters line up at a communal water-tap several blocks away. After waiting more than an hour, they stagger home with sloshing pails of water on their heads: a day's supply for bathing, washing, cooking, drinking and making tea. There is also a public toilet several blocks away, but using it costs more than the family can afford.

The family moved to Bombay from a dusty, sleepy village in eastern India five years ago. Bilkish's mother now works as a servant whenever her frail health permits, which is not often. The child's father works as a day laborer on construction sites, but he suffers from tuberculosis, a common complaint among slum dwellers the world over. His working days are numbered, so to make ends meet, the children are sent out into traffic to beg. Soon Bilkish will start working as a servant. She has never been to school.

This family's situation is multiplied by hundreds of millions in cities throughout the developing world, from Rio de Janeiro to Nairobi to Manila.[27]

By the year 2025, about 61 percent of the world's population will live in urban areas, compared to 45 percent in 1995. The urban population will increase by 1 million people per week, from 2.5 billion to 5.1 billion.[28] This urbanization is taking place mostly in developing countries, where urban poverty and hunger are also increasing (see Figure 1.5 and Table 1.5).

Although the proportion of hungry people living in rural areas remains high in the developing world as a whole, in some developing countries, urban malnutrition rates exceed those of rural areas (see Figure 1.6).[29] Slum dwellers are especially susceptible to malnutrition; in Bangladesh, the infant mortality rate in urban areas is 70 per thousand live births, while the rate is 138 in slums, where government services are virtually nonexistent. In Manila, the slum rate is three times greater than that in non-slum areas.[30] In Washington, DC, the infant mortality rate is 18, but it is eight for the United States as a whole.

Urban poor people in the developing world live in "life-" and "health-threatening" conditions in overcrowded huts that lack basic services. Miserable sanitation and other aspects of urban slums sometimes make urban health and nutrition qualitatively different from the rural situation. Strategic policies are needed to grapple with these problems.[31]

FIGURE 1.5

The Changing Face of Poverty

In 1990, the world's poor people were concentrated in rural Asia. Compared with 1970, however, poor people were:

MORE likely to be	LESS likely to be
African	Asian and Latin American
Children, urban women and, recently and in some regions, elderly people	Other adults
Landless	Small farmers
Living in resource-poor areas	Living in resource-rich areas
Urban	Rural
Refugees or displaced people	Settled

Source: Michael Lipton and Simon Maxwell, The New Poverty Agenda: An Overview *(Brighton, UK: Institute of Development Studies, University of Sussex, 1992).*

TABLE 1.5

Urban Poverty Rates by Region, 1996

Region	Urban Poverty Rate (percent)
Sub-Saharan Africa	41.6
Asia	23.0
Latin America	26.5
Middle East and North Africa	34.2
Developing Countries	27.7

Source: UNFPA.

FIGURE 1.6

Urban and Rural Malnutrition in Selected Developing Countries
1971-1981

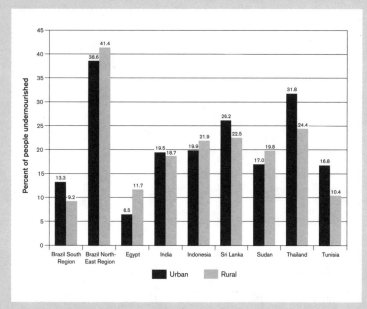

Source: *Joachim von Braun* et al., Urban Food Insecurity and Malnutrition in Developing Countries: Trends Policies and Research Implications *(Washington: IFPRI), 1993.*

Hunger in Complex Emergencies

Complex emergencies, caused mainly by civil wars, are the main cause of today's famines. These situations often lead to starvation and life-threatening disease by displacing people on a large scale and causing economic, political and social institutions to fail. These situations also intensify population pressure on available resources and contribute to environmental degradation. In some cases, natural disasters such as drought aggravate the problems. Bread for the World Institute's *Countries in Crisis: Hunger 1996* showed that undernutrition, illness and micronutrient deficiencies are widespread among uprooted people.[32] According to the U.S. Mission to the United Nations, 41.5 million people are at risk of starvation and death due to complex emergencies in 1996.[33]

The story of Maria Ingabire Uwamahoro is all too typical. A refugee from Rwanda, she is walking with thousands of others to Zaire. Only three of her five children accompany her. She fears for the two oldest, who were away gathering firewood when she was forced to flee her home suddenly to protect herself and the younger children. The older ones may have made it to a refugee camp or may be dead. Her husband, Minani, was killed while working at the tea factory.

On the day Maria left home, she had been weeding her fields of sorghum and beans. Her farm was one of hundreds crowded together in a patchwork quilt of small squares that covered the sloping hills and mountainsides. Most of the trees that once protected the topsoil had been cut down. The family had been given that rocky piece of land because Minani was the youngest brother of eight; after the family land was subdivided, this small plot was all that was left. Even before the war everyone in the area was desperate. There was simply too little land and too many people.[34]

The number of people currently affected by complex emergencies declined from 45 million in 1993-1994, but it is still 60 percent higher than 10 years ago. Countries with the greatest number of people at risk are shown in Table 1.6.

In light of "donor fatigue," emergency aid is under threat. The prospects of meeting emergency food needs are not bright. By 2005, emergency needs could grow to between 5.7 million and 6.2 million metric tons of food, according to U.S. Department of Agriculture estimates. When this is added to chronic food aid needs for food deficit countries, total food aid requirements could reach 26 million metric tons by 2005. But only 10.6 million metric tons of grain may be available for both purposes at that time.

Hunger Deaths[35]

Malnutrition is a significant factor in approximately 16 million deaths a year, or about one-third of all deaths. Particularly in Africa, total malnutrition-related deaths are increasing, and moderate malnutrition results in more deaths than does severe malnutrition. Many deaths related to hunger and poor nutrition occur beyond those resulting from the emergencies that receive the most attention. The urgent need for primary health care and nutrition – a need which governments must help address – for many of the world's most vulnerable groups exists not only during, but also before and after humanitarian emergencies. UNICEF and the World Health Organization (WHO) estimate that 12.4 million children under 5 die annually from malnutrition and preventable diseases.

But *starvation* accounts for just 150,000 to 200,000 deaths a year, or less than 0.4 percent of approximately 46 million global deaths in a routine year. During the second half of the 20th century, annual average starvation deaths have declined, although the number of disasters has apparently increased. This results largely from improvements in health science, a shrinking world, due in part to improved communications and trade, and the timely availability of aid. Since 1960, the largest famines have claimed several hundred thousand lives, but not millions, a fact not well known. The lowering of starvation deaths over time may be viewed as a success of public policies, human development and international cooperation. Given current trends, starvation deaths could continue to decrease over the next decade.

However, other potential trends could cause increased starvation: possible technological and industrial disasters, genocidal activities, complex emergencies, nuclear terrorism or the breakdown of nation-states. Public health emergencies that disrupt societies and cut vulnerable groups off from support could also accelerate starvation.

TABLE 1.6

Countries in Crisis, 1996

Country	Population in need (millions)
Afghanistan	4.0
Sudan	4.0
Bosnia and Herzegovina	3.7
Ethiopia	3.0-4.0
Angola	2.5
Rwanda	2.5
Sierra Leone	1.8
Liberia	1.5
Iraq	1.3-4.0
Haiti	0.9-1.3
Eritrea	1.0
Somalia	1.0
Tajikistan	1.0

Source: U.S. Mission to the United Nations.

Does the World Have Enough Food?

Between 1969-1971 and 1990-1992, the amount of food available for each person in the world (measured in calories) increased 11 percent, from 2,440 to 2,720 calories per day. Thus, average food availability exceeds minimum needs of 2,350 calories per person per day. In other words, if the world's food supplies were evenly distributed, there would be enough for every human being to meet minimum needs.

But in the least-developed countries (low-income countries with a per capita gross national product of $695 or less in 1993 and suffering from long-term handicaps to economic growth), availability was only 2,040 calories per person per day (see Figure 1.7). Moreover, food availability has stagnated in these countries over the past 20 years, suggesting that poor people have not been able to increase their food consumption. In sub-Saharan Africa, per capita

FIGURE 1.7

Per Capita Food Supplies

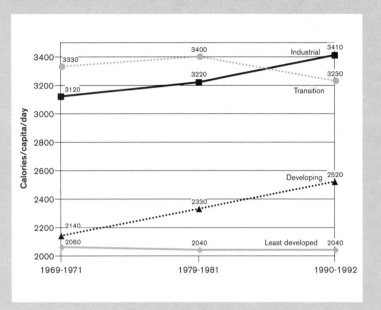

Source: FAO.

FIGURE 1.8

Per Capita Food Supplies, Developing Regions

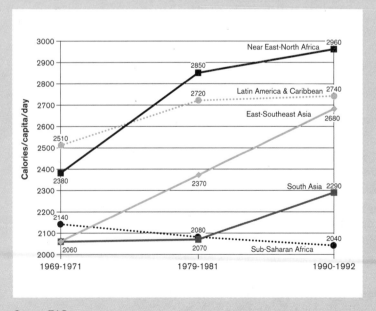

Source: FAO.

supplies have declined since 1969-1971 (see Figure 1.8). Even where average availability has improved, averages often mask severe inequalities in access to food with rich people consuming much more than their share, leaving poor people with even less.

Total world food production continues to grow, but the growth rate dropped from 3 percent annually in the 1960s to 2 percent in 1980-1992. International agencies are optimistic that food production will outpace population growth for the foreseeable future. But other analysts, notably Lester Brown of the Worldwatch Institute, are more pessimistic. Considering such factors as increasing scarcity of water, the declining effectiveness of additional fertilizer applications, falling fish catches, the cumulative effect of soil erosion, the apparent rising of global temperatures and the associated crop-withering heat waves, and social disintegration in many developing countries, he fears that food production will fail to keep pace.[36]

In the short term, grain supplies have without doubt been declining. Stocks have fallen below the alarming level of the 1970s that led to the 1974 World Food Conference. Grain prices have risen sharply over the past year. In 1996, prices were 50 percent to 100 percent higher than a year earlier, and will likely remain high until 1997 harvests, or beyond. FAO forecasts improved production in 1996, but not by enough to restore stocks to safe levels. This will affect poor people everywhere, but especially in the developing countries, where low-income households spend up to 80 percent of their income on food, mostly grain. Global food aid has dropped to 8.4 million metric tons of grain in 1994-1995 from a peak of 15.2 million metric tons in 1992-1993.

Conclusion

Hunger has declined globally over the past two decades. But in several regions, it persists on a large scale or is growing. In order to eliminate the scourge of hunger from the world, governments must do their part – create economic opportunities, especially for poor people, and maintain safety nets for vulnerable groups.

In Africa, hunger is pervasive and increasing. This is due partly to the continent's armed conflicts and political crises. Other factors include high population growth, coupled with harsh trade and aid policies on the part of the United States and other industrial countries. In many cases, it is because African governments are weak and sometimes corrupt.

The countries of South Asia have made steady, if slow, progress against mass hunger. Effective government programs have made a big difference for millions of people. But millions more remain undernourished, including a very high proportion of the region's children.

In the newly independent states of the former Soviet Union and some countries in Eastern Europe, people have suffered great hardships in the process of transition from a planned to a market economy. As in Africa, armed struggle contributes greatly to food insecurity in some countries.

Finally, too many children in the United States are hungry or at risk of hunger. As later chapters show, this is partly due to changes in the economy. Political decisions to reduce government assistance to poor and hungry families have also played a role. The next two chapters discuss recent cuts and the future of U.S. "welfare reform."

DR. MARC J. COHEN *is senior research associate* and JASHINTA D'COSTA *is an intern at Bread for the World Institute.*

CHAPTER 2

From the *War on Poverty* to the *War on the Poor*

by Teresa Amott, Marc J. Cohen and Don Reeves

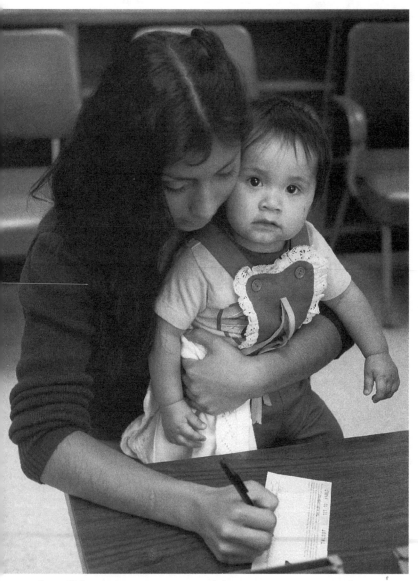

Some U.S. government programs provide temporary support to needy Americans. At-risk, low-income mothers and their infants receive cost-effective nutrition and health assistance through the Special Supplemental Nutrition Program for Women, Infants and Children (WIC). USDA

The 104th U.S. Congress (1995-1996) set out to make sweeping changes in the roles of the federal and state governments. It sought to balance the budget in seven years, cut taxes for middle- and upper-income families, increase military spending and slash spending on programs to help poor people.

The Onslaught Against "Welfare"

As a central feature of its efforts to shrink the federal government, Congress passed several versions of welfare "reform." An initial version, rejected by President Bill Clinton, would have turned several anti-poverty programs over to the states as "block grants" – federal lump sum payments. The proposed block grants would have substituted for Medicaid, which provides access to health care for low-income people; nutrition assistance; and welfare. By eliminating federal standards and guarantees, block granting will almost certainly lead to increased hunger in some areas.

The Clinton administration also favored less spending on anti-poverty programs, but sought somewhat smaller reductions. Aid to Families with Dependent Children (AFDC, the main federal welfare program), food assistance and Medicaid all combined were less than 9 percent of federal spending in fiscal year 1994. In contrast, military spending, interest on the national debt and the predominantly middle- and upper-middle-class entitlement programs, Social Security and Medicare, together accounted for 62.5 percent of the federal budget.

In July 1996, Clinton and Congress agreed on an election-year welfare reform deal. It preserves the federal Medicaid entitlement. Thanks in part to strong grassroots lobbying efforts, it does not block grant nutrition programs. But the legislation converts AFDC to block grants, ends the federal guarantee of cash assistance to all poor children, requires recipients to go to work within two years and puts a five-year lifetime limit on benefits. It requires unmarried teen-age recipients to live with an adult and imposes a "family cap," denying additional benefits to welfare mothers who have further children. Clinton had earlier imposed the work requirement and the residence restrictions on teen-age AFDC mothers by executive order.

The legislation reduces spending by about $60 billion over six years, with substantial cuts in food stamps and child nutrition programs and severe restrictions on benefits to legal immigrants. The bill will push an estimated additional 1.1 million children into poverty, increasing the already unacceptably high levels of hunger among children.[1]

Many states have undertaken welfare reforms of their own during the 1990s. Some of their policy changes attempt to regulate poor people's behavior, e.g., requiring teen-age mothers to live with adults and establishing family caps. However, other proposals seek to increase earnings and savings. These changes – and provisions encouraging education, training and work – could improve the well-being of low-income families.

By July 1996, the federal Department of Health and Human Services had approved 69 AFDC waiver applications (i.e., permission to deviate from federal requirements) from 41 states. Since early 1995, 11 states have requested that they be allowed to end welfare eligibility after two to five years.[2]

At the same time, many states have implemented or are considering their own cuts in anti-poverty programs. By 1992, 44 states had frozen or reduced AFDC benefits. New York has proposed cutting AFDC benefits 26.5 percent in 1996; California, up to 15 percent; New Mexico, 13 percent; and Rhode Island, 11 percent.

In early 1996, New York, Pennsylvania, California, Maryland and Washington had proposals before their legislatures to cut programs for low-income people while cutting taxes (and therefore their revenue base) for business and upper-income people. For example, California proposed a 15 percent cut in personal and corporate income taxes over three years, with most of these savings going to the 9 percent of Californians earning above $100,000 annually. Cuts to AFDC in the state in 1989-1990 and 1995-1996 have reduced benefits by 26 percent after inflation. An additional 5 percent reduction is under consideration.

Quite a few states have drastically reduced spending on programs under their exclusive control. One-third of the people in the country who were receiving state-financed General Assistance (aid to non-elderly, low-income adults without dependent children) have had benefits cut or eliminated altogether.

The onslaught against government programs designed to reduce poverty has been remarkable. Against a backdrop of growing hunger and inequity in the United States, the attack on anti-poverty programs is at least incongruous – and in our view, downright immoral (see The *War on the Poor*, pages 28-29).

The debate is far from over. Even as President Clinton signed the welfare bill, he said he would propose legislation to reverse some of its most onerous features. And, state legislatures were gearing up to respond to an unprecedented increase in responsibility to help meet the needs of low-income people – whether through direct assistance or programs that would prepare them for decent employment. At the same time, many state legislators are anxious as to whether states have sufficient revenues, staff and the political will to respond to the changes in national policy.

The *War on the Poor* by Jim Hug[1]

The *War on Poverty* has been transformed into a *War on the Poor*. The reality is that blunt and outrageous. Under the cover of *fiscal* responsibility and balancing the budget, the U.S. Congress is shedding its social responsibility and further destroying the already tenuous and faltering balance in and among our communities. The fundamental national guarantee that people of the wealthiest nation on the planet will have at least the minimal basic necessities for survival is being eliminated. Federal funding for social needs is being cut back seriously and sent as block grants to the states with few if any strings attached to prevent the extensive abuses at the state level that led to federal programs in the first place.

"Compassion" has been slandered as a tragically naive attitude. As embodied in federal programs, the argument goes, it has created welfare dependency. It is the "enabling behavior of a well-meaning but co-dependent" society.[2]

Private charities are being asked to replace impersonal government bureaucracies with the kind of personal involvement that changes people's lives. That seemingly idealistic challenge begs two important questions. How realistic is it to expect private charities, which now, all together, provide $8 billion annually to the poor, to make up for a projected federal cutback of $57 billion in its services to those same poor? And what is the appropriate responsibility of a government as the final guarantor of the well-being of all its people?

What About Jobs?

The original justification for these cuts claimed that government borrowing necessitated by the deficit absorbs too much of the nation's available capital. It is hampering the economic growth that would provide jobs and get people off welfare.

That rationale has dissolved. The December 1995 Congressional Budget Office forecast for the economy over the next seven years predicts increased corporate profits in the sixth and seventh years of the process and a decline in the rate at which people join the work force.[3] In other words, the cuts in social programs will not translate into jobs for the working poor and middle classes. They will translate into greater corporate profits.

Corporate leaders show little inclination to reinvest those profits in creating jobs. The stock market has been breaking historic records practically every day. Those skyrocketing profits are not being used to create new jobs at any significant rate. The wealthy are consolidating wealth and power rapidly. Where profits are rein-

vested, they more often go for machines that replace workers or to move production to places where labor costs are lower and regulation lighter. As the United Nations Development Programme *Human Development Report 1993* showed, from 1975 to 2000 and beyond, economic growth will continue to be strong while the production of jobs will remain nearly flat everywhere. And the continuing pace of technological innovation suggests that we are in an early phase of a process in which more and more people's work and livelihoods will be taken over by a silicon chip or a machine logic.

Poverty's Causes and Cures

Historically, there is a link between the public analysis of the causes of poverty and the types of anti-poverty programs embraced.[4] With the discovery of the depressing environment of ghettoes and slums, the nation set about building more humane housing environments. When unemployment was discovered to be a structural problem, public works and other government programs mushroomed.

Now the reigning political "wisdom" proclaims these programs failures, identifying the real cause of poverty as spiritual and moral. Poor people are trapped in a "culture of poverty," a culture of dependency fostered by those who tried to help them through government programs. Poverty will never be overcome, the argument goes, until the poor themselves assume responsibility for their own lives. Morality and spirituality are equated with personal responsibility.

False and Simplistic

This position reflects several false assumptions that undermine constructive public dialogue on these issues.

Have both the *War on Poverty* and the government social programs of the last 60 years *really* failed? Susan Mayer, professor of public policy at the University of Chicago, and Christopher Jencks, professor of sociology at Northwestern University, argue that the government's own data show that the major anti-poverty programs have basically done what they were meant to do:[5]

- Before 1965, the poor made 20 percent fewer doctor visits a year than the wealthy despite being sicker. By 1980 Medicaid eliminated that gap.

- Within seven years in the 1970s, the Food Stamp Program cut in half the negative effects of family income on food consumption and made hunger and malnutrition much harder to find.

- According to the Census Bureau, nearly every measure of poor families' housing conditions has improved since 1970.

- The proportion of 17-year-olds with very low math and reading scores has dropped substantially in the last 25 years, suggesting the success of programs like Head Start for low-income populations.

- The poverty rate among the elderly has fallen since the early 1970s – which was the goal of Supplemental Security Income and Social Security.

- Aid to Families with Dependent Children (AFDC) benefits have never been adequate to raise people out of poverty. Does it foster illegitimacy as claimed? The birth rate among teen-agers fell in the years when anti-poverty spending rose the fastest and rose when AFDC benefits fell.

None of these programs is perfect. Poverty still exists and is growing. But that is not so simply or clearly due to the "failure" of these programs.

Secondly, to argue that the cause of poverty is spiritual *rather than* structural is simplistic. The causes of poverty are complex. They are indeed spiritual; they are also structural.

Every day newspapers and business journals are full of discussions of the structural changes sweeping the planet. New technologies and globalization processes are restructuring the work place. Unskilled manufacturing jobs have been lost to machines and/or cheap labor in other parts of the world. Corporations, claiming pressure from international competition, have down-sized their operations, laying off full-time workers with benefits and rehiring them as part-time or contingent workers at greatly reduced pay and without benefits. Approximately 40 percent of the U.S. work force is now "contingent" in this way. And 46 percent of U.S. companies are using or studying "variable pay plans," which would further endanger employee pay. Under these schemes, company profits are made more secure, skilled specialists improve their income and lower-income households find themselves more insecure.[6]

Structural changes require programmatic responses. We must not force poor people off welfare rolls, demanding that they "become responsible and get jobs," if there are no jobs produced for which they qualify. Maryland has reported that the average number of families on AFDC in the state in 1994 was 79,317. That same year the private sector added only 5,690 jobs for which those families could compete – and these were principally minimum wage jobs currently incapable of raising a family out of poverty. The 38,725 other jobs created in the state required college or advanced degrees.

A Spiritual Problem

Structural problems are not the only ones that plague us, however. There *is* a spiritual problem at the heart of our current economic situation. It is more serious and corrosive than the irresponsibility of the relatively small percentage of poor people succumbing to welfare dependency. It is the social irresponsibility of those responsible for structuring the economy so that people are squeezed out and communities devastated in the pursuit of greater profits for a few or "economic efficiency" in the system.

Let me emphasize this point. The current public debate reflects a simplistic identification of "spiritual" and "moral" with an individualistic emphasis on "personal responsibility." The profound social dimension of every major world religion is being shrouded in silence. When Jesus' command to "love one another as I have loved you" gets translated into "tough love" so tough that it allows the homeless to wander and freeze on the streets until they "get their lives together" and leaves children to go hungry, Jesus – and every other major religious figure – has been betrayed. His mission is to bring good news to the poor and proclaim the year of jubilee when the resources God has given humanity are redistributed justly so all have what they need to flourish.

In the light of that mission, it is truly a major spiritual crisis when those who have more than they need rest comfortably while those who lack basics struggle and suffer: the spiritual crisis of the comfortable.[7]

JIM HUG, S.J., *is director of the Center of Concern, which engages in analysis, reflection and advocacy on issues of global development, peace and social and economic justice.*

1 Slightly adapted, with permission, from *Center Focus*, January 1996.

2 This is Marvin Olasky's argument in *The Tragedy of American Compassion*, reportedly given to each member of the U.S. House of Representatives by Speaker Newt Gingrich.

3 *Washington Post*, December 12, 1995.

4 Malcolm Gladwell, "The Failure of Our Best Intentions," *Washington Post*, Outlook Section, December 3, 1995.

5 Susan Mayer and Christopher Jencks, "War on Poverty: No Apologies, Please," *New York Times*, November 9, 1995.

6 "Unstable Pay Becomes Ever More Common," *Wall Street Journal*, December 4, 1995.

7 In the full article, Father Hug concluded with a strategy for "turning back this well-organized 'war' on the middle class, the working poor, and the most vulnerable." For full details, contact Center of Concern, 3700 13th St. NE, Washington, DC 20017; (202) 635-2757.

Bread lines of the Great Depression helped spark New Deal government programs to lift out-of-work people from poverty.

Library of Congress

The Congress that starts in January 1997 may or may not be better for poor people, depending on whom the voters elect. The next Congress may push to further weaken nutrition and other anti-poverty programs, or may find ways to add funding and provisions that will help state welfare reform to reduce poverty and hunger.

There will also be intense debate in many states during the next several years about how to reform welfare. State experience will need to be monitored as a basis for future revisions of national policies.

This chapter reviews the long-term growth of federal anti-poverty programs, the history of the main programs attacked by "welfare reform" and political developments of the 1980s. The next chapter outlines key arguments in the welfare reform debate and the sort of welfare reform that could move employable people into jobs and reduce poverty.

The Mixed Economy

For nearly 60 years, the United States and other industrial countries have tended toward greater reliance on government programs and policies to keep hunger, poverty and unemployment in check. As Massachusetts Institute of Technology economist Lester Thurow has observed, the welfare state permitted the political egalitarianism of democracy and the economic inequality of capitalism to maintain peaceful coexistence.[3]

But since the 1980s, the consensus has shattered to the point where James Pinkerton, who worked in the Bush White House, could recently assert, "The general proposition that unites most Americans is that government is too big and spends too much."[4] President Bill Clinton seemed to agree when he stated in his 1996 State of the Union address, "The era of big government is over."

All contemporary economies are mixed economies, with a major role for government alongside the market. Throughout the 20th century, government has played a growing role. But the tension between proponents of greater government regulation and intervention and proponents of unregulated, or "free market," economics is a source of ongoing political and philosophical debate.

Free market proponents believe that limiting government interference will provide the maximum consumer choice, offering the widest variety of products at the lowest possible prices and the highest possible quality in comparison to an economy in which government regulates markets. However, even the godfather of free-market theory, Adam Smith, believed that there were important economic roles for government: to establish a legal framework that protected property rights, uphold contracts and deeds, enforce laws banning theft and prevent collusion that would inhibit competition. In this sense, markets are in themselves partly the creation of government policy. And markets depend on government-established physical and social infrastructure – roads and waterways, education to prepare a work force and the absence of armed conflict.

In the centuries since Smith wrote, the public and private sectors have become intertwined in the mixed economies of the industrial world. In practice, it is often difficult to distinguish between the public and private sectors. For instance, in the United States, private charities often rely heavily on government commodities and funds.

Economists generally agree that there are cases in which a free-market economy cannot provide the most desirable outcome for a society. The case for government intervention begins with the problem of market failures, which arise when a market has special characteristics that prevent efficient, competitive operations. A classic example is environmental pollution. In the absence of government regulation, a polluting firm can offer cheaper products, and will have a market edge, but to the detriment of society. Mainstream economics teaches that, in such cases, government intervention will produce more efficient and competitive outcomes than would a laissez-faire approach.

In addition, economists have studied the ways in which government policy can stabilize the economy, targeting desirable levels of employment, growth and inflation through the use of tax, spending and credit policies.

Finally, if society deems that certain market outcomes lead to economic injustices, public policies can correct those outcomes. Notably, government can use tax and spending policies to redistribute income and provide goods and services to those who cannot secure them through the private market. All industrial societies decide what is required for a just society through the political process, and then allocate public resources to ensure that members of that society have access to those goods and services even if they cannot purchase them in the market.

Most of the world's religions and ethical systems demand that a hungry person be fed, and that a person not be denied food simply because he or she lacks the income to buy it. In the United States, we recognize that the private market and private charity cannot solve the hunger problem. Therefore, we take public action to feed hungry people through food stamps and other government programs. Most industrial-country governments also provide basic income security to those who cannot work or who reach the age at which the society says a person should be able to retire. Finally, most industrial societies regulate the labor market, setting into place a minimum wage and rights to organize unions and work in a safe environment.

There are differences among the industrial nations in what is considered an essential element of a decent standard of living. All industrial societies agree that access to health care should not be determined solely by income. In 1965, the United States enacted the Medicare and Medicaid programs to provide government subsidies so that retired, disabled and poor people have access to health care. But other nations have gone much further, providing universal access to health care.

According to economic historians Robert Heilbroner and Aaron Singer, in the 19th century, the U.S. federal government saw its role as a:

> promoter of business, underwriting "internal improvements," granting land to railroads and helping infant industries to take root. A second stage was the emergence of the government in the latter half of the century as a regulator of the economy, using its powers to assure the orderly workings of individual markets or industries…. With the Employment Act [that committed the federal government to stabilization policies to promote full employment] came a third stage. The government now took on the function of guarantor, taking as its prime objective the maintenance of socially acceptable rates of growth and levels of employment.[5]

Beginning with the New Deal of the 1930s, the government took on the regulation of the labor market. In the 1960s, the federal government waged a *War on Poverty*, leaving some long-standing programs as a legacy. In the 1970s, major federal legislative initiatives regulated environmental and consumer product safety.

Background on Federal Poverty and Hunger Programs

The federal government has established a broad array of programs aimed at reducing hunger and poverty. These include 16 food assistance programs, medical assistance through Medicaid, housing assistance, education and job training. Low-income single parents (and unemployed married couples with children) have received AFDC.

Before the Great Depression, the traditional system of aiding poor people through families, voluntary organizations and local governments proved totally inadequate. The New Deal created a federal social safety net, including Social Security for elderly and disabled people and AFDC (originally called "Aid to Dependent Children" and included in the Social Security Act of 1935).

During the Johnson administration, the government considerably expanded federal housing and urban development programs for low-income communities. During the 1960s, anti-poverty programs seemed to be working well.

AFDC

AFDC has provided cash payments to families of needy children lacking adequate income because of parental incapacity, death, absence or unemployment. The federal government has provided a major share of the funding and sets broad eligibility rules. However, states have also helped finance the program and administer it. They have had great discretion to determine additional eligibility requirements and set benefit levels.

Program Growth. Contrary to stereotypes, AFDC rolls did not grow dramatically in recent years. In 1972, 5.1 percent of the total U.S. population received benefits, compared to 5.3 percent in 1992. The proportion of poor children receiving benefits actually declined, from 75 percent in 1972 to 63 percent in 1992. In 1993, 14 million people lived in AFDC families, including 9.5 million children. But the total poverty population included 39.3 million people, of whom 15 million were children.

AFDC has not been as costly as people may imagine. In 1993, it cost the federal and state governments $25 billion for benefits and administration. The federal share was less than $14 billion, or under 1 percent of federal spending.

The purchasing power of the average monthly AFDC benefit declined 45 percent between 1970 and 1993. The average annual benefit was $4,476 per family in 1993, or just 38 percent of the poverty-level income for a family of three.

Between 1975 and 1993, federal spending (adjusted for inflation and population growth) on AFDC and child support enforcement combined grew by 0.1 percent annually. The average growth of all anti-poverty programs during the same period was 3.9 percent, while farm price supports grew 11.7 percent.

A recent reunion of former AFDC recipients in South Dakota suggests how distorted stereotypes can be. Among those attending:

- a family counselor in private practice;
- two state legislators;
- two retired social workers, one of whom was also a past American Legion Post Commander; and
- an attorney.

Critics argue that AFDC has created work disincentives. There is some truth to this view, although it is the labor market itself more than welfare that discourages work. Full-time minimum wage employment does not pay enough to lift a typical family above the poverty line, and most low-paying jobs do not include health benefits, access to child care or much job security. AFDC recipients, in contrast, receive Medicaid and food stamps, and sometimes are eligible for housing, education, child care benefits and additional food assistance. Recipients lose benefits when they go to work, and face additional costs for transportation, child care and clothing. Staying on welfare is often not so much a matter of lacking a work ethic as having a desire to maintain family livelihood security.[6]

Food Assistance Programs[7]

Modern federal food assistance began in the 1930s. It allowed the federal government to accomplish two objectives through public food distribution: reducing hunger and disposing of farm surpluses.

During World War II, the federal government stopped giving states money to distribute commodities. States required counties that wanted the commodities to spend their own tax dollars on distribution. Many of the poorest counties withdrew from the program even though their citizens remained hungry.

During the war, the armed services rejected many poorly nourished recruits. Recognizing the importance of good nutrition to national defense, Congress passed the National School Lunch Act in 1946 to ensure that all children, regardless of their parents' income, have access to a nutritious meal at school.

Between 1964 and 1974, states and counties had the option of not participating in the Food Stamp Program, and states determined eligibility rules. The federal government set benefit levels from the program's beginning in 1961. In 1970, Arizona, Delaware, New Hampshire and Oklahoma did not participate at all, and many other states did not offer the program in every county. Many participating states had extremely stringent maximum income eligibility standards. In three states, families with incomes at just 50 percent of the federal poverty line did not qualify. Thirty-eight of the 45 participating states excluded families when their incomes reached 75 percent of the poverty level. Nationally, more than 20 million people with incomes below the poverty line – 76 percent of the total population living in poverty – did not receive food stamps. In Florida, Idaho, Kansas, Maine, Massachusetts, New York and Texas, 90 percent of the people in poverty did not receive food stamps.

Similarly, in the early 1970s, local school districts set eligibility standards for the School Lunch Program. It was not available in many of the poorest schools. One study showed that fewer than half of 6 million low-income children got free or reduced-price meals.

Public Opinion and Hunger

Inadequacies in some welfare programs, especially Aid to Families with Dependent Children (AFDC), made them vulnerable to cutbacks in a time of fiscal restraint. Unexpectedly caught in the rush to "end welfare as we know it" were the federal nutrition programs, which have significantly improved the diets of low-income people in the last 20 years.

The effort to radically scale back federal food programs occurred with little public debate or support. Recent polls show that the voters are concerned about hunger and poverty. In a 1995 poll commissioned by Second Harvest, the national food bank network, 84 percent of respondents wanted the federal government to maintain or increase spending on food assistance. A Nielsen survey taken late that same year found that 95 percent of respondents rated the importance of hunger and poverty issues as equal to health care, a balanced budget and employment.

A 1996 survey conducted by *The Washington Post*, Harvard University and the Kaiser Family Foundation found that there is a strong concern among disaffected Americans (31 percent of the populace) about the widening gap between the rich and the middle class. They believe that government is increasing the gap by lowering taxes for the wealthy while doing too little for poor and hungry people. According to one veteran pollster, this group of disaffected Americans is the most important segment of the electorate in 1996.

In keeping with the civil rights consciousness of the 1960s, anti-hunger advocates accused the federal government of failing to protect the rights of citizens to due process and equal access to benefits. A broad coalition, including religious groups, labor unions, foundations and anti-hunger organizations, sought to expand eligibility for, and access to, federal food programs, upgrade benefits and provide recipients with legally enforceable rights to receive assistance. The public was incensed about reports of rampant hunger, Congress was prepared with data and new ideas about what would work, and President Richard Nixon was willing to expand food assistance.

Congress made school breakfast a permanent program and set federal standards for free and reduced-price school meals. Participation quadrupled over the next decade. Today, low-income children depend on the School Lunch Program for one-third to one-half of their daily nutrition. Children who participate in the School Breakfast Program have significantly fewer absences from school and score much better on standardized achievement tests than nonparticipants.

In 1971, the federal government established uniform food stamp eligibility rules and required every political jurisdiction to participate in the program by 1974. The Food Stamp Program became an "entitlement," meaning that the federal government has to provide adequate funding so that everyone eligible receives food stamps.

Food stamps increase the nutritional quality of poor children's diets by 20 percent to 40 percent. And, food stamps play an important role when the economy turns sour. The program served an additional 5 million people between 1990 and 1992, when the national unemployment rate increased from 5.1 percent to 7.7 percent. Herbert Stein, the chairman of the Council of Economic Advisers under President Nixon, says that the program serves the overall economy. The increase in benefits to poor people during recessions gives unemployed workers the means to purchase necessities and thus boosts the businesses that provide those services. According to the U.S. Department of Agriculture (USDA), every $1 billion of additional food stamp spending during a recession produces about 25,000 jobs.

In 1972, the government established the Special Supplemental Nutrition Program for Women, Infants and Children (WIC). WIC is the only federal food program targeted on the basis of nutritional vulnerability, as well as income. It offers nutrition education and prescribed supplemental foods (milk, juice, eggs, cereals, beans, peanut butter, etc.) to improve the diets and health of participating pregnant and nursing mothers, infants and children under 5. Studies have shown that WIC reduces infant mortality and anemia,

and increases cognitive performance. Each dollar spent on WIC for pregnant mothers saves up to $3.50 in Medicaid and special education costs by increasing birthweight and length of pregnancy. Although a few critics claim WIC fosters dependency,[8] the fact is that it uses short-term intervention to positively influence lifetime health and nutrition behaviors.

But unlike AFDC, food stamps or school nutrition programs, WIC is not an entitlement. It depends on annual appropriations for funds and currently can only enroll 72 percent of those eligible.

Like Medicaid and AFDC, the food programs are run as a partnership among the federal, state and local governments. The money comes from Washington, DC, but state governments administer food stamps and WIC. Local school districts run the school meal programs. This partnership has generally worked effectively, with each level of government making an appropriate contribution to the success of the programs.

Federal nutrition assistance has significantly improved the nutritional status of low-income people, particularly children. At present, nearly three out of every four beneficiaries of federal food programs are children.

In the 1960s, a team of doctors visited Appalachia and the southern United States. They discovered widespread malnutrition among children. Large numbers of children were apathetic and stunted, with swollen bellies and poorly healing wounds. In 1979, the Field Foundation found that the expansion of federal food assistance had significantly helped to reduce malnutrition. The following year, the Presidential Commission on World Hunger praised food assistance programs, but argued that they do not "reach the root causes of hunger."[9] The commission pressed for a national policy to ensure balanced growth and full employment as the best means to eliminate hunger permanently.

The Struggles of the 1980s

Ironically, despite evidence of the effectiveness of these programs, the federal government began to retrench on its commitment to end childhood hunger. In 1980 Ronald Reagan became president and many welfare critics gained power in Congress. These forces sought to reduce social spending, including food assistance. Congress significantly reduced funding for food stamps and school lunches.

The congressional cuts, combined with a deep recession and structural changes in the economy, led to a marked increase in hunger and poverty since 1979. As the federal social safety net eroded, individuals, religious congregations and charities began to step in. Food banks were set up all over the country, and the number of pantries and soup kitchens skyrocketed.

By the mid-1990s, a huge volunteer food assistance movement existed, with 150,000 private agencies providing some $3 billion to $4 billion in food to hungry people each year. The government provides these agencies with both surplus food and funds for distribution.

Since 1982, the U.S. Conference of Mayors has reported annual increases in emergency food needs in 29 large cities. Sixty percent of the cities' emergency feeding funds also come from the federal government.

Private programs cannot, however, take the place of the federal government. The value of food distributed by all private feeding agencies in the United States is only about one-tenth of the federal food program budget.

Advocacy groups pressed to restore the reductions in government food program benefit levels. Legislation passed in the late 1980s and early 1990s expanded food stamp eligibility and benefit levels and increased funding for WIC. Even so, by 1994, combined AFDC and food stamp benefits for a family of four in the median state equaled just 65 percent of the poverty line, and in no state did they exceed 90 percent.

Great energies went into restoring the policies of the previous decade and building private food assistance institutions. Permanent healing of the wound of hunger upon the body politic would have to wait until the bleeding stopped. Public and private food assistance may have been Band-Aids, but they were necessary ones.

Beginning in the late 1980s, advocates turned again to more structural approaches to the problem. A grassroots movement, including service providers, anti-hunger advocates and supporters of local self-reliance, sought to assure community food security. Local organizations from around the country came together in the Campaign to End Childhood Hunger.

In 1990, national anti-hunger advocacy organizations coalesced around the Medford Declaration to End Hunger in the U.S., which 3,000 organizations and prominent individuals initially endorsed. The declaration calls for full funding and utilization of federal food assistance programs and insists on a wide variety of efforts to expand purchasing power, mainly through market-based employment that offers decent wages, along with supportive public training, tax and child care policies.

But bigger political developments once again put this long-term vision on the back burner. Bill Clinton campaigned in 1991 to "end welfare as we know it," and many members of the 104th Congress, which took office in 1995, wanted to end welfare altogether.

DR. TERESA AMOTT *is chair of the economics department at Bucknell University.* DR. MARC J. COHEN *is senior research associate and* DON REEVES *is economic policy analyst at Bread for the World Institute.*

CHAPTER 3

The Raging Debate About U.S. Poverty

by Marc J. Cohen and Don Reeves

Thirty-nine million people in the United States live below the poverty line – about $17,900 for a family of five. A full-time minimum wage worker earns a gross annual income of $8,500.

Joseph Crachiola

This chapter explores the raging debate about poverty in the United States. The welfare bill that became law in 1996 shifts more responsibility to state governments, so we include a section on the activities of state governments. We are convinced that welfare reform, as it is currently being pursued, will do much more harm than good. We close with an outline of the kind of welfare reform that would instead reduce hunger and poverty.

The Controversy

Few critics of government programs deny that hunger and poverty exist in the United States or say that they are unimportant. This is a welcome advance from earlier debates. Today's critics argue governments contribute to poverty, rather than alleviate it.

Points of Debate

● The critics argue that when government uses tax or spending policies to transfer income from more affluent to low-income people (a) investors and entrepreneurs have less incentive to invest and save because of the amounts siphoned off in taxes; and (b) low-income people become dependent on handouts. The critics believe that a healthy free-market economy generates jobs and income which, in turn, help reduce poverty.

In response, proponents of income redistribution point to a moral principle of economic justice articulated in religious and secular traditions. They also note that poverty is costly to a society, and that reducing poverty stimulates the entire economy. And, while they too may be uneasy about "welfare dependency," their strategy for changing it includes nutrition counseling, education, job training, health care and other programs that cost more in the short run.

● Critics of government programs point to the seemingly inevitable tendency of bureaucracies to expand; government's inefficiency in delivering goods and services, as compared to free markets; and the

penchant of special interests to capture the benefits of programs. The critique applies to virtually any government program, but is focused on efforts to end poverty and hunger. Commentator Rush Limbaugh has gone so far as to state, "With the exception of the military, I defy you to name one government program that has worked and alleviated the problem it was created to solve."[1]

There is some merit in the critique. But it also could be applied to agencies that serve business and other interests, not just those that serve poor people. Both major U.S. political parties in recent years have promoted initiatives to reduce the size and cost of the federal government and make it work more efficiently. Outside government, the marketplace has its own share of "rent-seekers": price-fixing cartels, exclusive contracting arrangements and other anti-competitive practices well known even in Adam Smith's day.[2] An engaged public, acting as citizens and consumers, offers the best antidote to public and private sector cronyism that works against the public interest.

Even opponents of the welfare state recognize that markets cannot solve all social problems. The solution, in the view of U.S. House Speaker Newt Gingrich, a leading welfare critic, lies in caring; volunteerism; "American values" (two-parent families and work); an emphasis on learning; and protection against violence and drugs.[3]

Bread for the World Institute also supports societal, cultural and spiritual changes that would enhance the quality of family and community life. Churches and other religious congregations must take the lead in encouraging personal responsibility by all people – rich and poor. Responsibility includes not only taking care of ourselves and our families, but also taking care of people in need. We engage in charity and also use our power as citizens to help establish just public policies. Such policies can enhance opportunities for families to earn secure livelihoods while ensuring their basic needs are met.

● Many critics of the federal government see decentralization – turning responsibility over to state and local governments, the private sector and especially community-based voluntary institutions – as a means to improve efficiency and save money. Institutions closer to the problems are more likely to come up with creative solutions; "closer is better." This anti-bureaucratic and more market-oriented approach to public services favors education vouchers, medical savings accounts and resident ownership of public housing. The goal is not simply cost savings and personal responsibility, but also increased empowerment and choice for all people.[4]

We subscribe to the "principle of subsidiarity" (see Introduction) – that decisions should be made as close to the people as possible. Some states may indeed find new and more adequate ways to carry out welfare programs. But social justice requires the federal government to take responsibility for assuring minimum standards so that children do not go hungry anywhere in the nation. Some states lack the resources to solve economic problems, and federal revenues are needed. If a state is very poor, then it cannot provide adequate services for poor people, and transfers of income from richer states are needed.

Another rationale for federal activity comes from the need for universal standards. In the debate over the Social Security Act, legislators recognized that if some states offered higher Social Security benefits than others, retired people would migrate to the high-benefit states. That is why a national benefit level was established.

● Markets sometimes do deliver goods and services more efficiently than government. For example, overnight delivery services, including that of the quasi-governmental Postal Service, have vastly improved due to the rigors of free-market competition. But markets deliver goods to people who have money. If some families who have cats have more purchasing power than other families with children, the cats

The State of Our Civil Union

by E. J. Dionne

We shift back and forth between talk about individualism and individual rights on the one side and talk about the common good on the other, as if these were contradictory notions...far from being contradictory, the insistence on the dignity of each individual and the belief that all of us have obligations to the common good are complementary notions.... All of us are inextricably social, with ties to our families, our friends, our neighbors and our fellow citizens. We want to set our own course, but we also know that course involves obligations and commitments to others....

By casting "government" and "the market" as the main mechanisms of social organization, the conventional political debate thus leaves out the most important institutions in people's lives – family, church, neighborhood, work place organizations and a variety of other voluntary institutions ranging from sports clubs and youth groups to privately organized child-care centers and the loose fellowships created at taverns like Cheers of television fame. All are places where... everybody knows your name.

Conservatives and Progressives

Conservatives, both new and old, have done a good job of reminding us of the progressives' sometimes excessive eagerness for replacing the mechanisms of private charity and communal responsibility – family, church and mutual assistance societies – with the often clumsier mechanisms of government. What conservatives, especially the new conservatives, refuse to recognize is the extent to which these organizations are effective precisely because they do not operate according to the logic of free markets, but according to an older moral logic that predated capitalism. [Sociologist Alan] Wolfe argues that capitalism has been successful so far because "it lived its first hundred years off the precapitalist morality it inherited from traditional religion and social structure."

Non-capitalist Values

Following Wolfe, one can begin to see how the roots of the moral crisis Americans are experiencing lie...in a society built on individualistic and market values that steadily cut away the bonds of solidarity, morality and trust. If profit is all that matters, film makers or music producers will not think twice about filling the marketplace with products that foster amoral or dysfunctional values among the young. If all personal ties between employer and employee are deemed to be "irrational" or "sentimental" when compared to the competitive needs of the marketplace, employers need not think at all about how work schedules might affect the ability of employees to rear their children or how cutbacks in medical coverage might affect their employees' lives. And if government gives no protection for those many employers who do care about such things, it risks forcing them out of business as they are undercut by competitors for whom cost and price are the only factors in business decisions. The central irony of our time that so many of the new conservatives wish to avoid is this: A capitalist society depends on non-capitalist values in order to hold together and prosper.

If the problem is cast this way, the purpose of progressivism is not to use government to undermine the free market, but precisely the opposite: to create the social conditions in which the market can work well in its proper sphere.

E.J. DIONNE *is a columnist with the Washington Post Writers' Group. Excerpted with permission from* Woodstock Report, *No. 46, June 1996.*

may get a higher protein diet than the children. Government needs to intervene even at some efficiency cost, for the sake of equity.

Even critics like James Pinkerton, who worked in the Bush White House, concede that the private sector could not have defeated Hitler or built the interstate highway system.[5] Similarly, Speaker Gingrich admits that only the federal government (as opposed to state and local bodies) had the ability to dismantle the Jim Crow system of racial segregation.[6] The U.S. elderly poverty rate has fallen dramatically since the indexing of Social Security benefits and the implementation of Medicare, Medicaid and Supplemental Security Income. Other highly successful federal government programs include environmental protection efforts, programs of the Centers for Disease Control and Prevention and the "GI Bill," which put higher education and home ownership within reach for millions of people.[7]

Ending hunger and dramatically *reducing poverty* in the United States should be a major national priority on the order of defeating fascism, banning racial discrimination, or achieving a well educated and decently sheltered populace. Hence, we believe that national goals and standards are imperative, although some strategies and implementation might well be better designed by, or in greater cooperation with, state and local jurisdictions and civic organizations (see "The State of Our Civil Union").

● Another point on which welfare critics make a strong case is the pervasiveness of crime and insecurity in low-income communities, what Pinkerton calls a culture of "dealers, dope and drivebys."[8] He writes, "We are disuniting into a society of program traders, Think Pads and the Internet at one extreme – and crack, Uzis and three-strikes-you're out on the other."[9] The U.S. prison population exceeds 1 million, the world's largest. Murder is the leading cause of death among African American males aged 18-34.[10] As troubling as these statistics are,

it is important to keep them in perspective. White collar crime and tax evasion cost the United States billions of dollars each year. Too many business people regularly skirt legal and ethical limits. Smoking is said to contribute to the death of 350,000 people in the United States each year. Alcoholism and other drug use impose huge costs on private and public health care resources. Poor people in inner cities are not the only people in the United States who need to behave more responsibly.

Pinkerton argues – correctly, in our view – that greater economic security is the key to breaking the links between poverty and vulnerability. Decent jobs, at decent pay, are at the heart of secure lives and secure communities (see Chapter 4). Pinkerton also calls for stronger law enforcement.[11] Equally important are efforts to engage people affected by crime in preventing it such as community policing (where police officers become an integral part of a neighborhood, working closely with residents) and neighborhood watch committees. Families, schools and communities have primary responsibility to educate and enforce norms of behavior.[12]

● Anti-hunger and poverty programs are expensive, although the Heritage Foundation's $5.4 trillion estimate of the cost of the *War on Poverty* is probably exaggerated.[13] Pinkerton chides welfare state supporters for arguing that anti-poverty programs are merely underfunded rather than acknowledging their failures.[14]

We concede little on arguments that anti-poverty programs have been allocated sufficient resources, or that they have in the main failed.

Federal food programs have reduced serious malnutrition in the United States, but food stamp allotments are still based on the miserly Thrifty Food Plan, which was designed to meet short-term food emergencies rather than provide adequate nutrition over an extended period. Numerous studies have praised Head Start and the Special Supplemental Nutrition Program for

Hunger is a problem which is easy in an industrial democracy to fix. Other industrialized democracies don't have a widespread hunger problem like we do, and if our politicians would stop all of the ideological bickering, and if they would actually provide leadership – Democrats and Republicans, the White House and Congress – we could come together and end hunger in America in a matter of six to eight months.

DR. J. LARRY BROWN *is director of the Tufts University Center on Hunger, Poverty and Nutrition Policy.*

Women, Infants and Children (WIC) as effective, but these programs still lack adequate funding to enroll everyone who is eligible. Even the much maligned Aid to Families with Dependent Children (AFDC) program continues to serve its original purpose – as a bridge across a family emergency – for the great majority of its recipients. Each of these, and other programs for low-income families, have flaws that need remedial attention. But to label them failures is wrong.

Relatively modest improvements in federal nutrition programs could virtually eliminate hunger in the United States – at a cost on the order of $10 billion per year. In 1996, Congress gave the Pentagon $7 billion more than it requested. That extra, unwanted dollop to the military would have contributed to wiping out much of the country's hunger for a year.

● Our sharpest disagreement is with critics who argue that welfare programs are a principal cause of poverty and hunger in the United States. The overwhelming evidence is that poverty creates the need for AFDC and other safety net programs, and not the converse. While a small number of parents may be "coasting" on AFDC, a large group of researchers concluded in 1994, "The empirical evidence shows that single-parent families are *not* a primary cause of poverty in the United States."[15]

The national debate, therefore, should focus on helping families to escape poverty – whether or not they are on welfare. Efforts in this direction include improved education and work skills, full-employment policies

and protection of worker rights, minimum wage policies or enhanced work subsidies, public service employment on useful projects, assured health care and a range of community services, particularly child care. This case is more fully argued in Bread for the World Institute's occasional paper, *Let's Get Real About Welfare.*[16]

The labor market does not and cannot meet everyone's needs. Some people have disabilities that make it impossible for them to support themselves. Some are too young or too old to earn their own way. Many of us believe that society would be better off if at least one parent could stay at home with infant children. With 5 percent of the work force officially unemployed – as a presumed condition for controlling inflation – it would be impossible to put to work all those on AFDC who wish to work unless governments became employers of last resort.

Two Views of Poverty[17]

Two views about the main causes of poverty underlie much of the current debate. On one side are those who see poor people's behavior, and particularly the rise in out-of-wedlock births among low-income young women, as the key issue. On the other side are those who see changes in the economy as most critical.

The Behavioral Argument

The behavioralists argue that since 1965, the United States has spent trillions of dollars on anti-poverty programs; the results: increased rates of out-of-wedlock births, higher dependency on welfare (one child in eight lives in an AFDC family) and escalating costs. The child poverty rate rose 63 percent between 1973 and 1993.

Critics say that welfare programs encourage the erosion of the work ethic and family values by subsidizing idleness and single parenthood. They also contend that welfare discourages people from accumulating savings and other assets. The critics see "illegitimacy" as the cause of poverty, crime, drug abuse, illiteracy and homelessness. Children who grow up in single-parent families, the critics claim, are more likely to do poorly in school, commit suicide, abuse drugs, have out-of-wedlock children of their own, receive welfare as adults and engage in criminal behavior. And, in this view, AFDC encourages out-of-wedlock births.[18]

Living in a single-parent household can certainly be hazardous to a child's well-being. Births to unmarried teenagers, especially, can frequently present serious economic and social problems for both mother and child. In 1994, the poverty rate for female-headed households was 35 percent, compared to the overall rate of 14.5 percent. Reasons for the gap include lower pay for women workers and an inadequate system for enforcing child support payments by absent fathers. The psychological and social consequences to which the critics point are also real.

Moreover, out-of-wedlock births *have* increased in the United States:

- Between 1970 and 1990, the out-of-wedlock birthrate rose by nearly 67 percent, the proportion of two-parent families declined from 87 percent to 72 percent and the proportion of female-headed single-parent families rose from 11.5 percent to 24 percent;
- Between 1976 and 1992, the proportion of never-married mothers nearly tripled;
- In 1993, 5.5 million children lived with never-married mothers; 7 percent of them lived with teen-age mothers; and
- Teen-agers gave birth to nearly 30 percent of the out-of-wedlock babies in 1992.

But the increase in out-of-wedlock births is a global trend, not limited to poor teen-agers in the United States. Moreover, more than 65 percent of the increase in U.S. single-parent families has occurred in households with incomes above the poverty line. Since 1970, the poverty rate for children living in single-parent families has remained virtually unchanged. Between 1982 and 1992, the proportion of never-married women with graduate or professional degrees who had borne a child nearly doubled; the proportion with bachelor's degrees more than doubled.[19]

Several social and economic factors may be contributing to the increase in single-parent families:

- Changes in social norms among all income groups have reduced the stigma of out-of-wedlock births;
- Labor force participation has increased and the economic status of women has improved; and
- Education and employment prospects have declined for low-income young people.

Studies have found that the rise in out-of-wedlock births to teen-agers stems partly from lack of faith in the future. When young people have reasons to view their futures with optimism, they are more likely to wait until completing school to marry or have children. But diminished employment prospects deter marriage and lead to higher rates of cohabitation and out-of-wedlock births. A study of 37 industrial countries found that higher poverty and income inequality in the United States accounted for the higher teen-age and out-of-wedlock birth rates. A study of female African American teen-agers found that awareness of future economic opportunities led to large decreases in out-of-wedlock birthrates.

Low-income men with a high school diploma or less education cannot earn enough to support a family or offset the loss of AFDC benefits that would follow marriage. Also, high unemployment and incarceration rates for African American males contribute to the African American out-of-wedlock birthrate of 67 percent.[20]

AFDC has a negligible influence on the growth of single-parent families. Out-of-wedlock birthrates are higher in states with lower AFDC benefit levels. Also, in countries with more generous family allowances, teen-age birthrates and child poverty rates are lower than in the United States.

There is no reliable evidence that AFDC recipients have children simply to obtain increased benefits. This is not surprising, since combined AFDC and food stamp benefits in the median state only brought a

FIGURE 3.1

Share of Aggregate Household Income
By Income Quintile, 1974-1994

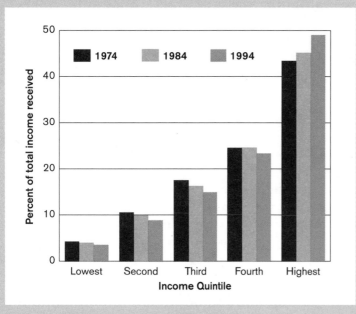

Source: Center on Hunger, Poverty and Nutrition Policy; U.S. Census Bureau.

FIGURE 3.2

Share of Aggregate Household Net Worth
By Income Quintile, 1984-1993

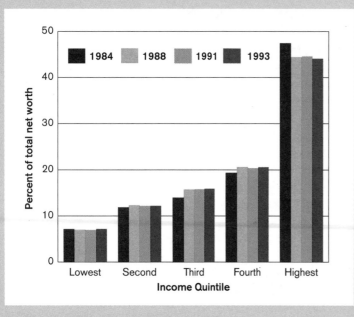

Source: Center on Hunger, Poverty and Nutrition Policy; U.S. Census Bureau.

family to 69 percent of the poverty line in 1994. The purchasing power of these benefits declined by 27 percent between 1972 and 1993. AFDC payments increase by an average of just $70 per month for a second or third child and less for additional children. A study of New Jersey's "family cap," which denies increased AFDC benefits to enrolled mothers who have additional children, found that it had no effect on birthrates. Contrary to stereotypes, about 75 percent of AFDC families nationally have only one or two children. Among low-income single women who were themselves raised in single-parent families, the size of welfare benefits has no significant influence on first births, subsequent births or out-of-wedlock births.[21]

In sum, efforts to restrict or sharply reduce AFDC benefits are unlikely to affect the rate of out-of-wedlock births. But such changes in policy *are* likely to cause increased poverty and vulnerability to hunger among U.S. children.

In any event, the majority of children of single parents do not succumb to the host of social pathologies identified by welfare critics. Most finish high school, remain law-abiding citizens and do not go on welfare. Few AFDC families become long-term dependents on assistance. Between 67 percent and 75 percent leave the program within two years, although they may return periodically between low-wage jobs or when confronted by medical emergencies.

The Economic Change Argument

The alternate view is that poverty stems from economic forces largely beyond the control of poor people.

Inequality Up, Wages Down. Both income and wealth distribution in the United States are glaringly uneven (see Figures 3.1 and 3.2):

- In 1993, the bottom 20 percent of income earners received 4 percent of all income and owned 7 percent of all wealth. In contrast, the top 20 percent received 49 percent of the income and owned 44 percent of the wealth;

- The income shares of the bottom 40 percent declined from 15 percent in 1974 to 13 percent in 1994, while those of the top 20 percent rose from 44 percent to 49 percent; and
- Between 1980 and 1990, the increased income of the wealthiest 2.5 million people in the United States equaled the total income of the poorest 50 million.

A variety of economic, social and demographic factors have affected the growth of inequality. These include the rise in the proportion of mainly female-headed single-parent families and declining real value of public assistance benefits noted above, as well as:

- Changes in labor markets, especially the long-term downward trend in the real wages of younger male workers;
- The continuing shift of jobs out of manufacturing into service industries, where most jobs available to less-educated, less-skilled workers are low-wage jobs;
- Within manufacturing, high rates of growth in high-technology industries that require highly skilled workers;
- The widening gap between the earnings of well-educated and poorly educated workers;
- Declining unionization and increased management control over decisions about the location of work and who gets hired or fired;
- Severe erosion of job security, with many jobs now part-time, temporary or contractual, without health insurance or other benefits;
- Greater globalization of labor and product markets, along with widespread relocation of production to low-wage developing countries, rapid growth in the world labor force and stronger preferences among U.S. consumers for low-priced imported consumer goods produced with low-wage foreign labor;
- Increases in the price of stock and other financial assets (which form the bulk of asset holdings of upper-income persons) relative to the price of houses and cars (the main types of assets owned by low- and middle-income persons); and
- An increase in the number of workers (because of immigration and the presence of "baby boomers" in the work force), which puts downward pressure on wages.

The decline in real wages and other economic factors related to employment, wages and attainment of work skills are the primary causes of poverty in the United States, not the rise in out-of-wedlock births.

During the 1960s, rapid economic growth and the expansion of the federal government's anti-poverty efforts led to a significant decline in poverty: from more than 22 percent of the population in 1959 to 11.7 percent in 1979. Child poverty dropped 45 percent between 1959 and 1969. However, since 1980, overall poverty has varied between 12.8 percent and 15.1 percent, generally lagging behind economic growth.

Between 1960 and 1991, the U.S. economy experienced six recessions. Normally, unemployment drops within 18 months of recovery from a recession. However, unemployment continued to rise during the 18 months that followed the 1990-1991 recession. Cutbacks in unemployment insurance in the 1980s at both the federal and state levels caused the proportion of unemployed workers receiving benefits to drop to record low levels.

Rising shelter and utilities costs have had a dramatic impact on U.S. livelihood security. In the 1970s, energy prices rose substantially, while in the 1980s, real estate speculation intensified rising shelter costs. Federal spending on low-income housing dropped by 80 percent between 1978 and 1988. By 1985, 45 percent of poor households spent 70 percent or more of their incomes on housing.

Rising health care and health insurance costs have also put a squeeze on low-income people, particularly working poor families. Only 22 percent of workers earning less than $5 per hour receive health insurance through their employer. In all, 42 million people in the United States lack health insurance.[22] Most jobs held by recent recipients of AFDC do not include health insurance coverage. While an adult might be willing to gamble with her health, few mothers are willing to deprive their children of access to health care.

Wealth Insurance. Government policies have contributed to the widening gap between rich and poor people, a clear affront both to economic and political justice, since money and power walk hand in hand. A just society seeks preferential treatment of people who have been disadvantaged, rather than those who have enormous advantages.

The Federal Reserve Board (the U.S. central bank) aims to keep at least 5 percent of the work force unemployed, because it gives lower priority to jobs and growth than to low inflation and high interest rates. This helps keep the nation competitive in the global economy. Low inflation and high interest rates are also especially important to people with money, while a full-employment economy is especially important to people who have a hard time finding a job that pays a living wage. Chapter 4 shows how governments establish competitive policies in order to bring in investments. Some of these policies are self-defeating. The chapter argues for more cooperation among governments and policies that, at the same time, support long-term economic growth and decent incomes for all people.

Federal tax policies likewise benefit middle-income and wealthy people, as well as corporations. Taxpayers are allowed to deduct from their taxable income mortgage interest paid for owner-occupied, rental and vacation homes and defer capital gains on home sales. Nearly 90 percent of mortgage interest deductions go to taxpayers with annual incomes over $50,000. Wealthy individuals and families also claim large deductions annually for charitable contributions, employer contributions to health care, contributions to retirement accounts and state and local property taxes. Corporations deduct large sums in the form of depreciation and capital gains deductions.

In 1993, tax deductions, credits and deferrals cost the federal government an estimated $400 billion in revenues, equivalent to 29 percent of federal government spending. The eight largest of these "tax expenditures" were the deductions for mortgage interest, capital gains, pension contributions and earnings, real estate taxes, state and local taxes, charitable contributions, medical expenses and employer health insurance contributions that, together, totaled $216 billion. One-third of these benefits went to the wealthiest 5 percent of taxpayers, while just 7 percent went to the bottom 52 percent.

That same year, the federal government spent nearly $600 billion on programs that mainly benefit non-poor, middle class and wealthy people. These include Medicare, Social Security, government retirement benefits, Unemployment Compensation, farm price supports and veterans' benefits. This spending accounted for nearly 43 percent of federal outlays.

In contrast, spending on benefits for poor and near-poor people amounted to $162 billion, or 12 percent of federal outlays, and went to 26 percent of the U.S. population. These programs included guaranteed student loans, Medicaid, food stamps, child nutrition programs, the Earned Income Tax Credit (EITC), Supplemental Security Income for disabled and elderly people, Child Support Enforcement and AFDC. Forty percent of those receiving assistance were children and 43 percent lived below the poverty line.

Finally, the federal government helps protect some of the assets of people who have them. The Federal Deposit Insurance Corporation protects depositors' accounts and reduces the disruptions caused by bank failures. The Securities and Exchange Commission has broad powers over public stock offerings and markets.

For many of the millions of people with incomes near or below the poverty line, savings and investment are luxuries. For these families, almost all income pays for the basic necessities of life. Typically, poor households lose their eligibility for federal assistance if they save more than $1,000 or have any significant tools or equipment to help them make a living.

The Role of Charities and Public-Private Partnerships

Some argue that it is the role of religious congregations and charities, not the government, to ensure that all our nation's children are fed. In fact, despite enormous growth in nonprofit organizations that serve hungry people, churches and charities cannot muster sufficient resources to address the magnitude of the problem.

People in the United States now support more than 150,000 private feeding agencies and give millions of volunteer hours to soup kitchens and food pantries. Congregations and private charities are unable to meet current needs, let alone to make up for the onslaught of demand that will be brought on by further cuts.

According to the U.S. Department of Agriculture (USDA), the cuts in food stamp funding included in the 1996 welfare bill were five times larger than the value of food distributed annually by Second Harvest, the national food bank network.

Congregations and charities are already swamped by ever-expanding needs. They have come forward to warn Congress that they will not be able to handle the numbers of requests for

emergency assistance expected if the federal government curtails its benefits for poor people.

The Salvation Army, which served some 70 million meals in 1995, warned:

> We are aware that our programs are supplementary and complementary to government hunger programs that are working…. No private charity or consortium of private charities could match the current government nutrition programs' yearly expenditures….

A recent study of the trajectory of current giving patterns in the United States says that "the most optimistic estimates predict that contributions to charities might make up for only 5 percent of the federal cuts"; and even if charitable giving rose, only a small part would go to help poor people.[23] Well-off people give mainly to nonprofit organizations that serve their own purposes – their own congregations, schools and universities.

The 1996 welfare bill cut $3.5 billion from child nutrition programs and close to $28 billion from food stamps over six years. Anti-hunger and farm groups prevented block granting of school breakfast and lunch programs.

William Mills/Montgomery County Public Schools

Charitable contributions have accounted for 2 percent of personal income annually for many years. Critics insist that lower taxes, perhaps combined with enhanced tax incentives (credits as well as the present deduction) for charitable donations, could boost contributions. In the past, however, changes in economic conditions and tax policy have not influenced the rate of giving.

Also, charities presently rely heavily on federal dollars for their work. Almost half the $87 billion charities will spend in 1996 will come from federal funds. So federal cutbacks would most likely lead to reduced services from charities.

The Temporary Emergency Food Assistance Program (TEFAP), for example, has already been providing commodities and funds to private feeding programs for more than a decade.

Religious institutions cannot pick up the slack either. The 350,000 local places of worship around the United States would each have to raise $171,000 during the next six years to make up the cuts in the 1996 welfare bill. This average figure understates the problem, since the heaviest burden is likely to fall on low-income, inner-city congregations. Also, when congregations are compelled to focus on feeding people and helping them obtain other basic necessities, they are distracted from fostering spiritual growth, cultural critique, political education and helping people cope with personal crises.

Critics call federal anti-poverty programs inflexibly rule-bound, controlled from afar and impersonal. But federal programs are not as soulless as the critics claim. For example, Head Start, the federal early childhood education program for low-income children, has a strong emphasis on volunteerism and community participation. No federal anti-poverty program is run day-to-day from Washington.

The federal government should expand its partnerships with nonprofit programs. It should also offer increased flexibility to the nonprofit organizations to carry out appropriate and holistic community-based programs.

The federal government has also sponsored an extremely creative effort to increase poor families' market-based food choices through the WIC Farmers Market Program, which allows WIC families to buy fresh produce using government coupons. This also boosts the income of often struggling family farms. States can choose whether or not they wish to participate.

Some other examples of partnerships, large and small[24]:

- Focus: HOPE, a civil rights organization in Detroit, has established one of the most remarkable job-training programs in the United States. It has taken over a block of abandoned factories, and, mobilizing millions of dollars in federal government funds (from the Departments of Commerce, Labor and Education), has converted them into ultramodern robotics factories where city youngsters – mostly from poor, African American neighborhoods – learn advanced technical skills that will make them competitors for high-skilled, high-paying jobs. Graduates emerge as skilled technician-engineers, competent to operate, maintain, repair and modify the most modern automated manufacturing systems. Retired machinists help run an apprenticeship program, which trains young workers in precision machining and metal working. A Focus: HOPE factory employs single mothers to rebuild automobile transmissions for a profit. The organization also offers participants opportunities to gain college degrees and remedial mathematics and literacy training. It provides surplus federal government food to over 70,000 low-income senior citizens, mothers and young children, along with nutrition education.

- "Shop and Ride" in Knoxville, TN, links nonprofit organizations, business and the city's federally funded transit authority. Anyone taking the bus to a grocery store may ask for a voucher. When stamped to prove the purchase of $10 worth of groceries, the voucher provides a free bus ride home. This helps low-income people afford to travel beyond the small, poorly stocked and overpriced stores in the inner-city to large suburban supermarkets.

- In New York City, the Food and Hunger Hotline has established One City Cafe, which offers low-cost, nutritious meals to both food stamp and cash customers; most restaurants will not accept food stamps. The program also offers job training and employment for homeless and formerly homeless people.

- The National Hunger Clearinghouse, funded by USDA, is a new project of World Hunger Year. It will connect thousands of groups working on hunger, food, nutrition and agriculture issues, with an emphasis on self-reliance as a permanent remedy for hunger and poverty. Using modern computer and telecommunications technology coupled with the personal touch, the clearinghouse will develop a database of over 30,000 organizations, government entities and individuals. The database will be accessible through the Internet, on the World Wide Web and by an "800" number.

Shifting Control to the States

The 1996 Welfare Act

This law will shift federal AFDC dollars to state governments as block grants. The states have considerable freedom to use this money in different ways. The bill encourages states to try to move people from welfare to work, so many states will curtail outright assistance to help subsidize employment – job training programs, for example, or payments to companies that hire welfare recipients. The limits that this law places on the states are mainly restraints on generosity. They have to stop assistance to 80 percent of welfare recipients within five years, for example.

Anti-hunger and farm interests worked together in 1995 and 1996 to protect the federal nutrition programs from block granting. Food stamps are the biggest federal nutrition program, and they will continue to provide a minimal "safety net under the safety net" as states experiment with welfare. Families get about $1 more in food stamps for every $3 cut from AFDC. So if welfare "reform" leads to increased poverty, as we expect, federal spending on food stamps will increase sharply.

It will take some years for the effects of the 1996 welfare bill to become fully apparent. It mandates spending cuts of $60 billion over six years, with the cuts increasing in size each year. Federal AFDC payments will, in fact, go up in 1997, because they will be based on an average of payments to the state over the previous four years. It will then take state governments some time to decide what to do with their new freedom, and there is always a lapse between political decisions and their implementation. No one can fully predict how state governments will modify assistance to poor families over time. The law's supporters are optimistic that state governments will be creative and responsive to local circumstances. But the historical record (see Chapter 2) is that states varied widely – and that many did poorly – before national standards and funding began.

We expect that many states will use their flexibility under the new welfare law in ways that will further hurt poor people. Some states are likely to be especially harsh. So the welfare bill of 1996 may well contribute to substantial increases in hunger.

What States Have Done So Far

Over the last few years, the states have already moved ahead with their own versions of welfare reform. They have changed or cut their own programs, and the Clinton administration has granted many waivers from federal requirements to encourage state experimentation.

A number of states have already cut their own assistance programs. The results have been documented in Michigan, for example.

Michigan Ends General Assistance.
Michigan ended its state-funded General Assistance program in 1991. Despite claims that recipients would find employment and private support, self-sufficiency has proved elusive. Only 38 percent of former recipients interviewed for a recent study found formal employment, at an average wage of $5.56 per hour for a 35-hour work week. Recipients are vulnerable to food and livelihood insecurity. Only half had health benefits, and half indicated that their health had deteriorated following the loss of assistance. About 67 percent were able to continue receiving food stamps, however. Only a third received help from private charities, usually for food. Demand for space in homeless shelters in Detroit greatly outstripped supply.

The study concluded that

> the vast majority of former recipients were still living on the edge of subsistence. By any stretch of the imagination, these people remain exceedingly poor, and their economic precariousness is complicated further by significant health and psychological deterioration.[25]

AFDC Waivers.[26] The state welfare reform plans that have been approved or proposed to the federal government are a mixed bag for poor people. Some states have sought time limits on benefits, a ban on increased benefits to children born to welfare mothers and the curtailment of state help with child care, education and job training. These provisions reduce families' incomes and make it harder for them to develop assets that they need to escape poverty. States have also obtained waivers from the federal government enabling them to reduce or eliminate benefits if recipients fail to comply with various requirements. If not implemented carefully, these provisions are also likely to do more harm than good.

On the positive side, some states have sought to permit AFDC recipients to earn and save more without losing benefits and to obtain education and job skills. Proposed and approved waiver provisions of this sort include:

- Providing child care benefits for recipients attending school, undergoing job training or working (including for some time after AFDC eligibility status changes);
- Using AFDC and food stamp benefits to supplement wages;
- Easing restrictions on asset ownership and the value of cars;
- Letting recipients create special accounts to help finance education or job searches;
- Providing incentives for the start-up of small businesses (Virginia and New York); and
- Requiring recipients to enter into contracts or plans to achieve self-sufficiency.

The area of most prolific state experimentation is the transition from welfare to work. Twenty-one states have sought permission to impose sanctions on AFDC parents who fail to comply with work requirements. Several states are seeking to extend supportive services such as job training, education and child care beyond federal time and income limits once recipients begin working. Importantly, 10 states want to continue Medicaid or other health care services.

Six states want to extend job-related services to non-custodial parents of AFDC children. Such a provision could increase recipient families' overall earning capacity by making child support payments more stable.

Whether waiver provisions have beneficial effects on the lives of recipients will depend on the states' commitment to provide the services and resources necessary for the measures' success. Most waiver programs seem to be premised on the continuing availability of Medicaid, food stamps and other federal entitlements that can help AFDC parents make the transition into the work force. Drastic federal cuts will make the state experiments much less likely to help people get out of poverty.

Virginia Independence Plan. Virginia enacted one of the most comprehensive state-level welfare reforms, the Virginia Independence Plan, and received federal approval to implement the waivers in July 1995.[27] It bars increased benefits to additional children born to welfare mothers; requires most minor parents to live with their own parents or other relatives; insists that welfare mothers identify their children's fathers; requires absent parents (if not in school) to pay child support; and mandates school attendance for AFDC children and minor parents. The program relaxes restrictions on AFDC benefits for two-parent unemployed families. These provisions went into effect immediately on a state-wide basis. Mothers unable to identify their children's fathers brought a successful court challenge to the state's efforts to deny them benefits.

Over four years, the state will phase in a work component, the Virginia Initiative for Employment, Not Welfare (VIEW). VIEW took effect in the Washington, DC, suburbs (home to 25 percent of Virginia's population, including 12,000 welfare recipients) in April 1996. VIEW limits AFDC benefits to two consecutive years and a lifetime total of five years. Medicaid and food stamps can continue beyond these limits. AFDC parents must participate in work activities within 90 days of receiving benefits. These include unsubsidized private employment, subsidized employment reimbursed from AFDC and food stamp funds, part-time or temporary employment or unpaid community work experience. Localities may provide child care, Medicaid and transportation assistance if necessary for the parent to work. These services can continue one year beyond AFDC benefits. VIEW participants must sign a personal responsibility contract.

Welfare workers say that VIEW has changed their relationships with recipients. "I like very much the feeling that we're responsible together and that [the recipients] and I are going to come up with a plan" for self-sufficiency, said Karen Roberts, a Fairfax County caseworker. "Before, people come in and you ask them if they have their pieces of paper." She added that "most women are insisting they do want to work." Roberts worried about some aspects of the new policy such as permanent loss of benefits for women who fail to name their children's fathers and sanctions on those who leave jobs. Also, job options may be limited. "If you get a $5-an-hour job, you are going to have to take it," she told a former temporary agency manager who went on AFDC to support herself and her teen-age daughter after the agency went bankrupt. The woman hopes to find work paying at least twice that much.[28]

Community Ministry, an association of Northern Virginia churches engaged in advocacy on behalf of low-income people, is seeking to involve area congregations in mentoring welfare recipients. The program links recipients with small teams of mentors who provide counseling and other support for the transition into the work force.

Wisconsin Works. In April 1996, Wisconsin passed legislation called Wisconsin Works ("W-2"), aimed at abolishing AFDC in the state by 2000. Congressional Republicans' pressure on President Clinton to grant waiver approval to W-2 was a factor behind the federal welfare deal. The Wisconsin plan limits AFDC benefits to two consecutive years and a lifetime total of five years, with a family cap. Able-bodied parents must work or obtain job training in order to receive aid. The law provides for subsidized employment for many participants at sub-minimum wages. The state will provide child care and health care, depending on income levels. "The days of something for nothing are over," said Republican Wisconsin Governor Tommy G. Thompson at a bill-signing ceremony. Supporters say the program will encourage self-sufficiency in place of dependency. Critics say W-2 forces welfare recipients into low-paying jobs and their children into substandard day care.[29]

Milwaukee's Catholic Archbishop, Rembert G. Weakland, who himself grew up in a welfare family, denounced W-2, calling it "not welfare reform but welfare repeal." Weakland said that not everyone who wants to work will be able to earn "a family wage." Under such circumstances, he added, "[I]t is unwise and unjust for the federal government to abandon its commitment to the poor."[30]

The implementation of a welfare-to-work "demonstration project" in Milwaukee suggests that W-2 is neither flexible nor empowering for poor people. One recipient, Colleen Braam, enrolled in a medical assistant training course, but lost her AFDC benefits because she did not attend a "job orientation" class sponsored by the county. Linda Wernette worries about how she will juggle work and caring for a disabled son. Brenda Dates lost one job for failing to list a nine-year-old welfare fraud conviction on her application, and was rejected for a new job when she did mention the conviction. Her "crime": failing to tell welfare officials that she had a $50-a-week cleaning job while on AFDC.

Strategies to Defend Poor People

People living in poverty are politically weak. Passage of the welfare law of 1996 suggests that low-income people and their allies have lost some of whatever influence they once had.

The law makes it yet more difficult for low-income people, and their allies, to defend their interests. It scatters the debate about poverty among state and territorial governments, as well as the national government. Prosperous people and well-funded interests can defend themselves in state legislatures. But poor people will not be well represented during many crucial decisions ahead.

There is a great need for concerned people to redouble their political work, adapt to the current political environment and maximize their effectiveness.

Speaking Up in State Capitals

In general, low-income people are even less well represented in state capitals than in Washington, DC.

Some low-income community organizations and welfare rights groups encourage low-income people to speak for themselves in state capitals. Many churches, synagogues and charities support low-income interests. The Roman Catholic Church and ecumenical Protestant organizations are often active, and the Lutheran church also maintains a network of state advocacy offices. There are hunger coalitions and child advocacy organizations in many states. In some states, assistance agencies have formed coalitions.

The accompanying case study looks at the Pennsylvania Coalition on Food and Nutrition (see page 51). Because of a reduction in federal funding for nutrition education, they must cut back on their activities. But they have decided to focus a larger share of their reduced budget on advocacy.

A recent study of state level advocacy for children shows that many state legislators are ill-informed about the situation of children and families in their states and about policies and programs that could help. Legislators are not very aware of child advocacy groups either.[31]

About 45 state-level hunger organizations and 90 local leaders and organizations are part of the Campaign to End Childhood Hunger, in partnership with the Food Research and Action Center (FRAC). These groups have won legislative victories in Washington and in some states. They have recently formed regional coalitions to strengthen their work, and they are developing model state legislation and methods to measure the impact of welfare reform on hunger.

Some national organizations provide various types of information and assistance to state-level advocates. These include FRAC; the Center on Hunger, Poverty and Nutrition Policy at Tufts University; the National Association of Child Advocates; the Center on Budget and Policy Priorities; and Bread for the World Institute.

Speaking Up at the National Level

Passage of the welfare law dramatizes the need for a stronger voice for hungry and poor people in national politics. Further attacks on federal efforts to assist low-income people are in the offing. On the other hand, national leaders could make positive changes. They could correct mistakes in the welfare law of 1996 or, in other ways, help to overcome hunger and poverty.

In recent decades, myriad interests have organized themselves to influence Washington decisions. Washington is now a honeycomb of lawyers and lobbyists, associations, pressure groups and ideological think tanks. About 8,500 of the 12,000 lobbyists, consultants and lawyers listed in *Washington Representatives* work for U.S. or foreign corporations. The main counterweight is a cluster of public interest groups who speak up for the environment and other causes. These include groups such as the World Wildlife Fund, Common Cause and Handgun Control. They also include organizations such as FRAC and the Center on Budget and Policy Priorities, which work on hunger and poverty issues.

Citizens and groups across the country who communicate with their own representatives in Congress are especially influential. They write letters, meet with their members of Congress, speak to churches and other groups, and get the issues covered by local media. Bread for the World is the largest grassroots anti-hunger advocacy network.

Electoral Politics

We must also elect representatives who are committed to overcoming hunger. Citizens can contribute time and money to parties and candidates – and then vote – with an eye to justice for poor and hungry people. Bread for the World's 1996 campaign, *Elect to End Childhood Hunger* (see page 8), has asked candidates for Congress to commit themselves to support legislation to help overcome childhood hunger.

Campaign finance reform has been repeatedly shelved in Congress. But reducing the

A Pennsylvania Case Study

by Kathleen Daugherty

A network of state advocacy organizations across the country helps to defend low-income people who are hungry or at risk of hunger.

The Pennsylvania Coalition on Food and Nutrition (PCFN) is Pennsylvania's statewide anti-hunger organization. It currently has a five-person staff that engages in advocacy, education and research within a network of human service providers and agencies, including religious organizations and denominations.

PCFN has mobilized its network around both federal and state legislation. Its state victories include Pennsylvania funding for the Special Supplemental Nutrition Program for Women, Infants and Children and a state fund for hunger relief.

Since its beginning in 1977, PCFN has been funded largely with federal dollars from the Community Food and Nutrition Program, a separately authorized portion of a federal block grant for community action agencies across the country. Its budget has been vulnerable to moods in Congress. PCFN is now struggling to make up for a swift cut in its federal funding, from two-thirds of its 1995-1996 budget to one-third of its 1996-1997 budget.

The likelihood of reduced federal funding for all human service work has convinced PCFN to spend more of its energy looking for local solutions to hunger and poverty. This includes efforts to empower low-income Pennsylvanians and to build new public-private partnerships. PCFN has cultivated a closer relationship with the office of the governor. This does not preclude disagreements with the administration, but it has created a relationship of trust within which disagreement can take place.

PCFN staff continue to work to increase public awareness of and participation in federal child nutrition programs such as the School Breakfast and Summer Food Programs. However, two new programs are commanding increasing levels of attention. "Super Cupboards" were invented in Pennsylvania, and PCFN is promoting the idea. A Super Cupboard helps regular clients for emergency food develop skills and attitudes for self-reliance. PCFN has also established a statewide "800" number telephone service to provide information on the closest emergency food sites and locations for the Summer Food Program.

KATHLEEN DAUGHERTY *is executive director of the Pennsylvania Coalition on Food and Nutrition and a member of Bread for the World Institute's board of directors.*

sway of moneyed interests would give politicians more incentive to pursue the common good.

It is also crucial to expand voter registration and political participation among the 24 million eligible voters with incomes below the poverty line.[32] Legislation on voting rights and eased registration rules have led to more widespread political participation. Eleven million new voters have joined the rolls since 1993, including 1.3 million who registered or updated their registration at public assistance agencies.[33] On the other hand, recent Supreme Court decisions on congressional redistricting have eroded the political power of racial minority voters, who are disproportionately low-income.

Shifting Effort to the Politics of Hunger

People in the United States are concerned about hunger. More than half contribute to hunger relief. More than a million volunteer in food assistance agencies. More than two-thirds of all the religious congregations in the country have programs to help hungry people. As the new welfare regime leads to yet more hunger and poverty – not immediately, but visibly within a few years – we can expect new rounds of "emergency" food drives.

Some of the effort devoted to helping hungry people would have more impact if it were redirected toward the politics of hunger. In *Transforming the Politics of Hunger: Hunger 1994*, Bread for the World Institute highlights seven high-impact areas for action:

1. Individuals and organizations that assist hungry people can expand what they do to influence government policies.

2. Religious communities can teach how social concern flows from a relationship with God and help motivate involvement in effective political action.

3. Low-income people's organizations can be strengthened, especially in their capacity to influence government policies that affect them.

4. Organizations that help low-income people can more fully engage people of color, especially in decision making.

5. The media can move beyond stories of pity and charity to explain the causes of hunger, and people and organizations concerned about hunger can make a bigger effort to influence the media.

6. People can expand and strengthen anti-hunger advocacy organizations.

7. People and organizations working against poverty and hunger can become aware of themselves as parts of a large, potentially dynamic movement.[34]

We have made some progress since 1994 in building cooperation among anti-hunger organizations. A number of the national anti-hunger networks expect to begin 1997 with a shared campaign of assistance, education and legislation to reduce hunger among U.S. children.

Toward Genuine Welfare Reform

Immediate Goals

Welfare reform at the state level, based on the experience of administrative waivers to date, should generate useful experiments in increasing employment and training opportunities and in improved delivery of services. State-level advocates and grassroots organizations can help develop positive innovations.

But most states will probably not provide enough resources to maintain adequate levels of assistance, let alone help employable people into jobs. Some states will further reduce already inadequate standards or introduce harsh provisions. Such negative decisions must be prevented, as states develop their versions of welfare reform and economic downturns intensify the pressure on resources.

At the national level, the continuing onslaught against government efforts to reduce poverty and hunger must be resisted. On the other hand, national leaders could moderate the welfare law of 1996. They should remove the ban on assistance to legal immigrants and restore the cuts in food stamps. Adequate funding for jobs programs would make the rhetoric about moving people from welfare to work a bit more realistic.

The federal government should monitor and evaluate how states respond to the welfare law of 1996 and its impact on poverty and hunger. Even supporters of the law admit that it is a massive and risky experiment, but the law made no provision for monitoring and evaluation.

Finally, there may be opportunities to expand effective federal programs – such as WIC, Head Start and Job Corps – that have not been block granted.

Ending Hunger and Reducing Poverty

The nation should commit itself to ending hunger and reducing poverty, and genuine welfare reform should move us in that direction. Individual and private voluntary activities make important and creative contributions to ending hunger and poverty, but cannot succeed on their own.

As Bread for the World Institute argues in *Let's Get Real About Welfare*, progress against hunger and poverty requires two types of government policies. First, government policies should establish a framework in which people can secure their own livelihoods; part of good governing is to create opportunity. Second, governments must ensure that basic needs are met for people who cannot secure their own livelihoods.

Creating Opportunity. Welfare critics are correct that poor people (along with everyone else) need to make good choices. Most poor people work hard to be self-reliant, but many cannot find jobs that support their families.

Overcoming poverty and hunger will require national economic policies that foster full employment and decent jobs. Reasonable taxes and regulations would give businesses more incentives to produce and generate jobs, and national economic management could also put more emphasis on full employment. Governments can also help make sure that it pays to work through further increases in the minimum wage and the Earned Income Tax Credit. Enabling low-income parents to enter the job market will also require public investments in education and skills training, child care, health care and assistance with transportation costs.

A Floor of Economic Justice. For those who cannot work, and especially for all children, the federal government has a central role in ensuring a floor of economic justice, especially assuring access to enough food. Most families need help only during an emergency, some on a continuing basis.

Fortunately, efforts to dismantle the national nutrition programs as part of "welfare reform" have been successfully resisted. At some point, the national government must also reestablish a guarantee of minimal cash assistance to poor families with children.

Both the necessary level of commitment and effective implementation of government policies and programs will require ongoing political participation of citizens, including hungry and poor people themselves.

DR. MARC J. COHEN *is senior research associate and* DON REEVES *is economic policy analyst at Bread for the World Institute.*

CHAPTER 4

Employment, Governments and the Global Economy

by Isabelle Grunberg

Everyone has the right to a standard of living adequate for the health and well-being of himself and his family, including food, clothing, housing and medical care, [education] and necessary social services, and the right to security in the event of unemployment, sickness, disability, widowhood, old age or other lack of livelihood in circumstances beyond his control.

United Nations International Covenant on Economic, Social and Cultural Rights, Article 11

This essay is adapted from a longer paper, "Rival States, Rival Firms, How Do People Fit In? The Global Unemployment Challenge," *UNDP/ODS Discussion Paper* No. 4 (January 1996), published by the United Nations Development Programme, Office of Development Studies. The views expressed here are the author's and do not necessarily reflect those of UNDP. The longer paper is part of a series published by UNDP/ODS, intended to stimulate debate and further research on policy measures that would help foster progress toward sustainable development. The series centers around two themes:

● Consistency among economic growth, social objectives and environmental concerns; and

● A new framework for development cooperation, including a new relationship between private finance and development.

The essay was the topic for an April 1996 consultation cosponsored by UNDP/ODS, the Friedrich Ebert Stiftung-New York Office and Bread for the World Institute.

For more information regarding the Discussion Papers, contact UNDP/ODS, (212) 986-0376; for a summary of the consultation, contact Bread for the World Institute, (301) 608-2400.

Hungry people are nearly always poor. Secure livelihoods – including having enough food to permit active, healthy lives – usually depend on employment or self-employment. Therefore a principal role of governments regarding hunger is, in cooperation with families, communities and nongovernmental civic organizations, to establish a framework in which people can secure their own livelihoods, while ensuring that basic needs are met for people who cannot meet their needs themselves.

But the economy has gone global. Things as basic as the food on the breakfast table and the clothes on your back can, and do, come from anywhere. An increasing portion of economic activity is carried out across borders. Most economies are more "open" than they were 30 years ago. This can be measured, for example, in the increasing value of international trade as a proportion of national incomes, in the increasing level of foreign direct investment or in the volume of foreign exchange trading (see Figures 4.1, 4.2 and 4.3).

In many respects, we all benefit from globalization. Food choices are greater. Many necessities cost less. According to the World Bank, the real cost of food has dropped by three-quarters over the past half century, in part due to global competition. On the other hand, new jobs created by increased trade or new technologies may not be located in the same place as the old ones, or yield the same rewards. They almost certainly require new skills. As jobs change and move from one community or nation to another, security of employment and livelihoods are threatened.

Virtually every nation now relies on markets as the principal means of allocating resources, goods and economic opportunity. The prevailing wisdom is that the route to prosperity and well-being lies in increased trade, more reliance on private rather than government entities, deregulated labor markets, control over inflation and balanced budgets, based primarily on reduced government expenditures. Under these conditions, usually described as *economic liberalization*, the expectation is that economies and new opportunities will grow – "a rising tide will lift all boats."

Globalization and increased trade are in fact associated with great reductions in poverty and hunger in a number of countries – particularly in East and Southeast Asia, where governments have played a very active role in setting and implementing national goals. But globalization and trade, and the usual package of accompanying economic reforms, are also associated with persistent and increasing poverty and hunger in other countries, long-term declines in the prices for raw materials and tropical crops, lack of secure or decent jobs, environmental deterioration, weakened safety nets, and breakdown of traditional cultures and societies.

The global economy shows bright promise, but mixed results. Does it constitute a good environment to foster human development – a process of enlarging the choices for all people?[1] Will it do so in the long term? Should developing countries plan to "go global" in the expectation that they will reap substantial benefits for their peoples in the process? Can people in industrial countries enhance the benefits and reduce the costs of globalization? What lessons does history teach us?

Background

In the 1950s and 1960s, nations, and to some degree even states and localities, could effectively shape their own societies toward greater equity and opportunity. Governments could mandate minimum wages and safe working conditions or block monopolies.

Such policy autonomy is no longer possible. Global competition is pervasive and ruthless, between both companies and nations. Even once-dominant economic powers, including the United States, appear driven by competitive pressures to adopt policies not in their own longer-term self-interest, and often not in the interests of their workers. In country after country, rich and poor, job security declines, wages stagnate or fall, income disparities increase between high-skill and low-skill workers, and poor working conditions persist.

The global economy shows bright promise, but mixed results.

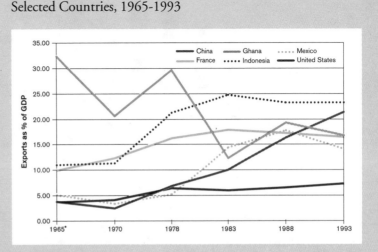

FIGURE 4.1

Increasing Trade
Selected Countries, 1965-1993

Indonesia data for 1967.
Source: World Bank; FAO.

FIGURE 4.2

Foreign Direct Investment
Selected Countries, 1965-1993

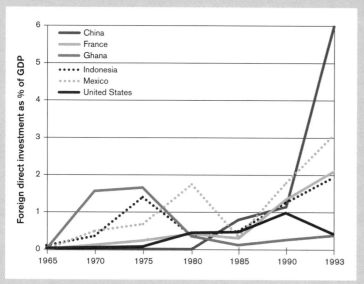

Source: World Bank.

FIGURE 4.3

Daily Global Currency Exchange Compared to World GDP
1977-1995

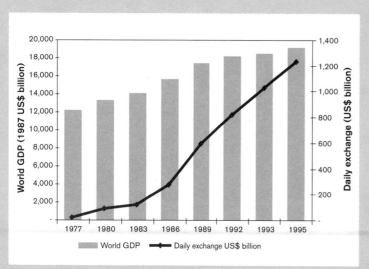

Note: 1995 GDP data estimated.
Source: World Bank.

In this setting, the need for effective government action to ensure that markets work efficiently, to minimize their ill effects and to create broader opportunities for secure livelihoods has increased, not diminished. Facing global competition and global corporations, new responses are both necessary and more difficult, since their success will require increased international cooperation among governments that are now in a competitive mode.

A Historical Perspective

The world was just as globalized at the end of the 19th century as it is now in terms of trade openness and international investments. In major industrial countries, for example, the ratio of merchandise trade to total production is often at a level similar to the one that prevailed in 1913. Between 1905 and 1914, capital flows in Britain were 6.6 percent of national income, larger than for any major industrial country in the 1980s and 1990s.[2] Why did we "go back" into a period of isolationism, with such disastrous consequences?

After World War I, governments tried to restore pre-war levels of openness, but without taking care of underlying imbalances — for example, the financial and monetary problems caused by debts and war reparations. In addition, no mechanism for coping with worldwide crises was operating. So a stock market crash in the United States degenerated into the Great Depression.[3] The collapse of most industrial economies led to widespread hardship and contributed to growing political extremism and nationalism, which eventually led again to global war.

Mindful of this last cycle of optimism regarding economic globalization, and the ensuing pain, is it possible to reap the benefits, and ensure that these benefits extend to everyone — particularly poor and hungry people? What are the real and suspected pitfalls or tradeoffs? How can they be avoided?

Globalization Since World War II

The process of economic globalization means that people take advantage of opportunities, hopefully to their mutual benefit. If money is scarce in a given country, yet could earn good returns because there are opportunities for business there, then allowing money to flow in will benefit everyone: the investor and the people who find employment in developing that business. If unemployment is high and wages low in an area, then moving garment production there creates needed jobs and lowers the cost of clothing for consumers, wherever they may be. The newly employed workers can afford more or better food, for example, or better schools and health care for their children. They may spend part of their new income on high-tech imports manufactured by better-educated former garment workers. Rapid economic change entails constant displacement, adjustment, mobility and retraining. But overall, the process should create a virtuous upward spiral.

And the fact is, since 1945, the world economy has grown at an unprecedented pace. Developed countries grew richer, and so did the developing world, including Africa. Remarkable gains were made in education and health care. For example, between 1960 and 1991, net enrollment in primary school in developing countries increased by nearly two-thirds – from 48 percent to 77 percent. The proportion of hungry people dropped by nearly half. Average life expectancy in these countries increased by more than a third between 1960 and 1993.[4] While far from universal, the benefits were widespread enough that most people were justified in bright expectations for their future, or at least that of their children.

Since the mid-1970s, however, strains have developed. The 1980s was a period of stagnation in most of Africa and Latin America, while the 1990s saw a dramatic fall in incomes in formerly communist countries. More than 100 countries, with populations totaling 1.5 billion people, experienced zero or negative growth of per capita income between 1980 and 1995.[5] There is no hard evidence that these strains are due to globalization per se, but serious questions have arisen about some possible consequences, or flaws, of globalization as it has developed.

Since World War II, the United States has enjoyed both economic prominence and political leadership. It engineered the postwar economic recovery, in particular through the creation of two international financial institutions during a conference at Bretton Woods, NH, in 1944. The International Monetary Fund was the main vehicle for maintaining currency values – principally in relationship to gold and the dollar – by making loans to countries that experienced balance of payments difficulties. The World Bank, created originally to reconstruct war-torn Europe, soon began making loans to poorer countries, many newly independent (see Chapters 5 and 6).[6]

As growth picked up, the world needed, and the United States issued, ever more dollars in comparison with the fixed amount of gold held in Fort Knox. The fixed gold-dollar parity became unsustainable. As a result, in 1971, the United States decided to de-link its currency from gold, in the process freeing all other currencies to float against each other. Thus ended the so-called Bretton Woods system. Even though that system was not sustainable in the long run, it provided, along with other national policies, a measure of predictability in international trade and finance. Shortly thereafter, in 1973, the Organization of Petroleum Exporting Countries (OPEC) dramatically raised the price of oil, which contributed to slower growth and inflationary pressures. Large oil revenues were deposited in Western banks, which in turn sought new venues for investment.

The World Bank and industrial-country governments encouraged poor countries to take out loans. Optimism prevailed about the benefits of increased world trade as the basis for making payments on the new loans. The seeds were planted for a massive debt crisis, which matured by the early 1980s.

The Successes of the Asian Tigers

Only a few developing economies were able to maintain the pace of widespread gains against hunger and poverty throughout the 1970s and 1980s, notably the "Tigers" of East Asia – South Korea, Taiwan, Hong Kong and Singapore – so called because of their aggressive pursuit of export-oriented economic growth. Their steady growth, which benefitted all their citizens, has been repeatedly pointed to as evidence that economic liberalization works.

The same set of policies are being held up as the model for three other groups of nations: (1) those that started the process somewhat later – Indonesia, Malaysia, Chile and Thailand, for example; (2) those that have gradually or abruptly abandoned communism and centrally planned economies – notably China, Vietnam, the former Soviet Union and Eastern Europe; and (3) those that floundered during the 1970s and 1980s – nearly all of sub-Saharan Africa and much of Latin America.

Yet a closer look at the Southeast Asian miracle shows that those countries adopted liberal economic policies incrementally. Repeatedly, especially during the early phases of their development, the central governments made crucial decisions, whether or not they matched signals from the global marketplace. They gave priority to heavy industries when assigning credit, for example, and maintained a strong emphasis on education for everyone.[7]

Increasingly, the conventional wisdom regarding liberalization – that "faster is better" – is being challenged. Other nations have suffered severely as they have attempted abrupt transitions to economic openness. Analysts point to two pairs of examples: Russia versus China among transition economies, and Chile versus Mexico among developing countries.

China, which has liberalized steadily but slowly since 1978, has not had any prolonged period of economic decline during its transition. It has enjoyed a more than 10 percent average annual growth rate in the last five years. Russia moved abruptly in 1989 and has seen a 9 percent average annual *decline* in the same period.[8]

Mexico, which completed liberalization of its economy in the second half of the 1980s, suffered a financial crisis in 1994. The economy has shrunk since then, and 40 million Mexicans were thrown into poverty (see Chapter 5, pages 75-78).[9] Chile, which has applied selective restrictions on short-term capital inflows since 1991, achieved exchange rate stability and average annual growth rates of 6.3 percent between 1990 and 1994.[10]

Beyond growth and other macro-indicators, how do globalization and liberalization affect the poorest people – those who have few assets, and whose income derives primarily from work?

Employment as a Key to Broader Social Concerns

Employment has a key place in social concerns, because it is the usual source of income with which people meet their basic needs, and also provides for social cohesion and individual accomplishment. Work often takes the form of self-employment, including activities in the informal sectors of the economy that may not be captured in official statistics.

There are many other social needs beyond full employment. Yet when employment is lacking, social instability threatens. Family and community bonds fray. The risk of crime increases. Employment is key to the capacity of governments to meet ongoing social needs such as education or safety nets for families unable to meet their own needs. If unemployment is high, tax receipts decline. Needs for social assistance rise.

At the same time, many resources that could be invested in education, infrastructure or permanent improvements are spent on meeting short-term needs or on unemployment benefits, if such programs exist. The countries of the European Union, for example, spend 2 percent of their gross domestic product (GDP) supporting unemployed people – nearly $150 billion per year. Unemployment payments alone account for almost half their budget deficits.

Public spending is necessary to ensure that markets work for people, not against them – for education and public infrastructure, for example, and not least for social safety nets. A competitive market economy creates winners and losers. It rewards the smartest and those who work hardest. Others fall behind. Real markets are often distorted to favor the rich and powerful. But people left out by the functioning or failures of the market should not be treated as "the worst human deadwood," to quote a recent article in *The Economist*.[11] This is dictated by compassion, by a moral imperative to respect all that is human, and pragmatically, not to waste human talents. Hence, in assessing the costs and benefits of globalization, it is important to focus on two main outcomes – employment and governments' capacities to alleviate social strains and poverty.

The Problem with Employment

Between 1960-1973 and 1988-1994, unemployment grew by a factor of 1.8 in Canada. It doubled in Italy and Japan, quadrupled in the United Kingdom, grew fivefold in France and increased by eight-and-a-half times in Germany.[12] The trend has been less severe in the United States, where the unemployment rate has fluctuated around 6 percent since the late 1980s. There, the loss has been qualitative, with a documented decline in real wages between 1990 and 1994, especially among lower-paid workers (see Figures 4.4 and 4.5).

FIGURE 4.4A

Unemployment
Selected Countries, 1960-1994

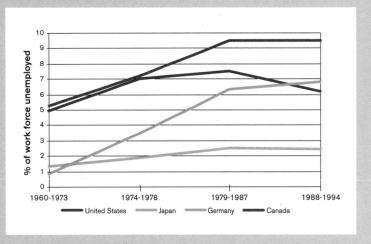

Source: United Nations.

FIGURE 4.4B

Declining Compensation
Selected Countries, 1961-1994

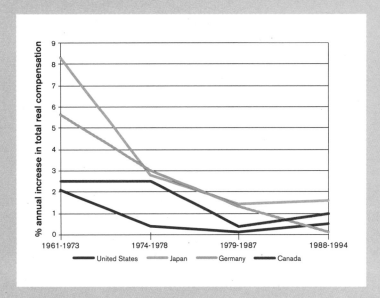

Source: United Nations.

FIGURE 4.5

Growing Wage Inequality
Selected Countries, 1979-1990

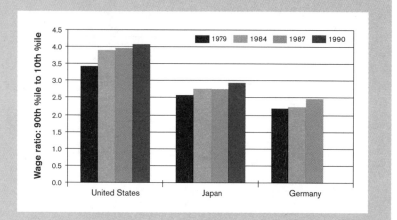

Note: 1990 data for Germany are not available.
Source: United Nations.

Five Causes of Slow Gains in Employment

Five factors have emerged as contributors or probable contributors to the stubborn persistence of unemployment in a global economy. The first two have had fairly broad attention and discussion: (1) lack of flexibility in labor markets – labor rules that were too rigid or too generous toward labor and thus discouraged new employment or the creation of new businesses; and (2) the combined effects of more competitive, expanding global trade and new labor-reducing technologies. Three other factors have received less attention: (3) uncertain and declining incomes leading to stagnating demand; (4) deflationary (growth-reducing) effects of governments' competition to gain market shares in the global economy and attract ever-mobile capital; and (5) the increasing volatility of interest and exchange rates.

The Myth of Labor Market Flexibility
Some argue that the cure for unemployment is increased labor market flexibility – letting minimum wages slip into irrelevance, for example, or a weakening of labor unions. That way, people would not price themselves out of work. Yet over the past 10 years, labor markets have become more "flexible" all over the world, with no overall improvement in employment rates. It seems that employment responds to many factors. Labor market flexibility may be one of them, but it is not the most important. In some instances it may be negligible. For example, Spain and Portugal have similar labor market regulations. Yet Spain has the highest unemployment rate in the European Union (24.4 percent), while Portugal has the second lowest (6.8 percent).

In instances where labor-related laws and regulations seem to have a role in explaining different rates of unemployment, these results have been obtained at a substantial social cost: declining wages for low-skilled workers in the United States and Great

Data on unemployment in developing countries are weak to nonexistent, but the best available estimates indicate similar trends. In sub-Saharan Africa, paid employment in manufacturing declined 0.5 percent per year during the 1980s. Urban unemployment now ranges between 15 percent and 20 percent, compared to around 10 percent in the mid-1970s. In Latin America, paid employment fell at a rate of about 0.5 percent annually during the 1980s.[13] Only Southeast Asian countries witnessed a consistent improvement in employment and workers' wages.

Throughout the world, high unemployment and underemployment have persisted. Often, the quality of employment has declined, even if employment figures remained stable. With a few exceptions, the bright promise of improved employment in a global economy has been slow to emerge, at best. What can account for this surprising fact?

Britain; increased income inequality, observed in most industrial countries and in Latin America; and increased job-related anxiety (see Figure 4.6). A U.S. pharmaceutical company has recently estimated that 25 percent of the U.S. work force suffers from stress-related illnesses.[14] A British study has found that such illnesses cost the U.K. economy $4.6 billion yearly. And a California study correlated overtime with a higher risk for heart disease.[15]

Particularly in many developing countries, where labor markets are least regulated, wages are often extremely low and work place conditions abominable. In 1994, an estimated 25,000 Brazilians worked in such poor wage and safety conditions that the Catholic Church called their circumstances slavery.[16] Long hours, poor wages and no bargaining power are the lot for many workers in Latin America and Asia. Even in the United States, the Department of Labor estimates that half of all sewing shops are breaking labor laws.[17]

Therefore, enhanced flexibility in the labor market seems to displace, rather than solve, the unemployment problem. The "European" disease of high unemployment with a highly regulated work place has its counterpart in countries with more flexible labor markets: growing numbers of working poor people, an increasing income gap and pervasive job-related anxiety.

If labor laws are not the main problem, what is?

Trade and Technology

International trade seems to cost jobs because firms move their facilities to areas with cheaper work forces, or emerging markets with growing demand. Technology also seems responsible for job losses, because more can be produced with less labor. In both cases, most economists expect that the losses experienced in one sector will be made up by gains in other parts of the economy.

Trade. Manufacturing jobs in industrialized economies are sometimes lost through trade with, and investment in, newly

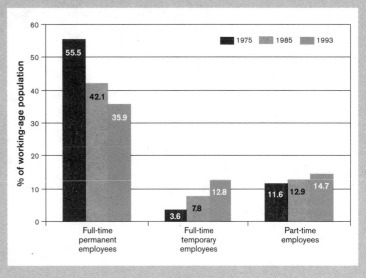

FIGURE 4.6

Declining Work Security
United Kingdom, 1975-1993

Source: Financial Times, *April 29, 1996.*

industrializing countries. But the newly industrializing countries will often buy more of the goods typically provided by industrial countries. These include technologically sophisticated and luxury goods.

In fact, Canada, France, Germany, Japan, Italy, the United Kingdom and the United States together enjoy a trade surplus with the developing world. Sales to the developing world explain why U.S. companies have fared so well in recent years despite stagnation in the home market. Boeing sells one in seven of its airplanes to China.

With the relocation of low-skilled, labor-intensive jobs to poorer countries, international trade has displaced lower-skilled workers in the North, although to a lesser extent than often assumed. Probably less than 20 percent of gross U.S. job losses are due to international trade.

Technology. It is difficult to assess the extent to which replacing workers with machines is responsible for unemployment. In theory, better technology means more wealth in an economy because more goods and services are produced by the same

Day laborers in Mexico City compete for scarce employment opportunities.

Ron Giling/Panos Pictures

Combined Effects of Trade and Technology.

Most economists blame technology more than international trade for eroding the wages of low-skilled workers, and even for unemployment.[18] While no consensus exists, it is clear that a combination of freer trade and displacement by technology puts pressure on wages and employment in the short term.

One important role for government under these circumstances is to more adequately train new workers and upgrade the skills of older workers, so they can participate in the new, emerging sectors of the economy. But can the high-growth sectors create enough good jobs? Only if these sectors are supported by a strong enough economy.

A quarter century into the era of globalization, it is becoming clearer that the dynamic effects of trade and technology have not been sufficient to overcome job losses. Could globalization undermine the very growth that is necessary for its "virtuous" effects to come into play?

Uncertainty, Declining Incomes and Weak Demand

One barrier to realizing the benefits from the presumed virtuous circle of globalization and trade appears to lie in the unsettling nature of changes in production and trade. A global economy means a constant reshuffling of resources and people. If a firm or a country in a remote part of the world becomes more competitive, all others have to adjust by vying to be more competitive, or by giving up that line of production.

More adjustments mean a higher turnover of firms and consequently a higher turnover of people – more job uncertainty. That may be true even though the total wealth created in the economy is increasing – consider the stalled income of U.S. workers in the face of steady growth in the overall economy.

Why do only 35 percent of those U.S. workers who lose their jobs find a similar or better position afterwards? U.S. workers laid off from a good-paying job take a pay cut of 10 percent on average, according to statistics

number of workers. Workers earn more for their firm and can be paid more because they produce more. Their extra income creates additional demand, boosting growth.

In addition, machines often lead to cheaper goods, making everyone "richer." From their savings, consumers can buy more and contribute to a buoyant economy – where workers can find new jobs or business opportunities.

Indeed, from 1946 to 1973, productivity increased rapidly, and workers' incomes kept pace in the industrial countries and many developing countries. The expected results generally came to pass. Since about 1973, however, productivity has grown more slowly. In many instances real wages have dropped. A boom in sales of high-technology goods and services has translated into higher profits, but not higher employment. Technology appears to have reduced the demand for low-skilled workers and lowered their wages, while increasing the demand and wages for higher-skilled workers and innovative entrepreneurs. The income gap between the groups has widened dramatically. More low-skilled workers are unemployed than in previous decades.

compiled by the President's Council of Economic Advisers.[19] If they are being shifted to more dynamic sectors of the economy, this should not be the case.

Globalization occurs in a context of weaker labor unions and labor laws. Imagine a situation where all firms laid off their workers at the same time, then re-hired them on less advantageous terms. There is little that workers could do about it. This is more or less what is happening, in particular with the advent of out-sourcing and subcontracting; large firms perform less themselves, but parcel out their activities to smaller suppliers. Hundreds of industrial-country firms now contract out for goods or services – components of manufactured goods, for example, or janitorial services – formerly handled within the company. In developing countries, most garments are produced through contractors. In either case, any obligation of the parent firm ends with the contract.

This creates a collection of small, vulnerable companies in keen competition with each other and unable to provide either benefits or security for their workers. Indeed, the smallest companies are often exempted from such obligations where they do exist.

Uncertainty, as an aspect of the race to the bottom, appears to be an insidious by-product of high turnover due to enhanced competition. It is less well-known or analyzed than bidding down wage rates around the world, which most people have in mind when they discuss the social effects of international trade. It may, in fact, be even more important. Both result from greater competition and weak or missing protective laws. As a result, wages can grow more slowly than productivity; people are asked to work harder, but the extra value goes to management and shareholders. This was the case in the United States between 1991 and 1994. In many low-income countries, real wage losses were even starker.

How does this feed into the general economy? Obviously, lower wages or shorter hours mean less available income, and less business for suppliers. But less security also means less purchases. Many durable and semi-durable goods require long-term planning for their purchase. When income is volatile, consumers delay such purchases, further weakening economic activity. So even when incomes look higher, demand may be stagnating, because volatile income does not readily translate into effective demand.

Recall that the "virtuous" nature of trade and technology operates by creating new markets, new products, new opportunities. This will not work well in an economy where people do not feel confident enough in the future to indulge.

Effects of Governments' Competition for Market Shares and Capital

Even though "competitiveness" is touted as the answer to economic problems, many public policies undertaken in response to global competition may actually be counterproductive.

For example, in times of economic stagnation, governments are discouraged from stimulating their economies – by public-spending projects, for example. They fear that investors will react by moving their investments to another country where the economy is "sounder." At the same time, there is no penalty, in terms of capital movements, for conducting contractionary ("anti-growth") policies. Quite the contrary. All the incentives are for governments to dampen growth.

The fact that capital can move so freely, "shopping around" for the most secure currency, always prone to panic and overreaction, is creating what some characterize as a deflationary bias in the world economy. The Bank for International Settlements, the major forum for central banks in industrial countries, sounded the alarm in its *1996 Annual Report*. It warns that increased global competition, wage flexibility and budget cuts pose new dangers of recession worldwide.[20]

In other areas, too, global competition provides incentives for governments to restrict the growth of their economies – or at least the growth in demand for goods and services. As competitors in the world market, each country seeks to offer cheaper goods to increase its share of global markets. If prices increase, domestic products become more difficult to sell abroad. To prevent inflation, governments implement policies that restrict domestic demand such as tighter budgets or less credit. With weaker demand, prices will fall and goods will sell better abroad, to the benefit of the exporting country.

Yet if most or all countries adopt the same strategy, the total size of the "global market pie" may shrink – or fail to grow – and country strategies will only offset one another. Combined with the effects of technology, this results in less demand for labor, which means either lower wages (the U.S. experience) or more unemployment (the European experience).

Most of the time, competition is healthy. When governments use macroeconomic policy to gain market shares, however, competition can be self-defeating.

Financial Volatility

One of the presumed benefits of globalization is greater opportunity for creating goods and services, and more opportunities for employment. Yet, it is not always easy to take advantage of even obvious opportunities. An interested entrepreneur will assess how profitable an opening appears to be. She will calculate likely returns. She will also estimate costs, of which interest on borrowed money is likely to be a major portion. If the interest rate is too high, she simply will not start up. Thus high interest rates can stifle economic activity.

Average, long-term interest rates have been much higher on most currencies over the last 15 years in spite of recent improvements. In the United States, for example, real long-term interest rates have averaged 5 percent since the beginning of the 1980s, while they averaged only 2 percent in the previous

three decades. This appears to be due to several factors linked to increased global competition.

Exchange rate volatility has increased. The returns on financial assets also fluctuate more widely – interest rate volatility has risen (though in both cases volatility plateaued a few years ago). In this unstable context, it is difficult to predict the future values of bonds and other financial assets. Hence, investors prefer to make short-term rather than long-term loans. Or if they make long-term loans or investments, they demand a much higher interest rate to compensate for the uncertainty. Money is more expensive for entrepreneurs to borrow.

Volatility has encouraged the growth of financial products that enable people to "buy insurance" and secure the value of their investments. For example, a farmer can sell a future contract, a promise by someone to buy his crop at an agreed price when it comes to the market. Other "derivatives" separate the relatively stable costs of doing business – cost of plant maintenance and labor, for example – from other uncertain aspects such as foreign exchange rates. They permit a business to cope with volatility by paying someone to assume the risk of great loss, with the possibility of large gains.

These financial tools also offer potentially lucrative rewards to whoever holds the slightest edge on information about changes in any aspect of economic life around the world: trends in the beef market, the value of Japanese real estate or public policies that might affect the exchange rate of a country's currency. Industrial firms often find that they can earn higher returns by investing in financial markets than by investing in their own lines of business in ways that would increase employment. Could this be a reason why investment – a key to growth and employment – has slowed down so dramatically since the 1960s? Between 1960 and 1973, investment in production facilities in industrial countries averaged 6 percent. From 1973 through 1990, it averaged 2 percent.

Firms have complained that this sluggish investment was a result of excessive taxes and wage demands that reduced profits. Yet a study of the United Kingdom found that, after taxes were reduced, profits were restored to their pre-1973 levels. Nevertheless, real investment failed to pick up.

These are long-term, underlying consequences of financial volatility. They may be at work in addition to the severe effects of financial crises such as that of Mexico.

In sum, increased labor-market flexibility plus trade and technology gains have not, on the whole, measured up to the bright promise of widespread increased employment and improved job quality. Part of the disappointment appears to spring from unanticipated effects of global competition: increased uncertainty of incomes and stagnant demand; fear of capital flight that leads to contractionary policies; deliberate constraints on consumer demand as a strategy for competing; and higher interest rates as a consequence of fluctuations in interest and exchange rates. Widespread creation of decent jobs will require policy responses to these issues.

Public Finance: Another Casualty of Globalization?

As we have seen, healthy public finances are necessary to deal with human and social needs, and to make an economy more productive through education, a good legal system, good infrastructure and good government services. Yet under global competition, as experienced, most governments are caught in a double bind – shrinking revenues and the need for expanded services.

Currently, most countries in the world are experiencing budget deficits. Increasingly, analysts link these deficits to some of the policy responses to globalization.

Higher interest rates, for example, are a prime suspect. Governments compete for a growing share of the available credit, helping drive interest rates even higher, thus spending ever more in interest repayments.

At the same time, governments are less able to find revenue from traditional sources such as taxes, since firms can easily move to low-tax environments. In fact, governments and local authorities often not only waive taxes to attract investors, they offer additional incentives and subsidies. Corporate taxes have dropped from 30 percent of U.S. tax revenue in 1960 to 3 percent today.

Faced with decreasing tax revenues from business, governments tax what is left: personal incomes. Compared to firms, people are less able or willing to move to lower-tax environments. In the European Union, for example, the overall tax rate on labor grew 20 percent between 1980 and 1993. In contrast, proceeds from capital gains taxes declined by 10 percent.

And of course, heavier payroll taxes mean that growth is less likely to create jobs, or that business opportunities will not translate into better wages or more employment.

Even as government revenues shrink as an indirect consequence of global competition, the demand and need for several categories of government services expand. As employment and business opportunities shrink, or fail to develop, more workers and their families need training and retraining, support during periods of unemployment, and safety nets to prevent hunger and poverty.

The U.S. federal government oversees critical safety net programs such as school lunch.
USDA

Standard Remedies

We can now look more critically at the remedies often prescribed for unemployment – labor market flexibility and cutting budget deficits to lower interest rates and enhance investment. Each creates economic difficulties for the poorest sections of society. We have seen that enhancing labor market flexibility will not help create more quality jobs.

What about cutting deficits? This could reduce the borrowing requirement of the public sector, thus cutting interest rates and boosting growth. Yet the idea of fiscal consolidation as a cure for unemployment rests on a few questionable assumptions:

- **It assumes that higher interest rates are mainly due to higher budget deficits.** In fact, financial markets and the effects of volatility may also be responsible, as discussed above.

- **It assumes that lower interest rates will suffice to spur investment and jobs.** Yet this is not true if demand is in the doldrums. Witness Japan's anemic economy, with a zero percent interest rate, or France's current morass in spite of repeated cuts. When markets are stagnant, business opportunities are rare, however cheap the credit. In fact, cheap credit is used for mergers and acquisitions, or for new investments that make firms leaner or more competitive, instead of producing more goods and creating more jobs.

- **It assumes that lower budget deficits will not hurt growth – and jobs**. Yet this assumption has been disproved in many developing countries that have cut public spending at the urging of donors. Growth-reducing effects have overwhelmed any dynamic effects.

Reducing budget deficits in an ad hoc manner will not address the deep, structural causes of fiscal crises. It will most certainly hurt poor people, who rely on public assistance, and create more poverty and hunger – hence an extra burden in the long run. It could also hurt the profitability of businesses by choking the provision of public goods such as education, good roads or less crime. The implications of this simplistic remedy have not been sufficiently thought through.

The Coordination Imperative

Coordination between governments on at least three fronts – social policy, macroeconomic policy and tax policy – are the main responses needed to make the most out of globalization.

In the relatively closed economies of the past, a balance between states and markets could be achieved at the national level. National authorities could reap the efficiency benefits of markets, while controlling, and compensating for, their potential divisiveness. But the economy is now increasingly international, while policy-making structures, including social organizations, are still largely fragmented among states. It is more difficult, in this situation, to provide the necessary environment for markets to work as they should – and to translate their benefits into human well-being.

Meaningful job training is an essential component of government strategies to reduce unemployment.

Home Builders Institute

An example of how markets do not function well in a legal and political vacuum is the need for antitrust policies. Competition needs to be nurtured, sometimes policed, if markets are to fulfill their "bright promises." When firms are so large that they overlap several jurisdictions, it is more difficult to monitor their behavior. Recently, for example, the world of business was quite stunned to hear that Asea Brown Boveri, one of the most respected firms in the heavy construction and machinery field, was under investigation at the European Commission for suspected collusion with competitors to maintain high prices.

The same thing could be said for financial investments; in the absence of worldwide deposit insurance, many investors fall victim to fraudulent companies. The U.K. Salvation Army, for example, suffered heavy losses in an international financial scam. When the heads of state of the leading industrial nations met in Lyon, France, in July 1996, they sounded a note of alarm over the rise of international financial fraud and organized crime.

Globalization means that business grows much larger than governments' capacities to uphold the rules of the game. So coordination among national governments is necessary. Yet coordination also means that more and more decisions will have to be made on the world stage, further and further away from ordinary citizens.

One can take a quick example from the experience of the European Union. To ensure the effective operation of a market, people have to be able to compare prices. Since one cannot compare apples and oranges, consumers have to be sure that what passes as an apple is really an apple – or what is offered as high-quality chocolate is indeed high-quality chocolate. When public authorities check for truth in advertising, it is easier to make price comparisons.

Also, consumers and producers of high-quality goods do not want unfair competition from substandard or dangerous products. Environmentally sensitive consumers do not want to accept products made in factories that pollute the environment. Workers don't want to compete with bonded child labor in South Asia, or with women workers who cannot organize or bargain collectively in Central America. Governments have to agree on common standards and guarantee that these standards will be enforced.

Yet this is where citizens often feel out of control, because they lack the ability to decide what the global standards should be. For example, the British consider raw milk cheese such as Camembert unsanitary and would like to ban such products from being sold in the United Kingdom. Yet they cannot, because they have agreed not to interfere with free trade with France. On the other hand, the French consider that English sausages do not contain enough meat to qualify as a "sausage." Since they cannot prohibit English manufacturers from using the name "sausage" (or block the importation of the dubious product), they have to put up with lower standards. Both ask why foreigners should decide what is considered good cheese or good sausage. Yet common standards are imperative if freer international trade is to work in practice.

Between protectionism and world government, one must find ways to harness global opportunities without too much loss of democracy.

Suggested Remedies

Policy responses will stem from what we suspect are causes of the current distortions. They can be summarized in five points:

- **Take the mysticism out of liberalization – be pragmatic in liberalizing trade and finance.** Liberalization is not a panacea that will guarantee success under every circumstance. The most successful economies have been those that have carefully weighed the costs and benefits of liberalization, and tailored plans to their particular circumstances.

- **Enhance or revive policies that protect families and workers in order to reduce stagnating demand due to income insecurity.** Governments are reluctant to maintain or strengthen social standards because of competition from other countries. Hence, social standards must become regular fare in international trade negotiations and agreements. But effective social standards cannot be imposed "from outside." They come only from a participatory process in each country – for example, bargaining between employers and employees.

  Standards can be used by industrial countries to block imports from developing countries. To avoid that, standard-setting should ensure participatory processes in which people help set the standards that will affect them.

- **Use existing mechanisms for international coordination to ensure a healthy, growing economy.** Governments now have little incentive to boost their economies in isolation, since the added demand "sucks in" goods from abroad, leading to trade deficits and a weakened currency. This would be eased if such stimulus were done simultaneously with other governments, particularly those of the dominant economies.

  More formal coordination – the creation of the European Monetary Union, for example – could also help ease the pressures of massive capital movement and its deflationary effects.

- **Coordinate policies on taxes and subsidies in order to cope with fiscal deficits.** Governments should coordinate their tax policies to ensure that they do not undermine one another by offering competitive incentives, and that they tax income from capital investments (despite its mobility) as well as from labor.

- **Citizens should be made aware that decisions made in international forums affect their lives and livelihoods.** Leaders of governments and civil society – journalists, teachers, politicians, academics, opinion-makers and especially grassroots organizers – should promote an understanding of global economic issues. An educated public can help ensure that the imperatives of human development and the value preferences of ordinary citizens guide global economic policy-setting.

Conclusion

We have seen that global markets are rich in promise. But this promise can only be fulfilled if the conditions are created for a real market economy to prevail. Paradoxically, this means more public policy, not less. Market economies need strong rules in order to function equitably and promote social stability. Agreeing on and enforcing these rules will be a major challenge of international cooperation.

Several signs indicate that the world economy is not quite functioning the way it should: employment is sluggish, less and less resources are available for social needs and people feel that their livelihoods are becoming more insecure. This could be the result of governments managing their own economies at cross-purposes, rather than together, for the mutual benefit of their peoples.

The fact that globalization was reversed once before, with disastrous consequences, should prompt us all to carefully study mistakes made and lessons learned.

Bright promise, mixed results, indeed. But most of all, formidable policy challenges.

DR. ISABELLE GRUNBERG *is a senior policy analyst at the Office of Development Studies within the United Nations Development Programme.* DON REEVES, *economic policy analyst at Bread for the World Institute, assisted with editing.*

CHAPTER 5

Governments and Hunger in Developing Countries: Case Studies

S ince the end of World War II, achieving an end to hunger and poverty in the developing world has had an important place on the international community's agenda. Industrial countries have provided billions of dollars in development aid, and some developing countries achieved rapid economic growth. Nearly all developing countries reduced child mortality and increased literacy and life expectancy. World hunger has declined.

Throughout this period, most development thinkers and policy-makers have held that governments had an essential role, working in partnership with markets and voluntary popular associations. The Indian scholar Amartya Sen has articulated the vision succinctly:

> Systematic public action can eradicate the terrible and resilient problems of starvation and hunger in the world in which we live. But…for this to be secure on a lasting basis it is important to integrate the protective role of the government with the efficient functioning of other economic and social institutions – varying from trade and commerce to the news media and political parties. It is also important to see public action in a broad perspective –

A self-financing fish-drying business, established by a Ghanaian women's group, provides employment in Accra.

Betty Press/Panos Pictures

involving active parts played by the public itself, going well beyond state planning and governmental actions.[1]

Clearly, governments helped reduce hunger in developing nations. India eliminated the scourge of periodic famines through government food distribution and public works employment programs.[2] Governments in countries as different as Chile, China, Cuba, Costa Rica and Jamaica "have used…much public intervention in securing health care, medical facilities and basic education across the population."[3]

Just as important as direct government interventions are the public policies that determine whether citizens have opportunities to secure their livelihoods through their own efforts – whether tax policies favor savings and investment; whether investments put people to work or save labor; whether jobs provide decent wages and working conditions; whether cheap food policies undercut the livelihood of farm families; whether economic policies are carried out in ways that do no harm to poor people.

Today, however, many developing countries are dismantling governmental institutions and relying more on markets. Especially since the international debt crisis of the early 1980s, the International Monetary Fund (IMF), World Bank and aid donor agencies have aggressively pressed developing countries to curtail government and rely more on markets in order to more successfully "adjust" to the global market economy.

The aid establishment has moderated its viewpoint somewhat. But the main thrust of "adjustment" continues to be a reduced role for government – lower spending, deregulation of businesses and labor markets and privatization of state companies. Reliance on the market and international trade are expected to generate economic growth, which, proponents argue, is a prerequisite to ending hunger and poverty. Some advocates of market-friendly development such as the Heritage Foundation argue that, almost automatically, the pursuit of economic freedom will lead to increased living standards, an end to poverty and greater political freedom.

This chapter consists of a series of short essays. Paul Streeten begins by setting the context within which three case studies in developing countries examine the effects of liberalization of their economies. Aloysius Prakash Fernandez says that the experience of liberalization in India is mixed and urges policy shifts and the incorporation of marginalized people in decision making. Carlos Navarro casts a critical eye on the effects of liberalization in Mexico. Anna Rich concludes that Ghana's shift from a heavily overregulated economy toward more reliance on markets has improved the economy and helped reduce poverty, but that the market alone cannot reduce poverty. Government policies and programs are also essential.

Bread for the World Institute believes that markets and governments both have a role to play in achieving sustainable development – the reduction of hunger and poverty in environmentally sound ways; that governments play an essential role in protecting society's most vulnerable citizens and assuring them economic opportunities.

What Can Governments Do About Hunger?

by Paul P. Streeten

The problem of hunger has not been primarily one of production, but mainly one of distribution between countries, regions and income groups, between the sexes and within households.

Part of the solution is the generation of adequate incomes among poor people, including both producing food for their own consumption and cash earnings to buy food in the market. For farmers, this means security of tenure or ownership of land, a regular outlet for sales and a supply of credit. For the informal sector, it means cessation of harassment and provision of credit, information and marketing. Public policies are critical. Also, various government public works programs and public employment generation schemes have been very successful: the Bangladesh Food-for-Work Program, India's Maharashtra Employment Guarantee Scheme and China's Yigong-Daizhen public works scheme, among others.[4]

Growth of income and of food production, important though they are, are not sufficient to eliminate hunger and malnutrition. The eradication of hunger and malnutrition is not just a problem of making the land more fertile and families less fertile. Receiving more food does not necessarily meet the basic nutritional needs of poor people; it may simply meet the basic needs of the parasites in their stomachs. Income may be diverted for debt repayment to parasitic landlords or moneylenders, or male heads of households may deprive their families of nutritional benefits.

It may not be more food that is needed for better nutrition, but education, safe water, medical services, reduced work loads, fewer unwanted pregnancies, shorter walks to and between work places, counter-pressures to advertisements or land reform. In all these areas, again, public policies play an essential role.

Nutrition policies for chronically malnourished people require a long-term, sustained effort. Government intervention can take the form of agricultural policy, supplementary feeding, food fortification programs, food subsidies and rationing, and complementary policies in non-food sectors such as employment creation or credit for the informal sector. Particularly important are policies for foreign trade and the exchange rate, which determine how much poor farmers get for their crops.

Rich countries tend to tax poor urban food consumers in order to subsidize relatively better-off farmers. Poor countries have tended to tax, often indirectly in a disguised form, poor farmers in order to subsidize food such as high-quality wheat and rice that is consumed by the better-off urban groups. But among the poorest people are rural landless laborers and urban dwellers who have to buy food and are sometimes helped by these subsidies.

So long as power structures and the alignment of interest groups deny poor people access to adequate food supplies, hunger will continue. In some conditions, however, the interest of the ruling group can be harnessed to alleviate poverty and hunger. Well-nourished, healthy and educated workers are more productive and, if decently paid, better customers. But while such interest can be mobilized for hunger reduction, in the last resort, it is access to political power by poor people and equitable distribution of assets (particularly land) that alone can guarantee adequate food supplies and the other measures. Ultimately, the problem of eradicating hunger is political, not nutritional, technical or economic.

DR. PAUL P. STREETEN *is a consultant to the U.N. Development Programme, having previously served in posts at Oxford, Sussex and Boston Universities, and at the World Bank.*

Privatization in India

by Aloysius Prakash Fernandez

A senior Indian government official recently asked me whether the new economic liberalization policy has adversely affected poor people. My response startled him. Poor people, I pointed out, have always lived in a privatized economy. They have paid interest rates that reflected the market rate of credit plus extortion, the size of which depends on their degree of vulnerability. They have not been organized, hence competition keeps their wages below the official rates; they work for daily wages, often through contractors, hence layoffs have not been an issue. They have coped daily with a situation of scarce resources and limited options for obtaining such essential items as food, transportation, education, shelter and health.

In all these areas, they have had poor access to resources. Where they have managed to obtain access, they often have had to pay for services that they should have received for free. In most cases the services were of poor quality.

Bombay's skyscrapers cast shadows over its urban slums, which increasingly are home to India's poor.

Ron Giling/Panos Pictures

The policy of liberalization, which increased the scope for privatization, started tentatively in the mid- to late 1980s. The 1990s saw rapid and visible progress as the policy became politically acceptable. Understandably, it means different things to different groups of people.

To industrialists, privatization means increasing freedom to bring in technology, capital and consumer goods, including luxury items, to cater to a relatively small, elite group. It also means a decrease in the government's licensing power and a decline in the monopoly status and privileges of public sector enterprises and major private firms. This opens up space for new business players.

To financial institutions, the new economic policy presents the opportunity to raise resources in the open market, to free lending polices to respond to the market both in terms of interest rates, which had been fixed at unreasonably low levels by the government, and to explore previously restricted avenues for investment.

To large farmers and those with access to irrigation, privatization has meant higher prices for surplus food (mainly wheat and rice), better quality seeds available from private producers, easier credit and increasing opportunities to invest in high technology, export-oriented products.

Liberalization policy has catered to the demands of well-off people for luxury goods, and opened up the world as a work place.

It has thrown up a large service sector for the middle class and released its potential for entrepreneurship, which had been bottled up and suppressed. Today, I do not experience the same deep concern among middle-class urban and semi-urban youth about their future as in the past. Those who are not employed are largely those who restrict their job options and location or are otherwise incapable of holding any responsibility. The middle class now enjoys wide choice among what it considers essentials such as milk and spices. As a housewife remarked, "formerly, if the milkman failed to turn up, we had to do without milk; now, we have several choices."

To landless rural people, privatization has provided opportunities for employment in the construction and agricultural sectors, particularly in areas with irrigation and where farmers have shifted to cash crops. For those landless people willing to migrate to work sites (about 15 percent to 20 percent of the agricultural labor force), wages have by and large kept pace with the cost of living.

For the media, privatization has opened up the airwaves as never before. Advertisements for consumer goods fill every channel (there are over 50 available), fostering change in food habits and behavior. The savings rate, which hovered around 24 percent of gross national product for many years, has declined to 22 percent. Frustration has increased around the country. This is partly due to the unbridled use of power by some politicians and bureaucrats. But frustration also comes from rising expectations fostered by the media. The media makes very visible the growing gap between the conspicuous consumption of the elite and the vulnerability of poor people.

To government, privatization has provided the rationale for cutting back on capital expenditures. Foreign capital is now expected to fill the gap. Liberalization was expected to attract private investment and large loans from multilateral and bilateral institutions for infrastructure. Private investors have preferred instead to put money mainly into the stock market for short-term gains and into the production of luxury consumer goods such as sophisticated cars and food.

Multilateral and bilateral investment has also been disappointing. This is partly due to local politics and to the time required to approve projects in an administrative culture accustomed to functioning in a closely regulated economy. Investment in infrastructure would have provided jobs to those with limited skills, largely landless and near-landless people, and increased their access to basics such as water, transportation and electricity. Liberalization has not opened up markets abroad as expected either. Protectionism in developed countries continues to grow under various garbs, including that of environmental protection. The net result of these disappointments has been the accumulation of a roughly $100 billion foreign exchange debt and an annual trade deficit of about $5 billion. The annual debt service obligation is now equal to the inflow of fresh foreign capital.

Most of India's people depend on small and marginal dry-land farming (no irrigation). This group has not benefitted in any way from the privatization policy. In fact, they have been affected adversely. Their vulnerability has increased during the past 10 years. In areas where rainfall is low and erratic, this vulnerability has increased significantly. Small farmers' food security has been undermined.

Landless people who have been unable or unwilling to migrate to new jobs have also been hurt. Their wages have stagnated and purchasing power declined. Privatization is not the sole cause. Bad management of vital sectors and poor implementation of anti-poverty programs also played a major role.

Both small farmers and landless laborers who stayed in their villages have undergone a shift in their food consumption over the past 10 years. They are relying less on locally produced items such as traditional staples and eating more foods that have a higher social status and take less effort to prepare such as rice or ready-made products. This shift has led to growing demand for cash, resulting in neglect of dry-land food crops, which were consumed but have no markets. As inflation raises the cost of food, these sectors of the population have become more vulnerable to market fluctuations.

Several factors behind this increased vulnerability flow directly from the macroeconomic policy adopted under liberalization. For example, government investment in agriculture has declined in real terms. From 18 percent of total gross domestic capital formation in 1980-1981, it has declined to 11 percent in 1991-1992. Moreover, government investment and services are still biased toward irrigated areas and crops. With one or two exceptions, research has not focused on dry-land production, either. Capital investment has neglected dry-land farming.

Since 1981, a large part of public expenditure went into higher subsidies for fertilizer, irrigation, electricity and credit. Among these, dry-land farmers use only fertilizer. During the past three years, the government has removed subsidies on potassium and phosphate fertilizers, causing sharp price increases of over 100 percent. Urea fertilizer, used largely in wheat and rice-growing areas that have assured irrigation or adequate rainfall, remains subsidized. Cultivators of such crops form a dominant political lobby. The result of the sharp price increases for potassium and phosphates will, in the medium term, reduce productivity on dry-land farms owned by poorer and less-powerful producers.

With the increase in prices of these fertilizers, horticultural farmers in the southern states have increased their use of cow manure. Farmers in adjacent areas find that the price for manure has increased and prefer to sell almost all the dung produced on their farms. This meets their demand for cash, but less organic material goes into their fields.

Thus, the dry lands will become increasingly unproductive. This will have serious repercussions on livelihoods and lifestyles, perhaps forcing small and marginalized farmers to migrate, and in any case undermining their food security. Reports from all project areas of Myrada, an Indian nongovernmental development organization, provide growing evidence of land sales by these farmers to larger-scale producers with the capital, skills and attitudes required to make these lands productive. This development contributes to the country's overall food basket, but it has increased the number of landless people and reduced the basis of their security.

In order to strengthen food security, development strategy needs to focus investment on the regeneration and management of natural resources. Success in this area creates the greatest potential for improving livelihood opportunities for poor people.

Agricultural policy and related laws need to change. For example, the law should allow common management (not ownership) of land within a defined watershed. This has proved effective to support sustainable increases in productivity.

Other policies and practices need to change:

- Agricultural extension strategy must shift from the present focus on specific crops to a farming systems approach, especially in dry-land areas, where farmers cultivate a mix of crops to meet their needs and insure themselves against the failure of any one crop;

- The information system must shift from the current top-down monopoly to a framework that actively involves farmers, private companies, traders, nongovernmental organizations and agencies dealing with agricultural inputs and markets;

- The emphasis on standardization of attitudes, extension skills and systems, which has a strong bias toward irrigated crops, must shift to a stress on differentiation, so as to meet the various needs of small and marginal farmers in dry-land areas;

- Research must shift from focus on a single crop under laboratory conditions to adaptive research under realistic physical and social conditions, including both dry-land farming field conditions and people's perceptions; and

- The approach to policy must shift from the culture of a "delivery system," assessed by targets that are easily quantifiable, to one that provides long-term support to farmers' institutions which design their own rules, sanctions and responsibilities.

In terms of extension organization and staff, there should be:

- Different norms for recruitment, compensation and incentives for staff working with dry-land farmers than for those working in irrigated areas;
- Decentralized finance and administration; and
- Adequate resources for research scientists, combined with the right attitudes and incentives.

Privatization has fostered a number of trends that need to be reversed. Subsidies for inputs in dry-land farming systems are necessary. Essential food items, including basic foods for children, should be subsidized for poor people. At the same time, poor people need to be given opportunities and make the effort to learn new skills. Finally, national reconstruction efforts must draw in youth who are wasting their time on gambling and other anti-social activities. This phenomenon is on the increase, particularly in rural areas.

The results of privatization are mixed. The country may become increasingly vulnerable, with its poorer segments suffering the most, unless problems are addressed. Steps should be taken to correct excessive consumption, foster savings, invest heavily in dry lands, change the bias in agricultural research and extension toward dry-land farming systems, increase productivity (especially in the public sector) and strengthen institutions, particularly among marginal groups. A true democracy must incorporate marginal groups into the mainstream.

ALOYSIUS PRAKASH FERNANDEZ *is the founder of Myrada, an Indian nongovernmental development organization.*

Privatization, Crisis and Food Security in Mexico

by Carlos Navarro

Beginning in the early 1980s, the Mexican government undertook profound changes in economic and agricultural policies. The purpose was to transfer some of the government's control over the economy to the private sector, in order to attract fresh investment. The policies included privatization of hundreds of state enterprises and a fundamental shift in the government's commitment toward the agricultural sector.

Mexico had been forced to default on its foreign debts in 1982. The resulting flight of capital threw the economy into deep depression. Privatization was part of Mexico's strategy to recover from that crisis.

Between 1982 and 1994, the government sold about 1,000 properties. These ranged from pineapple plantations and sugar processing plants to huge monopolies such as the national telephone company and the nationwide television network, Televisa. President Carlos Salinas de Gortari, who held office from 1988 to 1994, also reprivatized the nation's banks, which the government had nationalized in the 1970s. The current president, Ernesto Zedillo, is proceeding with privatization of the handful of remaining government companies such as the national railroad line, sea ports and airports and the country's petrochemical plants.

A large number of the companies that the government sold to private investors were in dire need of fresh capital to modernize their operations and expand. But a major problem with the privatization process was that "increased efficiency" almost always implied a reduction in operating costs, which frequently translated into a reduction in personnel. Therefore, privatization has contributed to a surge in poverty over the past decade.

While few statistics are available on the total number of workers who lost their jobs due to privatization, informal estimates suggest a figure in the hundreds of thousands. Mexico's largest labor organization, the Mexican Workers' Confederation, says that in 1993 alone, the government's efforts to downsize, which include both privatization and the elimination of some government agencies, cost 395,000 jobs. More than one-third of these job losses were in the manufacturing sector, where unemployment also means loss of health, retirement and other government benefits.

Employment losses related directly to the transfer of government enterprises to private investors may pale in comparison with indirect effects of the privatization philosophy. A recent estimate by a private business organization suggests that 2 million Mexicans lost their jobs in 1995 because of the country's current economic crisis. In turn, the crisis stemmed indirectly from the Salinas administration's economic policies, which attempted to promote economic development partly by attracting massive amounts of "soft" foreign investment by offering exorbitant interest rates on government bonds.

This policy of artificially propping up the Mexican economy came back to haunt the government in 1994. The uprising of the Zapatista National Liberation Army in Chiapas, one of the poorest of Mexico's 31 states, was followed by the assassination of the ruling party's presidential candidate and its general secretary. Investors decided that the political climate was becoming too "risky."

The short maturity of the government bonds allowed the private investors to withdraw their money from the Mexican economy and still reap huge profits from the high interest rates. Because of the massive flight of foreign and some Mexican capital, President Zedillo was forced to devalue the currency in late 1994 and take stringent measures to attempt to restore economic stability, including sharply reducing government spending.

The U.S. government, the IMF and other multilateral institutions insisted on the policy changes as a condition for Mexico to receive about $50 billion in loan guarantees in early 1994. Reduced social spending hurt Mexico's poor people.

For much of its 67 years in power, the ruling party has used efficient, well-managed social welfare programs and patronage spending to undercut political challenges.[5] Salinas had provided generous community development funding to areas where the opposition had gained a foothold. But these programs were curtailed.

In addition to paring government spending, the Zedillo administration increased the value-added tax to raise government revenues. Since low- and middle-income people have to spend virtually all their income, a sales tax hits them harder than high-income people. In April 1995, when the tax increase took effect, the consumer price index rose 8 percent.

The hike in the value-added tax also forced some businesses to close, due to a sharp reduction in retail sales. According to an estimate by a private business group, domestic consumption declined by almost 13 percent in 1995, or twice the rate of decline reported in 1994.

The business closures contributed further to unemployment and were reflected in a contracting economy. Mexico's gross domestic product (GDP) declined by 11 percent in the second quarter of 1995, followed by a 10 percent drop in the third quarter. For the year, GDP fell almost 7 percent, and, by unofficial estimates, fell another 3 percent in the first quarter of 1996.

During 1996, the Zedillo administration has continued to carry out austerity measures. The government eliminated a price ceiling on dairy products and is considering taking the same action on tortillas. The policy is designed to help the dairy and corn milling industries survive. But it means a higher price for essential food items for Mexico's poorest people.

Most Mexicans are not able to grow food for themselves. Although 60 percent of Mexicans lived in rural areas in 1950, today 72 percent live in and around cities. Nearly 22 million live in the capital, Mexico City, more than half of them in shantytowns and slums. The city gains a million new residents each year through births and poor migrants from nearby rural states. Its streets are filled with vendors, many of them children, and beggars – many of them, too, are children. Professor William Whitaker, who has studied Mexican social welfare policies, calls it "a city of contrasts, a city of diversity… opulence and poverty…. A city of people on the move…. A city with children everywhere…. Dreams and dreams denied in its markets, parks, streets…."

The Zedillo administration insists that a sustained recovery will begin by the end of 1996 or the beginning of 1997. Notwithstanding the rosy official forecast, the reality remains quite grim. According to a recent report from the United Nations Economic Commission on Latin America and the Caribbean, at least 50 percent, and probably a higher proportion, of Mexico's population is now "poor" or "very poor." A study released by a special commission of the lower house of the Mexican Congress reported that the number of poor people stood at about 60 million (67 percent of Mexicans) at the beginning of 1996.

Beyond increasing the number of poor people, recent policies of privatization also created a new class of super-rich Mexicans. According to a report in *Forbes*, there were 24 billionaires in Mexico as of 1994, compared with only two billionaires when Salinas took office in 1988. Because of the economic crisis, the number fell back to 10 in 1995.

The move toward privatizing government operations will probably not affect the basic foodstuffs processing and marketing agency CONASUPO, which provides many forms of direct assistance to poor people. However, other changes that have occurred in Mexico's food production policy have placed a greater burden on subsistence farmers and on rural poor people.

Under Salinas, the government implemented a set of changes in agriculture that sacrificed the principle of food self-sufficiency in favor of encouraging domestic and foreign private investment in the agricultural sector. Salinas pushed for these changes in part to comply with the North American Free Trade Agreement (NAFTA) and the world trade pact. The government's long-standing policy of buying corn and other basic crops from farmers at artificially high prices was not compatible with these agreements.

Instead of offering price guarantees to farmers for corn, the government implemented a system of direct production subsidies. This had the effect of rewarding the larger and more efficient farmers, while reducing assistance for the least efficient subsistence producers. More importantly, Salinas' policies encouraged the use of land for crops for export to the United States and Canada such as fruits and vegetables. This reduced the acreage farmers used to grow food for the domestic market and for themselves.

Following NAFTA, Mexico also began to phase out barriers to imports of U.S. corn and other basic crops. In 1994, the year NAFTA took effect, Mexico increased basic grain imports by 27 percent. In 1996, Mexico is expected to import 10 million metric tons of basic foodstuffs, including corn and beans. As recently as 1990, Mexico proudly promoted its ability to grow enough food on its own to feed the country's population.

While the changes in subsidies and increased international trade have deeply affected production of basic grains in Mexico, other factors have had an even more devastating effect on the agricultural sector. The lingering economic crisis has increased interest rates to exorbitant levels and worsened an already-difficult credit situation for most agricultural producers. A large percentage of farmers are in arrears on their debts, so they cannot obtain new loans for necessary fertilizers, herbicides and seed.

On top of all these problems, agriculture in the northern areas of Mexico has suffered from an extended and severe drought. The reduced capacity of reservoirs in northern states has forced farmers to abandon up to 2.5 million acres of land in 1996 alone. The drought has lingered in some areas of northern Mexico for as long as four or five years.

The Zedillo government has made some efforts to provide assistance to the agricultural sector. These include debt-restructuring programs, financial assistance for production and a drought assistance program for the northern states. But this assistance is minor in relation to the problems that have put thousands of small Mexican farmers out of business.

CARLOS NAVARRO, *a staff writer at the Latin American Institute of the University of New Mexico, is a member of the board of directors of Bread for the World Institute.*

Structural Adjustment in Ghana

by Anna Rich

In 1983, Ghana's economy was on the brink of collapse. Long-term economic decline, triple-digit inflation, deteriorating terms of trade, drought and political instability combined to force the Ghanaian government, headed by Flight Lieutenant Jerry Rawlings, to accept the World Bank and IMF's conditions for assistance. The international financial institutions (IFIs) helped design a structural adjustment program that would bring Ghana's desperate economy back into the global market. In the years following, Ghana went along with the IFIs' plans for reforming its economy more consistently than any other sub-Saharan African country, making it the "most structurally adjusted" country in Africa.

The initial assumption of the structural adjustment program was that the market, rather than government actions, would return prosperity to Ghana. The IFIs' primary emphasis was on "getting the prices right." Removing governmental price and distribution controls would spur the needed economic turnaround. The goals of adjustment included devaluing the overblown exchange rate (to make exports more competitive), removing governmental controls on domestic prices, privatizing state enterprises, stabilizing inflation and decreasing government spending.

In response to these policies, economic growth rates rebounded, from a –1.3 percent annual average during 1973-1983 to 5 percent a year since 1983, a period when many other African economies stagnated or deteriorated. Inflation fell, exports increased and in flowed foreign aid. Ghana became the World Bank's "star pupil," touted as an example of the benefits of increased reliance on market mechanisms and a decreased governmental role in the economy.

Ghana's economic improvements, while welcome, have not yet significantly improved the lives of a majority of Ghanaians. Serious and complicated challenges, some even created or exacerbated by economic reforms, continue to stand between Ghana and widespread prosperity.

Despite increases in economic growth, other key indicators of development do not show sustained improvement. Population increases have diluted the effect of the strengthened economy – yearly per capita economic growth has stayed around 2 percent. Inflation, though down from its high of 123 percent at the beginning of adjustment, averaged close to 40 percent for much of the 1980s. Interest rates remain prohibitively high. The government budget deficit persists, despite the firing of more than 100,000 public employees.

Perhaps most critically, the investment crucial to long-term success has failed to materialize. Government has kept its own spending on public investment low, relying on foreign aid to provide most of the funding. But private investment has not expanded; instead, it declined for most of the 1990s. The ratio of investment to national income is lower than it was 20 or 30 years ago.

Charles Abugre, a Ghanaian analyst, believes that the main constraint to investment is "not macroeconomic uncertainties or government bureaucracy or even lack of technical assistance, but factors which arose directly from the adjustment process itself." For instance, in an attempt to limit inflation, the government imposed credit ceilings and high interest rates. A World Bank survey showed that 100 percent of small firms and 89 percent of all firms cited this higher cost of credit as a major barrier to expansion. Until investment picks up, Ghana's prospects for long-term growth remain dim.

Massive amounts of foreign aid have been vital to Ghana's growth so far. Foreign aid donors have rewarded Ghana for its adjustment faithfulness, but aid-driven growth may not be sustainable. Development assis-

tance accounted for 11 percent of Ghana's national income in 1994, almost double the figure for 1984-1987. Aid to Ghana has increased at a time when aid to Africa as a whole was being cut.

Much of the aid and donor influence has gone into export activities such as gold mining, timber and cocoa. Exports have contributed the most to economic growth during the adjustment period, while agricultural production has risen only 2 percent a year (below the 3 percent annual rate of population growth) and manufacturing has grown only slightly more. But Ghana's export orientation may not be the best strategy for sustained growth. Gold is a nonrenewable resource, logging is causing rapid deforestation and cocoa earnings depend on volatile world prices.

Meanwhile, Ghana has neglected domestic food production, including staples such as cassava, yams, plantains and cocoyams. Non-export agriculture employs 45 percent of Ghanaians, so its development could provide a base for growth with equity. Small investments to improve the traditional methods and simple hand tools used in farming could have a big impact on food availability and incomes.

Much of the aid has come as official, low-interest loans, so external debt has almost quadrupled since 1980. Debt service payments ate up 27 percent of all Ghana's exports in 1994. Since 1987, Ghana's repayments to the IMF have exceeded receipts.

In the early stages, adjustment did not address the human costs of market liberalization and decreased government spending. Increased fees for health and education services made it harder or impossible for the poorest Ghanaians to gain access, for example. Because of government cutbacks, there was only one physician for every 23,000 Ghanaians in 1989-1994, compared to one for every 15,000 in 1980-1985.

The need for attention to human costs was first acknowledged in 1987 with a "Program of Actions to Mitigate the Social Costs of Adjustment." This package aimed to help those who had lost their jobs in the civil service or state-owned enterprises, low-income groups suffering from increased prices for basic necessities and decreased value of wages, and the "structural poor," those, particularly in the north, who traditionally had few opportunities to earn money.

Foreign aid donors committed funds for community projects and help for redeployed and retrenched labor, rehabilitation of basic social services and food-for-work programs. Unfortunately, the promised aid was very slow in arriving, and most funds that did come through ended up in the cities, buying vehicles and office equipment.

Nevertheless, the percentage of Ghanaians living below the poverty line decreased from 37 percent to 31 percent from 1988 to 1992. This was mostly due to economic and financial recovery and good weather, rather than social programs. Growth was concentrated in rural areas. In Accra, the capital, poverty has increased dramatically, from just 7 percent in 1988 to 21 percent in 1992.

So while Ghana's adjustment has moved the country away from a desperate economic crisis, a 1996 World Bank review of development in Ghana correctly warned against "overselling Ghana as a success story."

Ghana has also moved from authoritarian rule to democracy, and that may make it more difficult to impose further dramatic adjustments.

A new 17 percent value-added tax (VAT) provoked widespread protests last year. Eric Aseidu Gybi, a teacher participating in an anti-VAT demonstration, explained that the government had not yet followed through on its promise to raise teachers' salaries by 20 percent in an attempt to keep up with inflation. "Only God knows when it will be given to us," he said, "but meanwhile prices of goods continue to go up." Popular pressure forced the government to repeal the VAT.

Hunger and malnutrition are still widespread. Twenty-six percent of children under 5 are stunted, 27 percent underweight and 11 percent wasted.

In February 1996 Ghana launched its first-ever attempt to integrate national policies relating to food and hunger. Its outlook is multisectoral, recognizing the interrelationships among agriculture, health care, nutrition and governmental policy in improving food security and reducing malnutrition.

In sum, Ghana's shift from a heavily overregulated economy toward more reliance on markets – aided by foreign donors – has improved the overall economy and may have helped reduce rural poverty. But Ghana is finding out that the market alone cannot reduce poverty; government policies and programs that address social problems are also essential. Ghana's adjustment experience also shows that a strong government is crucial to creating an enabling environment for private market growth as well as in directly meeting social needs.

ANNA RICH *is studying political science at . Swarthmore College and was a summer intern at Bread for the World Institute in 1996.*

Conclusion

India, Mexico and Ghana have all moved dramatically away from government-dominated economies toward more reliance on markets. In each case, they were pushed in this direction by serious economic problems – for India and Ghana, slow economic progress over many years; for Ghana and Mexico, a severe economic and financial crisis. They were also pushed or encouraged by international institutions or aid agencies.

In each country, economic liberalization has yielded significant economic improvements, especially for the national economy as a whole. But the shift has been turbulent, and each country still faces serious economic problems.

Also, the shift toward markets has, in each country, imposed heavy costs on many poor and hungry people. Each government has felt compelled to complement liberalization with new social programs, and, in each case, much more should be done. The biggest challenge is to adopt development strategies – such as promotion of dry-land agriculture in India or domestic food production in Ghana – that will open better opportunities for poor families to participate in private sector growth.

These case studies confirm the wisdom in UNICEF's call – since early in the 1980s – for deliberate programs and policies to deal with social issues during adjustment.

Lack of commitment to social policies during the process of market-oriented reforms can lead to hardship, especially for children. UNICEF has found that nutritional levels and school enrollment declined in many African countries that undertook such reforms at the behest of foreign aid donors.[6] According to Lance Taylor and Ute Pieper, scholars at the New School for Social Research, poverty and hunger have often worsened in countries that relied entirely on the market to steer the economy:

The beneficiaries of reform have been households in the top 10 percent to 20 percent of the income distribution who could afford an ample array of new consumer goods in a liberalized trade regime and a local economic technocracy to put the new policy packages in place. The losers included people in the bottom 80 percent of the distribution....[7]

Some countries have managed to combine structural adjustment, economic growth and sustainable development. Examples include Botswana, Peru and Zimbabwe in the 1980s. In order to achieve this, a number of elements seem to be necessary:

- policies to promote economic growth rather than austerity;
- policies that protect vulnerable groups from the adverse consequences of economic change;
- explicit and high priority to education, health and nutrition;
- broad access to productive assets and social services;
- gender equity;
- relative equality in the distribution of income and opportunities;
- open, honest and competent governmental institutions; and
- political participation by an active civil society.[8]

Clearly, governments and civil society remain necessary complements to markets in achieving sustainable development.

CHAPTER 6

Development Aid and International Institutions

by Marc J. Cohen and Don Reeves

Development assistance improves the lives of poor people, in part by improving access to nutritious, affordable food.

The industrial countries, led by the United States, are cutting aid to developing countries. The cuts are deepest in aid to very poor countries and poverty-oriented programs. For fiscal year (FY) 1996, the United States cut its development aid by 22 percent. The prospects for further cuts in FY 1997 are likely. The United States also slashed funding for international aid organizations such as the World Bank and U.N. agencies by more than one-third. The United Nations is in crisis because the United States and other nations are not paying the shares that they promised.

Some market-oriented ideologues justify reduced aid by claiming that aid only spawns counterproductive programs anyway. The "reduce government" school of politics is especially disparaging with regard to the United Nations and other international institutions.

This chapter first discusses the decline in aid, one influential justification for it and our view that development aid should be maintained and reformed. The next section discusses achievements and needed reforms in international institutions. Finally, we sketch an agenda of policies to promote sustainable development that will further reduce global poverty and hunger.

Cuts in Aid[1]

In 1995, aid from the main industrial country donors totaled $59 billion. In real dollar terms, this figure represents a decline of 9 percent from 1994. For the poorest countries, aid declined 8 percent between 1990 and 1994. In 1995, the percentage of national income devoted to aid declined for 16 of the 21 major aid donor countries. Bilateral aid to sub-Saharan Africa, where hunger and poverty are especially severe, fell by $670 million between 1991 and 1994.

The United States has made the deepest cuts. In 1995, the United States ranked dead last among donors in aid as a percent of national income. And, although the United States provided the highest dollar volume of development aid from 1945 until the early 1990s, it has fallen behind Japan since then. In 1995, both France and Germany also provided more assistance than the United States. Total U.S. foreign aid, including funds for export promotion and military assistance, accounts for about 1 percent of U.S. government spending, despite widespread public perceptions that the figure is in the range of 26 percent. Development aid accounts for less than one-third of 1 percent of federal spending.

The deep U.S. cuts for FY 1996 fell hardest on poor people. Development aid to Africa was 22 percent below the previous year's level. Refugee assistance remained at fiscal 1995 levels, and the budget for disaster assistance increased. But allocations of aid to such critical sustainable development sectors as agriculture, environmental protection and democratization declined by more than one-third. The food aid budget fell 7 percent, and food aid tonnage will drop more because food prices are rising (see "Food Aid and Food Security...," page 87).

For political reasons, Congress and the administration made no reductions in aid to Israel and Egypt, which exceeds $5 billion annually. This includes most U.S. military and security aid, which increased. FY 1996 foreign aid legislation also maintained or modestly increased narcotics control assistance and aid to promote U.S. business overseas, forms of aid that do not contribute to sustainable development and poverty alleviation.

Some foreign aid critics justify these deep cuts in aid. In a series of reports that were taken very seriously in the U.S. Congress, the Heritage Foundation agreed that cutting aid is actually the best way to help eradicate poverty.[2]

"The more government interferes in the free market," says a Heritage report, "the more it hampers economic growth and lowers the standard of living of its citizens."[3] The pursuit of economic freedom will, according to Heritage, almost automatically lead to increased living standards, an end to poverty and greater political freedom.

In Heritage's view, government-to-government transfers have promoted unworkable government enterprises and programs, and have actually made many countries worse off. The foundation argues that the United States has provided $500 billion worth of aid to developing countries over the past 50 years, but poverty has increased in many major recipient countries.

Despite decades of aid, critics argue, "[T]he Third World has experienced social disintegration, economic stagnation, debt crises and, in some regions, declines in agricultural production and incomes."[4] Especially in Africa, they say, aid has fueled corruption, repression, violence and the creation of a few showcase projects that benefit few people.

Bread for the World Institute and other nongovernmental organizations (NGOs) have argued with some success for a shift in the emphasis by official aid agencies from economic growth to sustainable development, by which we mean the reduction of poverty and hunger in environmentally sound ways. The Heritage Foundation calls sustainable development a smokescreen for state management of the economy, environmental regulation and industrial subsidies. In this view, aid's inevitable consequences are economic stagnation and poverty.

Heritage notes that 70 percent of aid does not reach poor people, and that much U.S. aid goes into the pockets of suppliers and consulting firms based in the United States.

But the foundation's studies' main point is that aid distorts resource allocation and suppresses thrift, industry and self-reliance. Hence, they conclude, aid is pointless: countries that pursue pro-growth policies don't need it, and those that do not pursue such policies don't deserve it.

These sweeping generalizations require serious qualification. As Chapter 5 showed, there is no automatic connection between free markets and equity, well-being and democracy. But in fact, the aid agencies, led by the International Monetary Fund (IMF) and World Bank, have consistently and successfully promoted free markets in the developing countries. In the 1970s and, to a lesser extent, in the 1990s, aid agencies have moderated their enthusiasm about markets with caveats regarding "investment in people," "safety nets" and now "participation." But the aid agencies have never swerved from their efforts to promote and condition assistance on fiscal discipline, markets and international trade.

The critics are correct, however, that too much U.S. aid goes to U.S.-based consulting firms and subsidizes U.S. industries. For example, a major portion of the U.S. Agency for International Development's (USAID) budget for child survival activities goes to for-profit consulting firms, even though nonprofit groups operate in a more cost-effective manner and are more likely to develop effective partnerships with local communities. We discuss this more fully in our occasional paper, *Putting Children First*.[5]

Most importantly, the Heritage Foundation is right that most U.S. aid has not adequately benefitted poor and hungry people. Through the Cold War, aid went primarily to "friendly governments," regardless of whether they were honest or democratic. Bread for the World Institute estimates that in FY 1994, only 17 percent of the $15 billion U.S. foreign aid budget went to programs focused on reducing poverty and hunger in environmentally sound ways.[6] But it is precisely these programs that have been hardest hit by recent cuts in U.S. aid. These programs should instead be expanded.

Aid Can Work

Despite the failings of aid, the Heritage portrait of it is far too bleak. Assistance from UNICEF and USAID contributed in a major way to remarkable progress in reducing child death rates over the past 15 years (see Figure 6.1). Child vaccination rates in developing countries rose from 25 percent in the early 1980s to 80 percent by the end of the decade. The strong commitment of many developing-country governments (often including the personal attention of heads of state and government) and the intense involvement of communities in carrying out programs were also crucial factors. The market alone would not have led to these dramatic successes in saving children's lives (see Figure 6.2).

Aid has also provided significant support for dramatic gains in life expectancy and educational achievement in many developing countries.

Aid to agriculture, including support for research on how it increases yields (see "Aid to Agriculture," page 86), has played an important role in reducing hunger and boosting incomes among poor rural people. Intensified agricultural research, especially in developing countries, is critical to maintaining the adequacy of world food supplies. But U.S. aid cuts are also falling on agricultural research.

USAID has recently made credit for microenterprises in developing countries – very small businesses owned by low-income entrepreneurs – a major focus of its work. Such aid *supports* thrift, industry and self-reliance, and seeks to enable some of the world's poorest people to become players in the market.

The critics' deep pessimism about Africa is unwarranted, even though hunger and poverty have grown on the continent. Many African countries such as Benin, Zambia and South Africa have moved decisively from dictatorship to multiparty democracy. Botswana and Zimbabwe, both democratic since independence, have managed to avoid famine during periodic droughts because of effective public programs.[7] Zimbabwe and Namibia have demonstrated that peaceful, democratic and multi-ethnic states are possible in Africa. Popular organizations seeking a role in planning and implementing development activities have proliferated rapidly throughout the continent.

Aid can play a critical role in helping Africans to achieve their aspirations. For example, U.S. aid to Kenya supported new technology, created in collaboration with Africans, that allowed corn production to double and improved rural nutrition. In Niger, microenterprise funds from USAID provided new economic opportunities to more than 100,000 families. Ninety-five percent of the loans made to these enterprises were repaid. Such investments in long-term development help poor people to become self-reliant and prevent humanitarian crises. Since 1981, USAID's Development Fund for Africa ensured a stable funding base for sustainable development in the region. But in 1996, Congress eliminated the fund as a separate account within the foreign aid budget.

About 29 percent of U.S. relief and development aid is actually administered by private voluntary organizations (PVOs) such as Catholic Relief Services, CARE and World Vision. This is a long-standing example of partnership between the U.S. government and charities. There is bipartisan enthusiasm about PVO effectiveness, but cuts in official aid are affecting PVO programs too (see "Food Aid and Food Security...," pages 87-89).

The head of USAID, J. Brian Atwood, has made the case for reversing the drastic cuts in aid to sustainable development:

> The United States cannot afford to become isolationist. The best way we can protect ourselves from a host of diseases and other ills that plague Third World countries is to work in partnership to help eradicate them. We need to understand that foreign

FIGURE 6.1

U.S. Funding of Child Survival
Fiscal Years 1984-1996

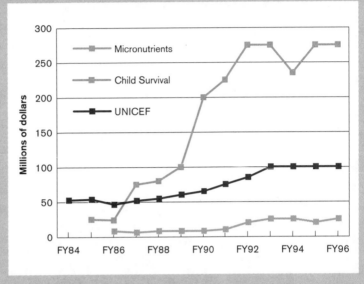

Source: Congressional Appropriations Committees; USAID.

FIGURE 6.2

Under-5 Mortality in USAID-Assisted Countries

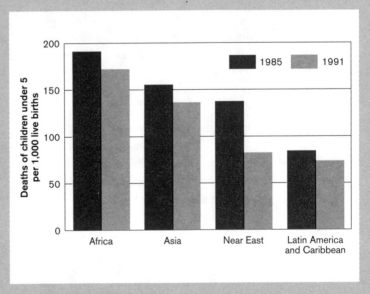

Source: USAID.

Aid to Agriculture

In the early 1970s, Vellore Ramanathan and his wife, Lakshmi, were poor farmers living in the North Arcot region of South India, where Hindu temples dotted the landscape and vibrant green crops grew in vast tracts during the rainy season. They grew rice and peanuts and were trying to support Vellore's mother, three daughters and one son on 2.5 acres of land. They consumed most of what they grew, but sold enough to pay for the upkeep of the farm, hire laborers to help harvest the rice and to buy food, clothes, kerosene and other household essentials. To support the family income, Lakshmi and the two older daughters also worked hard as laborers on other farms when they could.

Vellore was constantly nagged by worries about the future. Would the family be able to eat and survive each year on its scant income? If another drought came, how would the family cope? How would he find dowries for the marriages of his quickly growing daughters? How would he be able to provide land for his son, who wished to marry and remain in farming?

One day the extension workers in the area told Vellore and Lakshmi about a new kind of rice, developed with the help of foreign aid donors. The extension workers said it yielded more and grew faster than what farmers in the area were currently using. It was hard for Vellore and Lakshmi to consider changing seed varieties. If the seeds failed, the family might go hungry. Yet they began to see other farmers adopt the new rice, and these farmers told them of great harvests in a short amount of time. Finally, they planted the seeds and saw their harvest go up. They marveled at their good fortune. Because the new rice variety grew so rapidly, they were able to grow an extra crop each year with the help of irrigation water from their well.

They also adopted new peanut varieties that not only were more tolerant of poor rains, but also increased their yield. Because neighboring farmers began to need more labor to help with their bountiful crops, Lakshmi and her two older daughters were able to earn twice as much income as laborers. Vellore and Lakshmi gave some of their land to their son while increasing their total rice production on their own smaller parcel of land. By the end of the decade, Vellore and Lakshmi's total rice production was double what it had been 10 years earlier.*

*According to the International Food Policy Research Institute's initiative, *A 2020 Vision for Food, Agriculture, and the Environment*; see *Feeding the World, Preventing Poverty, and Protecting the Earth: A 2020 Vision* (Washington: IFPRI, 1996).

aid is a form of defense spending that protects our national security — and at considerably less cost, by the way, than the $30 billion that Congress is currently spending for 20 B-2 bombers.[8]

Trade and Investment: A Road to Development?

Many aid critics rally around the slogan "trade, not aid" and argue that private investment flows will do more to reduce hunger and poverty than aid from governments. Under current trading rules and policies, however, there is no way for most poor countries to trade their way into prosperity. Trade barriers in industrial country markets cost developing countries about $100 billion annually, or nearly double what they receive in official development assistance. The forces that are pushing most developing countries to adopt export-oriented policies have not convinced the industrial countries to eliminate barriers to key developing-country manufactures such as textiles. The global trade liberalization agreement that was recently concluded could *cost* Africa $2.6 billion a year, because of rising prices on imported food and lower prices for African export crops.[9]

While developing countries in Asia and Latin America are increasingly exporting manufactured goods, Africa continues to rely heavily on primary commodity exports such as unprocessed agricultural products and minerals. The terms of trade have consistently been against these goods in recent years. Global trade liberalization and donors' pressure on developing countries to boost exports in an uncoordinated manner will drive prices down further.

U.S. trade with developing countries is substantial. The developing world provided 41 percent of U.S. imports and purchased 39 percent of U.S. exports in 1991-1992. However, much of this trade is with higher income developing countries. Low-income countries supplied just 8 percent of U.S.

Food Aid and Food Security in an Era of Downsizing

by Jindra Čekan and Kimberly Miller

The U.S. commitment to reducing global hunger and food insecurity is part of an integrated strategy and vision for sustainable development. Since 1990, U.S. food aid has, by law, focused primarily on promoting food security in recipient countries. Much of the U.S. government's food aid activity is carried out by private voluntary organizations (PVOs) and cooperatives. U.S. PVOs generally target relief and development projects to poor households and communities. These projects seek to reduce chronic poverty, the root cause of hunger. PVOs work closely with local institutions and secure funds from private donors to complement U.S. government resources.

Yet this effective public/private partnership is in jeopardy. The United States has lowered its food aid tonnage drastically. The U.S. Agency for International Development (USAID) has reduced its overseas presence substantially, limited the range of projects eligible for funding and stressed immediate proof of "results" for Congress, all of which can jeopardize the quality of assistance to the most chronically vulnerable people.

Food Security Defined

USAID defines food security as a situation in which "all people at all times have both physical and economic access to sufficient food to meet their dietary needs for a productive and healthy life." *Sustained* food security includes immediate food consumption, as well as the means by which people assure diversified sources of agricultural production, income, health, water, sanitation and education.

Food insecurity is not only a question of poverty, but the proportion of income households devote to food. The poorest people in the developing world spend 80 percent or more of their earnings on food. Food insecurity is caused by natural as well as human-made disasters, and people can be either transitorily or chronically food insecure.

PVOs and Food Security

Catholic Relief Services (CRS) and other PVOs use food aid for both emergency relief and long-term development. Food aid has helped to keep people alive in disasters such as the Ethiopian famine of the mid-1980s, the Somali famine of the 1990s and refugee crises in Cambodia, Kurdistan, Rwanda and Haiti.

Long-term dependence on food aid is neither sustainable nor desirable, and U.S. law requires that food aid projects not create a disincentive to local agriculture. PVO development projects use food rations as both nutritional supplements and incentives. Health projects targeted at malnourished children and their mothers combine feeding with training in improved child care practices. Food-for-work projects, in which workers are paid partly or wholly with food, improve agricultural productivity and physical infrastructure, and conserve natural resources. Other food aid projects enable school children to be fed, the handicapped to be rehabilitated and refugees to be resettled.[10] The rations rarely cover more than half of an individual's minimum daily food intake, but the projects promote self-development and eventual self-sufficiency.

Such targeted non-emergency uses of food aid are not long-term solutions to the ecological, political or macroeconomic ills of recipient countries, but if appropriately used, they can help alleviate acute short-term hunger and foster development for those in chronic need.

PVOs pursue the goal of food security through projects that enable people to not only satisfy immediate and longer-term consumption, but also generate buffers against shocks such as drought and enhance their quality of life through access to land, safe water and personal safety.[11] It is important to build people's ability at all levels, as people are often forced to choose among eating three meals, selling their assets, remaining healthy or paying their basic expenses. Being forced to make such tradeoffs jeopardizes prospects for sustained development.

PVOs buttress food security through non-food resources as well. Projects address malnutrition and promote healthy growth of children through education of mothers, which increasingly is based in communities and provides training *without* food (except for therapeutic feeding of severely malnourished children). Most PVOs seek to enhance small-farm agricultural production through training in improved agricultural production and natural resource management.

Many PVOs also try to help poor communities boost their incomes to diversify their sources of food security. For example, CRS and other agencies offer small loans to poor people, mostly women, who invest in very small-scale, non-farm business activities – often employing only the borrower herself – such as processing and selling food, making clothing and fattening and reselling small livestock. These are known as "microenterprises." The loans are often as small as $30 for six months, but the repayment rates exceed 90 percent.[12] Incomes for food purchases are particularly important for urban food security.

Cuts in U.S. Aid

In spite of growing needs, U.S. support for humanitarian and development assistance has reached a 50-year low. Funding for U.S. international food aid has fallen by 30 percent over the past three years, with total tonnage declining by 50 percent. In March 1995, the United States announced that it would unilaterally reduce its annual pledge under the international Food Aid Convention by nearly one-half, from 4.47 million metric tons to 2.5 million.

Poverty-focused programs have borne the brunt of cuts in foreign assistance spending. Budget cuts will likely force the continued downsizing of USAID, including the closure of even more field missions in poor countries.

Ironically, all this has happened as USAID has pledged to increase the level of aid implemented through local and international PVOs. Congress, too, has consistently expressed support for maintaining or increasing PVO involvement in programming of development and humanitarian assistance. Yet resources allocated have been shrinking, and aid programs that help poor people have sustained the deepest budget cuts.

PVOs bring a number of advantages to relief and development work. They tend to work at the community level, operate in a cost-effective manner and stretch development dollars by leveraging significant private funding. PVOs commonly carry out programs in partnership with indigenous non-governmental organizations. Many PVOs consider local capacity-building as important as service delivery, unlike some contractors and "for-profit" consultants.[13] PVOs are accountable to their private supporters across the country and engage them in education and advocacy campaigns on world hunger and poverty. For many of the poorest people, PVOs provide their "voice."

Effects of Downsizing

Yet budget cuts have forced USAID to pull out of Burkina Faso and Togo, two of the poorest countries in Africa. By suspending USAID funds for PVO development projects in these two countries, as well as others without USAID missions, the agency is jeopardizing food security investments that PVOs have made there over the last 30 years. For example, CRS has carried out a lunch program for over 300,000 children in the most vulnerable areas of Burkina Faso, and is pressing USAID to allow this effort to continue. There are encouraging indications that this policy may still change.

USAID had also limited the definition of food security to using food aid to support only agricultural production, health and nutrition. In spite of households' need for *income* for food security, the agency does not want to allow PVOs to sell food to finance microenterprise loans. The overall aid budget is declining, and other funds for these purposes are now scarce. Yet households' needs to produce food, utilize it and gain access to it through income remain the same.

Food aid has provided vital assistance to institutions that serve handicapped, ill, aged and displaced people, as well as orphaned and malnourished children from destitute families. The institutions rehabilitate handicapped people, educate orphans, train their parents and provide other services to the poorest of poor people. Yet, USAID plans to phase out these sorts of programs over the next two to five years in Haiti, Kenya and Burkina Faso. This is ironic, given that the very self-sufficiency that USAID wants to promote is being sacrificed in the name of budget cuts.

Funding cuts and threatened further downsizing have caused USAID to press PVOs for proof of program impact. PVOs *should* have to demonstrate that U.S. government investments of food and dollars have had a measurable, positive effect on recipients.[14] PVOs have begun devising impact indicators for development programs such as decreases in severe malnutrition and increases in agricultural yields and school enrollment and attendance.

However, pressure to demonstrate immediate, positive results may be counterproductive. If the results are to inform future funding decisions, then the projects chosen may be in higher potential areas. These areas are likely to prove positive impact more reliably, rather than more marginal and needier areas and economic sectors that take longer to rehabilitate but whose food security problems are more dire. Also, in the rush to prove impact, USAID may be compromising PVOs' ability to learn from their mistakes.

Conclusion

Clearly, situations where people are extremely food insecure are unlikely to disappear without continued intervention by a wide array of national and international donors, implementing agencies, local governments and indigenous PVOs. Mustering the political will to end global hunger will require concerted effort by both the public and private sectors.

The U.S. government, for its part, needs to reverse the downward trend in bilateral and multilateral development and humanitarian assistance to the poorest people and countries. It must also press forward with reform efforts, including putting "partnership" language into practice and finding ways to effectively work with PVOs in a manner that capitalizes on their value-added, unique organizational identities and respects their need for substantial autonomy, independence and flexibility in assessing needs and carrying out programs with local counterparts.

PVOs, for their part, should:

- continue to hone and strengthen their capacity to conduct performance-based programs, remaining in dialogue with USAID concerning appropriate impact indicators;

- continue to push for the retention of assistance to food insecure countries and vulnerable populations, particularly in Africa; and

- step up their own advocacy activity around hunger and poverty issues, including increased efforts to educate and activate their constituencies on these concerns.

DR. JINDRA ČEKAN *is food security advisor at Catholic Relief Services.* KIMBERLY MILLER *was formerly director of public policy at CRS.*

imports and bought a mere 5 percent of exports during the same period. Sub-Saharan Africa supplied 2 percent of imports (mainly oil from Angola and Nigeria) and bought less than 0.6 percent of U.S. exports. Only 0.1 percent of the benefits under the Generalized System of Preferences (GSP), which provides duty-free treatment to developing-country manufactured and processed exports, go to the lowest-income countries. This is because GSP excludes textiles, footwear, clothing and leather goods, the products that the poorest countries are most likely to manufacture.[15]

Reliance on direct private investment alone is not a viable anti-hunger strategy for developing countries either. New corporate investment in the developing world – mainly from Western sources – increased by 13 percent in 1995, totaling more than $90 billion. But about 75 percent went to 12 countries, mainly in Asia. China alone received over one-third of the funds. Direct foreign investment in Africa increased from $1.4 billion to $2.2 billion from 1990-1992, but is still only about 2 percent of direct foreign investment in developing countries.[16]

Private investment seldom helps to meet basic needs of food, education, primary health care, family planning or sanitation. These remain areas where public action – and foreign aid – are essential.

New Hope from Civil Society

The worldwide spread of democracy since the early 1980s has allowed civil society organizations to flourish and to press for more people-oriented development policies. Many popular organizations are pushing their governments and aid donors to do more to overcome poverty and reduce hunger. These efforts hold out promise for transforming the politics of hunger internationally.

In Africa, for example, the Inter-Africa Group, an advocacy organization based in Ethiopia, has devoted considerable attention

to food security issues, including emergency response and prevention, as well as chronic hunger. It has encouraged NGOs in the Horn of Africa to engage poor and hungry people in devising and implementing development programs. The Inter-Africa Group also works creatively to promote conflict resolution and build democratic institutions. It has had some influence on U.S. aid in Ethiopia and on several international institutions.[17]

In Asia and the Pacific, representatives from 108 nongovernmental and people's organizations from 18 countries convened in Bangkok, Thailand, in April 1996 for a regional consultation in preparation for the November 1996 World Food Summit. They issued a declaration reaffirming "The strong conviction that food is the basic human right that supersedes property rights, commercial advantage, free trade and the dictates of the market." They called for "a new social contract…among Asian farmers, Asian peoples and Asian governments." It would include:

- decentralized and democratic control by people over food production and distribution;
- people's participation in policy and decision-making;
- recognition of the vital role of women in food and nutrition;
- effective agrarian reforms to benefit small-scale producers; and
- emphasis on sustainable agriculture and policies to preserve land for agricultural and food production.[18]

In Brazil, a popular movement against hunger has captured the imagination of Brazilians from all walks of life. Although the country has the world's 10th largest economy, 32 million people (more than 20 percent of the population) are hungry. In 1993, Brazilians established the Action of Citizens Against Misery and for Life. It includes more than 3,500 local committees around the country that focus on nutrition, employment, housing, education, health and sanitation. The committees sponsor communal bakeries, small vegetable gardens, microenterprises and paper recycling and production. The work emphasizes both emergency food distribution and job creation for the poorest Brazilians. Almost 3 million people have joined the committees, including doctors, lawyers, nutritionists, journalists, business people, workers, artists and students, as well as poor people. The campaign has forged strong links across lines of race and class.

At the national level, the Brazilian government agreed to establish a National Council for Food Security, composed of cabinet ministers and representatives of civil society. Its major responsibility is to assure that the government makes food security a key national policy objective, with adequate funding for anti-hunger initiatives.[19]

Bread for the World Institute networks with hundreds of NGOs around the world to push for reforms at the World Bank. NGOs have convinced their governments and the bank to make much more of the bank's analysis publicly available. This often gives citizens in the developing countries information that they did not have before about development problems in their country and their government's policy dialogue with the World Bank. Although bank and many government officials resisted this more open information policy, public debate about bank-related development activities has, in some cases, clearly improved their quality and chances for success.

International Institutions[20]

Cooperative action by governments and civil society will become increasingly important as the world becomes increasingly interdependent (see Chapter 4). Nations will also need to work together on factors that could reverse progress against world hunger: population growth to about 9 billion people by the year 2030 and increased fluctuations in the prices and supply of food because of recent trade liberalization in agriculture.

We must prepare now to feed about 9 billion people who will inhabit the world by 2030.

JACQUES DIOUF, DIRECTOR GENERAL, FOOD AND AGRICULTURE ORGANIZATION OF THE UNITED NATIONS

Presently, the institutions of international governance are weak in relation to sovereign states and global corporations. Nonetheless, the U.N. system plays an important role in transferring development and humanitarian resources from the industrial to the developing world, preventing and resolving violent conflicts between and within nations, identifying and helping solve international problems such as those related to the environment or women's special needs, and developing norms for international behavior. It is also a major storehouse of information about the well-being of the world's people. All these activities help reduce hunger.

The world body is an association of its member governments, dependent on them for decision making and resources. Its ability to influence the actions of an unwilling member state is quite limited. Nevertheless, examining instances when the U.N. system has helped resolve common problems may suggest ways to enhance its role in reducing poverty and eliminating hunger.

Probably the most helpful examples are those in which consensus and moral suasion have moved nations toward common action that they could not undertake individually. The success of the childhood immunization scheme referred to above entailed cooperation among UNICEF, governments in developing and donor nations and nongovernmental agencies. The World Health Organization led a similarly successful global effort that eliminated smallpox.

One of the longest-running efforts toward structural change is that of the International Labor Organization (ILO), which actually predates the United Nations, to persuade nations to voluntarily establish worker standards. More than 100 nations have adopted ILO conventions. They have pledged to permit workers to organize and bargain collectively, abolish forced labor and prohibit discrimination against women and minorities in employment and pay. What nations actually do often falls short of these commitments, but the ILO conventions have had a far-reaching impact on working conditions.

The Law of the Sea Treaty is one of the more complex consensual agreements negotiated under U.N. auspices. Hammered out during most of the 1970s, this agreement resolved several long-standing disputes regarding passage through international straits, zones of sovereignty and economic influence. It clarified rights to fish and to protect threatened species. The treaty sets up new mechanisms to allocate the resources under international waters, which were declared to be the heritage of all humankind. Although the United States finally signed the treaty in 1995, the Senate has not yet ratified it. Even so, the United States and most other non-signatories have honored virtually all its provisions since its completion in 1978.

The United Nations attempted to negotiate a Code of Conduct for Transnational Entities – both private and government corporations – for more than a decade before abandoning the attempt. The need for a code to regulate global corporations continues to grow.

The Food and Agriculture Organization of the United Nations (FAO) is convening the 1996 World Food Summit, which will attempt to "adopt a policy and a plan of action that would guarantee the fundamental human right to food in the world." Governments will be asked to make important pledges to develop and set aside resources for national food security plans, to strengthen coordination among the international agencies that deal with food security; to help countries where food security is deteriorating; and to encourage a greater role for civil society organizations. They may also look at negotiations on a code of conduct related to food security. NGOs have also proposed a Food Security Treaty, which seeks to make the abstract right to food into an enforceable reality.[21]

U.N. peacekeeping operations have great potential for reducing war-related hunger and poverty by preventing or shortening conflicts and reducing the likelihood of their recurrence. But such operations are usually contingent on negotiating consent of the relevant government(s) or major contenders. Two main exceptions: (1) when the richest and most powerful nations are willing to take action under a U.N. umbrella, as in the Persian Gulf in 1990-1991 when the United States, with limited participation by other countries, carried out U.N.-endorsed military activity, or similar action in Korea in the early 1950s; and (2) when there is no effective government, as in Somalia in 1992-1993.

The establishment of the International Criminal Tribunal for the Former Yugoslavia in 1993 may represent something of a breakthrough. It has the power to seek extradition of alleged war criminals from all member states, and to report noncompliance to the U.N. Security Council for possible sanctions. At least in theory, the International Force in Bosnia on behalf of the United Nations is supposed to assist the tribunal by detaining suspects. A similar panel exists to prosecute perpetrators of genocide in Rwanda, and there are proposals to establish a permanent court to try cases of crimes against humanity.[22]

The Yugoslavia tribunal, while not directly related to hunger, offers hope that new global bodies and agreements may emerge that could enforce the right to food. State sovereignty remains a problem in this regard, although international consensus is growing that sovereignty ceases to apply when governmental institutions collapse, as in some recent African crises, or when the government is directly involved in creating humanitarian emergencies.

Chapter 4 highlights the need for better international coordination in managing the global economy. The international economic institutions that do exist are dominated by the rich nations and tend to serve their interests. The Group of 7 (Canada, France, Germany, Italy, Japan, the United Kingdom and the United States), the world's richest countries, account for just 12 percent of the world's population, but their governments' annual economic summit is the single most influential global economic institution.

The General Agreement on Tariffs and Trade (GATT) has provided the framework for international trade. The most recent GATT agreement, signed by 124 nations in 1994, is the most far-reaching. It established the World Trade Organization as successor to the GATT, and greatly strengthened its dispute settling mechanisms, which in some instances may now lead to trade sanctions. It included agreements to reduce barriers to agricultural trade that will force adjustments in national agricultural policies. Africa will no longer have special access to European markets, and declining food aid will also add to hunger in Africa.

The GATT agreement will phase out the Multi-Fiber Agreement, which now restricts the sale of labor-intensive textiles and clothes. The phase-out will create new jobs in poor countries, but threaten some lower-skilled workers in industrial countries. The agreement also extends international protection of patents and copyrights. The industrial countries wanted this, while others see it as a threat to cultures and traditional plant varieties. The net impact of the GATT agreement on poverty and hunger will not be known for years. Many economists are optimistic, but many developing country NGOs think it will be sharply negative.

With the exception of forced labor, efforts to link labor rights to broad international trade agreements have been unsuccessful. Limited labor rights were addressed in a side agreement to the North American Free Trade Agreement among Mexico, Canada and the United States. Efforts are underway to bring labor rights onto the agenda of the newly created World Trade Organization.

International Financial Institutions

The international financial institutions (IFIs), including the IMF, the World Bank and related regional development banks, are the leading public source of development finance. Developing-country governments owe more than 2 trillion dollars in debt, much of it to the IFIs.

Debt has become a major cause of hunger and poverty in developing countries. It drains resources from efforts to achieve sustainable development and human well-being such as education, health care and good sanitation. In most indebted developing countries, poor people had no say in their governments' decisions to take on the debt burden. African countries spend more than twice as much on debt service as they do on health and primary education. In Zambia, malnutrition increased two and-a-half times within a decade after the country enacted austerity policies to curb its debt.[23]

Not only are the IFIs – especially the bank and the IMF – the "lenders of last resort," but their "seal of approval" concerning a country's economic policies is essential for attracting aid from governments and investment from private corporations.

Beginning in the 1980s, the World Bank joined the IMF in tying new or replacement loans to borrower governments' adoption of "structural adjustment" policies. Adjustment programs are designed to recover financial stability and economic growth. They include balanced budgets, privatization of government enterprises and currency devaluations, all focused on recovering fiscal strength, promotion of exports and increased market orientation. But resulting reductions in government spending and increased import costs have often hurt poor and hungry people.

Although the IMF and World Bank point out that they never "impose" conditions without the sovereign consent of borrower governments, financially strapped regimes are in an extremely weak bargaining position. Thus, these institutions, especially the bank, have enormous power to shape countries' development policies.

The bank has, in recent years, given more attention to the poverty alleviation impact of their operations, and is somewhat more open to participation by affected people in the decisions that will shape their lives. Very recently, the IMF and bank have entered serious discussions about reducing some of the debt of the poorest nations.

In the World Bank, the IMF and the regional development banks, voting power is based primarily on financial contributions. So the rich countries again dominate, although developing-country governments have some say.

Bread for the World Institute, through its Development Bank Watchers' project, has sought to encourage more participatory decision making by the World Bank and regional development banks, as well as developing-country governments. Although this will not redress the power imbalance, we believe it will lead to a stronger focus on reducing hunger and poverty. Our project has helped shape the World Bank's plans to promote more participatory development activities. It also helped get the bank to establish a fund that will provide resources to nongovernmental agencies to help finance microenterprises.

In February 1996, the project helped arrange a dialogue between the bank's top leaders and representatives of 400 African NGOs in Accra, Ghana. In 1996 and 1997, the project will focus on helping to empower NGOs in both wealthy and developing countries to influence the policies of their own and donor governments, as well as the IFIs, in order to achieve sustainable development.

Reform Proposals

Sir Hans Singer, British development expert, has recently proposed some additional reforms to help make the institutions of global governance more accountable to publics and more interested in eradicating hunger. He suggests somewhat more democratic decisionmaking in the World Bank and IMF, coupled with decision-making structures in U.N. bodies outside the Security Council that would more realistically reflect the power, wealth and population of different nations. Parallel to this, Singer recommends greater collaboration between the IMF and World Bank and the rest of the U.N. system, since it is increasingly difficult to treat economic, social, humanitarian and military issues separately. He believes that the U.N. Development Programme's holistic approach to "sustainable human development and human security" could help bring the U.N. system back into the focus on human problems for which it was originally designed.[24]

Conclusion: Toward a New Development Agenda

Bread for the World Institute supports the goal of sustainable development, the reduction of hunger and poverty in environmentally sound ways, in the United States and around the world. A sustainable system necessarily must be predicated on the actions of an informed citizenry, especially low-income people who experience problems in the system most intensely.

Hunger will persist in the developing world into the next century, and will worsen in sub-Saharan Africa. Actions taken now — by developing-country governments and civil society, both public and private aid donors and concerned publics in the industrial world — can do much to reverse current trends. But deep cuts in aid, especially poverty-focused development aid, will add to world hunger, especially in Africa. What is needed instead is to reform aid, so that more of it is focused on the kind of development that can overcome hunger.

Bread for the World Institute favors development aid that is equitable, environmentally sound and that recognizes poor people as critical stakeholders in all phases of the process. Such development must involve both market and public institutions. It includes public investment in human capital such as assuring broad access to health care and education. In addition, protecting vulnerable groups from the impact of economic change is essential. Most important, public policies must assure that all population groups benefit from economic growth and have equal access to economic opportunities. Increasingly, development of this sort is backed by local governments (especially in Latin America), with financial assistance from the central authorities.

Beyond aid, a comprehensive solution to the problem of growing unpayable developing-country debt is needed. New financial resources are needed, and debt relief conditions should be consistent with poverty reduction rather than placing new burdens on poor people.

The world trading system remains severely biased against the poorer developing countries. Those countries need mechanisms that will assure that global trade liberalization will not undermine efforts to achieve self-reliance, especially in food and agriculture. Also, industrial-country trade barriers and export subsidies continue to hurt developing countries. Developing countries need continued and expanded preferential access to industrial-country markets, as well as opportunities to export processed goods. Leveling the trade playing field is likely to require additional financial and technical aid:

- to cope with rising prices of essential imports during the process of trade liberalization;

- to improve internal marketing and transportation systems so as to better link domestic and world markets; and

- to improve product quality standards in order to take advantage of new market opportunities.

International institutions are important. They should be supported and made more effective, especially more democratic.

Though the road to sustainable development is a difficult one, we think it is the most hopeful alternative to a world sharply divided between haves and have-nots.

In any event, the United States and other industrial countries cannot afford to turn their backs on the developing world. Economic deprivation results in social upheaval and political extremism. Poverty and instability have effects that quickly cross national borders in the form of refugees, drug trafficking, terrorism, global warming, environmental degradation and AIDS. Also, developing countries are a fast-growing market for U.S. exports, and, with help, poor countries in Africa and elsewhere could also contribute to global prosperity.

Effective public institutions at the local, sub-national, national and global level all have essential functions in the task of ending hunger – one of humanity's greatest challenges in the 21st century.

Governments not only have a duty to protect the food security of vulnerable groups, but their actions are critical to expanding economic opportunities for poor and hungry people, for example by ensuring widespread access to credit. Most important, we believe, for guaranteeing that governments "get the policies right" is the active engagement at every step of the public, particularly poor and hungry people.

DR. MARC J. COHEN *is senior research associate and* DON REEVES *is economic policy analyst at Bread for the World Institute.*

CHAPTER 7

Call to Action

by David Beckmann and Larry Hollar

Joseph Crachiola

During the 1995-1996 congressional term, the U.S. government enacted policies that are likely to increase hunger in the United States and worldwide. President Clinton vetoed two very punitive welfare bills in 1995, but in 1996 signed welfare "reform" that is likely to be very harmful to hungry people. This law will take $60 billion away from poor people in the United States and end a 60-year guarantee of federal assistance to children in poverty. Congress also slashed U.S. development assistance, making the deepest cuts in poverty-focused programs.

Critics claimed that compassion, as it was exercised through federal programs, was expensive, flawed and counterproductive. In their view, government, and especially the national government, too often created costly programs that result in disempowerment and dependency. Many people across the political spectrum wonder what went wrong and what can be done.

This debate in the United States is part of a worldwide trend. Western Europe is stepping back from some welfare state commitments. Countries that once had communist governments have virtually all rejected those systems. Developing countries have also been reducing the roles of their governments. This is partly because financial problems and foreign creditors have pressed for such changes, but partly because many local people are convinced that a larger role for markets will better serve them.

In our view, the United States is not only turning its face away from hungry and poor people at home, but continues to default on its moral responsibility to respond internationally. The depth of malnutrition and poverty, the day-to-day human misery, the devastating and abusive effects of long-term deprivation are beyond the imagining of most U.S. citizens. Bread for the World Institute believes there should be more talk about the cost in human lives and well-being and less about budgets, especially since we are drowning in affluence.

Conclusions

Governments are under siege. Yet as the preceding chapters demonstrate, governments have crucial roles to play in reducing hunger and poverty. Hunger is on the increase in those regions where governments aren't working or where government efforts to reduce poverty are being curtailed.

Governments operate at various levels. Following the principle of subsidiarity, we believe that local *is* often better. Federally funded programs administered by states and localities such as the Special Supplemental Nutrition Program for Women, Infants and Children (WIC) provide hands-on and caring services.

But we wonder whether local governments have the infrastructure and cash flow to deal with the magnitude of the problem they will face. Local governments turn to state governments for money, even as state governments seek funds from the federal government. The $60 billion cutback in federal welfare and nutrition funding is like a noose around the neck of service providers.

Also, governments *are* limited in what they can do well. People who escape from poverty have had to work hard and smart – and maybe get some help along the way.

We believe that national governments have a distinctive role in assuring even-handed justice across state lines. The U.S. government should assure that children don't go hungry, whether they live in Mississippi or Minnesota. The federal government needs to provide funding to help lower-income states meet national standards. Some state welfare reform programs have creative elements, but their success depends on continued federal standards and funding. What's most important is ending hunger and poverty, not which level of government carries out the programs.

National governments also have international responsibilities. In our interdependent world, it is both wrong and short-sighted for the U.S. government to slash those foreign aid programs that help overcome poverty and hunger around the world.

Finally, there are some governmental functions that must be carried out at the international level. Chapter 4 argues that we need to strengthen international management of the global economy. Chapter 6 describes some necessary and effective international institutions. It also describes ways to improve the international financial institutions, especially their impact on poor and hungry people.

Governments have important roles to play in meeting basic human needs and enhancing the quality of our lives together. This report cites many examples from various countries' public programs that effectively and efficiently reduced poverty and hunger. Child survival and microenterprise programs are outstanding examples from developing country experience. Foreign aid has helped promote these approaches, which are now being copied in the United States and other industrial countries.

Chapter 1 notes that other industrial countries have much less childhood poverty than the United States, mainly because they have more extensive government programs in place to protect children. Chapter 2 shows that welfare and nutrition programs in the United States have worked fairly well, despite all the negative rhetoric aimed in their direction.

Participation of citizens such as these Indian activists is critical to the effectiveness of government anti-hunger efforts.

Suzanne Kinderratten

30 years. The bulk of those jobs will be in the private sector, mainly in the urban areas of developing countries. From the standpoint of hungry people, there's no substitute for a healthy, but fair, private sector worldwide.

Private charities also have a distinctive role to play in reducing hunger. They are humane, immediate and sometimes creative. But charities cannot do the job alone, as they readily admit. Governments must also do their part.

Some of the most effective approaches involve public-private partnerships. CARE and Catholic Relief Services have long used U.S. food aid to supplement community assistance projects, for example. Chapter 3 notes cases where low-income U.S. communities have organized to deal with their problems and received government assistance.

The active participation of citizens – including hungry and poor people themselves – is needed to ensure that government activities are effective. The best government anti-hunger programs engage the intended beneficiaries as active players, not passive objects, creating a sense of ownership and long-term viability. A good example is WIC's nutrition education component, which helps mothers and children keep themselves healthy long after they leave the program.

True, some government activities are inefficient or even corrupt. Too many well-conceived programs, in the United States and elsewhere, lack the resources to function as well as they could. Government programs often become the captives of special interests or powerful elites, at the expense of the common good and people in need. U.S. government farm programs are a classic example: established to preserve small family operations, the programs have provided large-scale farmers with the lion's share of the benefits. Similarly, food subsidy programs in developing countries frequently have catered to relatively well-off, politically powerful constituencies instead of hungry people.

The role of governments in reducing poverty and hunger is less visible than food banks and other private assistance programs. But governments can establish a framework within which nearly all families can earn their own livelihoods. High taxes and transfers of income can indeed reduce people's incentives to produce and earn income. On the other hand, public investments in nutrition and education are often necessary to give people from low-income backgrounds a chance to become fully productive and earn a decent income. Chapter 2 notes that nearly all countries have economies that are a mix of markets and governments. People of good will may disagree about how to get the balance right in specific cases.

Chapter 4 analyzes how economic globalization has limited what governments can do to provide a framework for jobs and sustainable development. It shows how globalization pushes governments to restrain growth and job creation. The solutions require increased cooperation among governments in managing the global economy in order to make that economy function better and to establish a more just world.

As noted in Chapter 1, the future extent of poverty and hunger in the world depends mainly on whether the world economy can create 2 billion new jobs over the next

Ultimately, the only way to assure that government programs are adequately funded and operated honestly, efficiently and in the public interest is for hungry people and their political allies to engage in vigilant monitoring and advocacy. Chapter 6 describes how grassroots groups have burgeoned in developing countries since the spread of democracy in the 1980s. Increasingly, they are holding their governments and international financial institutions accountable for how economic policy decisions affect poor and hungry people. Bread for the World's campaign, *Elect to End Childhood Hunger*, in the 1996 U.S. congressional elections is another example of citizen action to win government decisions that reduce poverty and hunger.

The political onslaught against government efforts to reduce poverty and hunger has done a lot of harm. Programs on which low-income U.S. families depend have been cut – in some cases, dismantled. In a number of instances, such as Michigan's retreat from General Assistance, the added pain and problems for struggling people have already been documented. Millions of poor people are suffering from similar actions by other governments. Chapter 5 documents the pain in India, Mexico and Ghana.

Yet the debate about the role of governments also holds some promise. Many government programs, both domestic and international, are in need of reform. Where hunger is on the increase – as in the United States – there is clearly a need for extensive public debate about causes of, and solutions to, hunger. If we can move beyond stereotypes and political ideologies to analysis and civil discussion, today's debate could identify more effective strategies.

Then, we can shift the focus of debate away from reducing what we spend on poor people. We should instead be debating how best to reduce poverty and hunger. And, we need to mobilize people of good will to contribute generously to charities and lobby effectively in state and national capitals.

Two decades ago, the World Food Conference issued the Universal Declaration on the Eradication of Hunger and Malnutrition, expressing widespread consensus that hunger could and would be ended by now. The governments of the world are preparing for a World Food Summit in November 1996. But the goal of ending hunger is certainly not driving political debate. For example, during the welfare reform debate in the U.S. Congress in 1995-1996, members of Congress discussed such issues as the federal budget deficit and turning programs over to the states. The debate largely ignored whether the changes would bring the nation closer to ending hunger.

If we can mobilize the will to overcome hunger, today's worldwide debate about governments' roles might help us get the job done.

Invitation to Leadership

The governance of a community is not synonymous with its government. A community acts together through a myriad of agencies, informal organizations and linkages. These relationships "govern" the community's sense of itself. The community uses government, and government also provides leadership in the community. But many

What Citizens Can Do About Hunger

- Learn the critical policy issues.
- Work to hold governments and other powerful institutions accountable.
- Vote.
- Join Bread for the World and other anti-hunger groups.
- Build anti-hunger coalitions.
- Volunteer in or contribute to direct anti-hunger services.
- Work with low-income people and organizations that seek empowerment for hungry people.
- Live a responsible lifestyle.

individuals and organizations outside government help to decide what the community's purposes and priorities are.

This is true of the international community, too, although the world's peoples are not as closely bound together as the families in one small town. Over the past decade, nongovernmental organizations that represent and articulate grassroots concerns have proliferated rapidly. For example, throughout Africa, such groups have offered new channels for Africans to express their aspirations. These groups exist in countries with repressive, nonrepresentative regimes as well as in democracies.

Government programs must continue to complement private efforts if we hope to overcome hunger.

William Mills/Montgomery County Public Schools

PLEASE SHARE FOOD WITH OTHERS

The work of Bread for the World Institute's Bank Watcher's Project has helped to show how such grassroots groups can network to claim a voice in major decisions made by international financial institutions and governments. It has also helped link groups across national and regional lines.

Everyone in a society – including those who do not see themselves as leaders in a traditional sense – has a key role in holding government and other institutions accountable to moral standards. Much of today's cynicism about governments' capacity to help poor and hungry people stems from growing frustration with government's unresponsiveness. In the United States, Bread for the World, as well as other anti-hunger and child advocacy organizations, environmental groups and citizens' associations help caring people make a difference. One individual feels isolated, but working together with like-spirited people across the nation and the world multiplies impact. Participation in building the common good can also be personally satisfying and contribute to one's own sense of wholeness, community and meaningful spirituality.

The challenges that face all grassroots advocacy organizations today are difficult:

- how to overcome apathy, cynicism and me-first-ism;

- how to make complex policy issues understandable to those who are not experts and relevant to those whose world views are narrow;

- how to engage technology in a way that's useful both for the grassroots and those on whom pressure is to be brought;

- how to encourage activism among younger people, low-income people and those stretched by competing demands for their time and attention;

- how to overcome undue pessimism about government and the widespread sense of disconnectedness between people and government; and

- how to weave disparate advocacy efforts into large-scale, lasting political change.

Governments today are more or less responsive to citizen opinion, depending not only on the form of government but also on the degree of citizen organization and commitment. In the United States, the country with the longest unbroken record of democratic rule, voter participation in most elections is shockingly limited. Polls show widespread disenchantment with government, and too many people are apathetic about civic matters.

Some think this reflects a spiritual crisis, or at least a loss of faith in society's structures and likely progress. Others see economic and social polarization in U.S. society and fear more fragmentation and violence. To some, government seems increasingly gridlocked and unable to resolve the issues society faces.

It is no wonder that many seek renewed security in families and religious faith to help address the spiritual crisis, or in institutions closer to home than a distant national government to solve grave social problems. *What Governments **Can** Do* shows, however, is that governments have an indispensable role to play in assuring the well-being of vulnerable people. But governments do not act alone.

In the United States, it is quite feasible to end widespread hunger. Government would have to play a modestly expanded role, but winning the necessary political support does not seem beyond the range of possibility. It also seems quite possible to win support for U.S. foreign aid and trade policies that would powerfully contribute to reduced hunger worldwide.

But these political changes depend on individuals and organizations committing themselves to help win them.

*What Governments **Can** Do* is, fundamentally, about companionship (Latin *cum* = with, *panis* = bread) in society. Governments can't do everything, but they play crucial roles in sharing our common bread so that all may have a decent life. And the only force that can guarantee responsive and effective government is concerned citizens who crave a just and companionate society.

DAVID BECKMANN *is president of Bread for the World and Bread for the World Institute.* **LARRY HOLLAR** *is a Bread for the World regional organizer.*

TABLE 1

Global Hunger – Life and Death Indicators

	Total population (millions) 1996	Projected population (millions) 2025	Projected population growth rate (%) 1995-2000	Projected total fertility rate 1995-2000	% population below age 15 mid-1996	% population urban 1995	Life expectancy at birth 1994		Infant mortality rate per 1,000 live births 1994	Under-5 mortality rate per 1,000 live births		Maternal mortality rate per 100,000 live births 1980-1992
							Male	Female		1960	1994	
Developing Countries	**4,633.4**	**7,055.9**	**1.8**	**3.29**	**35**	**38**	**62.4**	**65.3**	**68**	**216**	**101**	**346**
Africa (sub-Saharan)	**612.9a**	**1,285.5a**	**..**	**..**	**46**	**..**	**..**	**..**	**107**	**256**	**177**	**597**
Angola	11.5	26.6	3.3	6.69	45	32	47.4	50.6	170	345	292	..
Benin	5.6	12.3	2.9	6.60	47	31	47.2	50.6	85	310	142	160
Botswana	1.5	3.0	2.9	4.46	43	28	65.3	69.2	42	170	54	250
Burkina Faso	10.6	21.7	2.5	6.06	48	27	45.3	48.1	89	318	169	810
Burundi	6.6	13.5	2.8	6.28	46	8	49.4	52.9	106	255	176	..
Cameroon	13.6	29.2	2.8	5.30	44	45	57.0	60.0	69	264	109	430
Cape Verde	0.4	0.7	..	3.95	45	54	65.5	67.5	54	164	73	..
Central African Republic	3.4	6.4	2.4	5.29	43	39	47.8	52.5	103	294	175	600
Chad	6.5	12.9	2.8	5.51	41	21	47.9	51.1	119	325	202	960
Comoros	0.7	1.6	..	6.50	48	31	57.5	58.5	86	248	126	..
Congo	2.7	5.7	2.7	5.87	44	59	47.8	52.0	82	220	109	900
Côte d'Ivoire	14.7	36.8	3.2	6.88	47	44	48.6	50.5	90	300	150	..
Djibouti	0.6	1.1	..	5.39	41	83	48.7	52.0	113	289	158	..
Equatorial Guinea	0.4	0.8	..	5.51	43	42	48.4	51.6	114	316	177	..
Eritrea	3.6	7.0	2.6	5.34	44	17	51.4	54.6	117	294	200	..
Ethiopia	56.7	126.9	2.9	6.51	49	13	48.4	51.6	117	294	200	560
Gabon	1.4	2.7	2.8	5.70	34	50	53.9	57.2	91	287	151	190
Gambia	1.2	2.1	..	5.21	45	26	45.4	48.6	129	375	213	1,050
Ghana	18.0	38.0	2.9	5.53	45	36	56.2	59.9	76	213	131	390
Guinea	6.9	15.1	2.9	6.51	44	30	46.0	47.0	131	337	223	800
Guinea-Bissau	1.1	2.0	2.1	5.42	43	22	43.9	47.1	137	336	231	700
Kenya	29.1	63.4	2.8	5.76	48	28	53.0	55.4	61	202	90	170x
Lesotho	2.1	4.2	2.6	4.86	41	23	60.5	65.5	106	204	156	..
Liberia	3.1	7.2	3.2	6.33	44	45	56.0	59.0	144	288	217	..
Madagascar	15.2	34.4	3.1	5.65	46	27	57.5	60.5	100	364	164	660
Malawi	11.4	22.3	1.8	6.69	48	14	44.3	45.4	140	365	221	620
Mali	11.1	24.6	3.0	6.60	48	27	46.4	49.7	119	400	214	2,000
Mauritania	2.3	4.4	2.5	5.03	45	54	51.9	55.1	114	321	199	..
Mauritius	1.1	1.5	1.1	2.28	29	41	68.3	75.0	19	84	23	99
Mozambique	16.5	35.1	3.4	6.06	46	34	45.4	48.3	161	331	277	300
Namibia	1.6	3.0	2.6	4.90	42	37	60.0	62.5	62	206	78	230
Niger	9.5	22.4	3.3	7.10	49	17	46.9	50.2	191	320	320	590
Nigeria	115.0	238.4	2.8	5.97	45	39	50.8	54.0	114	204	191	800
Rwanda	8.2	15.8	2.6	6.00	48	6	45.2	48.0	80	191	139	210
Senegal	8.5	16.9	2.7	5.62	45	42	50.3	52.3	60	303	115	560
Sierra Leone	4.6	8.7	2.3	6.06	44	36	39.5	42.6	164	385	284	450
Somalia	9.5	21.3	3.1	6.51	48	26	47.4	50.6	125	294	211	1,100
South Africa	42.4	71.0	2.2	3.81	37	51	62.3	68.3	52	126	68	84
Sudan	28.9	58.4	2.7	5.37	43	25	53.6	56.4	74	292	122	550
Swaziland	0.9	1.6	..	4.46	46	31	57.7	62.3	74	233	107	..
Tanzania	30.5	62.9	2.8	5.48	47	24	50.2	52.9	105	249	159	340
Togo	4.3	9.4	3.0	6.08	49	31	55.2	58.9	83	264	132	420
Uganda	22.0	48.1	2.9	6.72	47	13	42.2	44.3	111	218	185	550
Zaire	45.3	104.6	3.0	6.24	48	29	50.4	53.4	120	286	186	800
Zambia	9.7	19.1	2.6	5.50	47	43	45.4	46.8	114	220	203	150
Zimbabwe	11.5	19.6	2.1	4.53	45	32	49.8	51.8	57	181	81	400
South Asia	**1,341.0a**	**2,072.8a**	**..**	**..**	**37**	**..**	**..**	**..**	**84**	**238**	**124**	**482**
Afghanistan	21.5	45.3	5.6	6.37	41	20	45.0	46.0	165	360	257	640
Bangladesh	123.1	196.1	2.2	3.90	40	18	58.1	58.2	91	247	117	600
Bhutan	1.7	3.1	2.3	5.44	39	6	51.6	54.9	125	324	193	620
India	953.0	1,392.1	1.8	3.42	36	27	62.6	62.9	79	236	119	460
Nepal	22.5	40.7	2.5	4.95	42	14	56.5	56.5	84	290	118	520
Pakistan	144.5	284.8	2.8	5.59	41	35	62.9	65.1	95	221	137	500
Sri Lanka	18.6	25.0	1.2	2.29	35	22	70.9	75.4	15	130	19	80
East Asia and the Pacific	**1,809.8a**	**2,345.1a**	**..**	**..**	**29**	**..**	**..**	**..**	**42**	**200**	**56**	**165**
Burma (Myanmar)	47.5	75.6	2.1	3.81	36	26	58.5	61.8	79	237	109	460
Cambodia	10.5	19.7	2.5	4.86	46	21	52.6	55.4	113	217	177	500

	Total population (millions) 1996	Projected population (millions) 2025	Projected population growth rate (%) 1995-2000	Projected total fertility rate 1995-2000	% population below age 15 mid-1996	% population urban 1995	Life expectancy at birth 1994 Male	Life expectancy at birth 1994 Female	Infant mortality rate per 1,000 live births 1994	Under-5 mortality rate per 1,000 live births 1960	Under-5 mortality rate per 1,000 live births 1994	Maternal mortality rate per 100,000 live births 1980-1992
China	1,234.3	1,526.1	1.0	1.95	27	30	68.2	71.7	35	209	43	95
Fiji	0.8	1.2	..	2.76	38	41	70.6	74.9	22	97	27	..
Hong Kong	5.9	5.9	0.3	1.21	19	95	76.2	82.3	5	52	6	6
Indonesia	200.6	275.6	1.5	2.63	35	35	63.3	67.0	71	216	111	450
Korea, N	24.3	33.4	1.6	2.23	29	61	68.7	75.2	23	120	31	41
Korea, S	45.4	54.4	0.9	1.80	23	81	68.8	76.1	8	124	9	26
Laos	5.0	9.7	2.8	6.03	45	22	52.0	55.0	94	233	138	300
Malaysia	20.6	31.6	2.0	3.24	36	54	69.9	74.3	12	105	15	59
Mongolia	2.5	3.8	2.0	3.27	40	61	64.4	67.3	58	185	76	240
Papua New Guinea	4.4	7.5	2.2	4.63	42	16	57.2	58.7	67	248	95	900
Philippines	69.0	104.5	2.0	3.57	38	54	66.6	70.2	44	102	57	210
Singapore	2.9	3.4	0.8	1.73	23	100	73.5	78.6	5	40	6	10
Solomon Islands	0.4	0.8	..	4.98	47	17	69.7	73.9	26	185	32	..
Thailand	59.4	73.6	1.0	2.10	30	20	65.2	71.6	27	146	32	50
Vietnam	76.2	118.2	2.1	3.51	40	21	64.9	69.6	35	219	46	120
Latin America and the Caribbean	**490.4**	**709.8**	**1.7**	**2.83**	**35**	**74**	**67.2**	**72.5**	**38**	**159**	**47**	**178**
Argentina	35.0	46.1	1.2	2.58	31	88	69.7	76.8	24	68	27	140
Belize	0.2	0.4	2.6	3.66	44	47	73.4	76.1	32	104	41	..
Bolivia	7.6	13.1	2.3	4.36	41	61	59.8	63.2	73	252	110	390
Brazil	164.4	230.3	1.5	2.65	34	78	65.5	70.1	51	181	61	200
Chile	14.5	19.8	1.4	2.44	30	84	71.1	78.1	13	138	15	35
Colombia	35.7	49.4	1.5	2.49	33	73	67.4	73.3	16	132	19	200
Costa Rica	3.5	5.6	2.1	2.95	34	50	74.5	79.2	14	112	16	36
Cuba	11.1	12.7	0.6	1.82	22	76	74.2	78.0	9	50	10	39
Dominican Republic	8.0	11.2	1.6	2.80	37	65	69.0	73.1	38	152	45	..
Ecuador	11.7	17.8	2.0	3.10	36	58	67.3	72.5	45	180	57	170
El Salvador	5.9	9.7	2.2	3.59	40	45	65.8	70.8	42	210	56	160
Guatemala	10.9	21.7	2.8	4.90	45	42	64.7	69.8	51	205	70	200
Guyana	0.8	1.1	..	2.32	38	36	64.4	69.5	46	126	61	..
Haiti	7.3	13.1	2.1	4.60	40	32	56.7	60.2	74	260	127	600
Honduras	5.8	10.7	2.8	4.30	45	44	67.5	72.3	41	203	54	220
Jamaica	2.5	3.3	0.8	2.10	34	54	72.4	76.8	10	76	13	120
Mexico	95.5	136.6	1.8	2.80	36	75	68.9	75.0	27	148	32	110
Nicaragua	4.6	9.1	3.1	4.50	44	63	66.6	70.3	49	209	68	..
Panama	2.7	3.8	1.6	2.63	33	53	71.8	76.4	18	104	20	75
Paraguay	5.1	9.0	2.5	3.92	42	53	69.4	73.1	28	90	34	300
Peru	24.2	36.7	1.9	3.11	36	72	65.5	69.4	41	236	58	200
Suriname	0.4	0.6	..	2.39	35	50	69.0	74.0	27	96	33	..
Trinidad & Tobago	1.3	1.8	1.1	2.25	31	72	70.5	75.3	17	73	20	110
Uruguay	3.2	3.7	0.6	2.25	26	90	69.7	76.2	19	47	21	36
Venezuela	22.3	34.8	2.0	2.98	38	93	70.0	75.7	20	70	24	..
Middle East and North Africa	**370.6a**	**630.8a**	**..**	**..**	**41**	**..**	**..**	**..**	**48**	**239**	**62**	**200**
Algeria	28.6	45.5	2.2	3.41	40	56	67.5	70.3	54	243	65	140x
Bahrain	0.6	0.9	..	3.42	32	90	71.1	75.3	17	203	20	..
Cyprus	0.8	0.9	..	2.35	25	54	75.6	80.0	9	36	10	..
Egypt	64.2	97.3	1.9	3.44	40	45	64.7	67.3	41	258	52	270
Iran	68.7	123.5	2.1	4.52	44	59	69.0	70.3	40	233	51	120
Iraq	21.0	42.7	3.0	5.25	47	75	66.5	69.5	57	171	71	120
Jordan	5.7	12.0	3.3	5.13	42	72	67.7	71.8	21	149	25	48x
Kuwait	1.5	2.8	3.2	2.90	29	97	74.1	78.2	12	128	14	6
Lebanon	3.1	4.4	1.8	2.75	33	87	68.1	71.7	33	85	40	..
Libya	5.6	12.9	3.3	5.92	45	86	63.9	67.5	64	269	95	70
Morocco	27.6	40.7	1.8	3.10	38	48	63.9	67.5	46	215	56	330
Oman	2.3	6.1	3.9	6.67	36	13	68.9	73.3	22	300	27	..
Qatar	0.6	0.8	..	3.96	30	91	70.0	75.4	19	239	24	..
Saudi Arabia	18.4	42.7	3.5	5.94	43	80	69.9	73.4	31	292	36	41
Syria	15.2	33.5	3.3	5.36	49	52	66.7	71.2	32	201	38	140
Tunisia	9.1	13.3	1.7	2.75	37	57	68.4	70.7	28	244	34	70
Turkey	63.1	90.9	1.8	3.04	33	69	66.5	70.7	47	217	55	150
United Arab Emirates	1.9	3.0	2.0	3.88	32	84	73.9	76.5	17	240	20	..
Yemen	15.1	33.7	3.2	7.14	52	34	51.9	52.4	78	340	112	..

	Total population (millions) 1996	Projected population (millions) 2025	Projected population growth rate (%) 1995-2000	Projected total fertility rate 1995-2000	% population below age 15 mid-1996	% population urban 1995	Life expectancy at birth 1994		Infant mortality rate per 1,000 live births 1994	Under-5 mortality rate per 1,000 live births		Maternal mortality rate per 100,000 live births 1980-1992
							Male	Female		1960	1994	
Countries in Transition	340.9a	334.8a	..	..	24	..	..	..	30	..	36	..
Albania	3.5	4.7	1.0	2.66	33	37	70.0	75.8	34	151	41	..
Armenia	3.6	4.7	1.2	2.40	31	69	70.3	76.3	27	..	32	..
Azerbaijan	7.6	10.1	1.1	2.30	33	56	68.0	75.5	35	..	51	..
Belarus	10.1	9.9	−0.1	1.65	22	71	64.5	75.1	18	..	21	..
Bosnia and Herzegovina	3.5	4.5	4.5	1.60	23	49	70.5	75.9	15	155	17	..
Bulgaria	8.7	7.8	−0.4	1.50	19	71	67.8	74.9	16	70	19	9
Croatia	4.5	4.2	−0.3	1.65	20	64	68.1	76.5	12	98	14	..
Czech Republic	10.3	10.6	0.1	1.83	19	65	67.8	74.9	9	..	10	..
Estonia	1.5	1.4	−0.5	1.61	20	73	63.8	74.8	20	..	23	..
Georgia	5.5	6.1	0.3	2.10	24	59	69.5	77.6	23	..	27	..
Hungary	10.1	9.4	−0.3	1.71	18	65	64.5	73.8	13	57	14	15
Kazakhstan	17.2	21.7	0.7	2.37	31	60	66.5	75.0	41	..	48	..
Kyrgyzstan	4.8	7.1	1.6	3.30	38	39	66.5	73.8	47	..	56	..
Latvia	2.5	2.3	−0.7	1.64	21	73	63.3	74.9	22	..	26	..
Lithuania	3.7	3.8	0.0	1.83	22	72	64.9	76.0	17	..	20	..
Macedonia	2.2	2.6	0.8	1.97	24	60	69.8	75.8	27	177	32	..
Moldova	4.4	5.1	0.3	2.10	27	52	63.5	71.6	31	..	36	..
Poland	38.4	41.5	0.2	1.88	23	65	66.7	75.7	14	70	16	11
Romania	22.8	21.7	−0.2	1.50	21	55	66.6	73.3	23	82	29	72
Russian Federation	146.7	138.5	−0.2	1.53	21	76	61.5	73.6	28	..	31	..
Slovakia	5.4	6.0	0.4	1.92	23	59	66.5	75.4	13	..	15	..
Slovenia	1.9	1.8	0.0	1.46	19	64	68.8	78.1	7	45	8	..
Tajikistan	6.3	11.8	2.7	4.50	43	32	68.8	74.0	63	..	81	..
Turkmenistan	4.2	6.7	2.1	3.62	41	45	63.5	70.0	70	..	87	..
Ukraine	51.3	48.7	−0.2	1.64	20	70	64.2	74.2	21	..	25	..
Uzbekistan	23.3	37.7	2.1	3.54	41	41	67.5	73.2	52	..	64	..
Yugoslavia	10.9	11.5	−0.3	2.03	22	57	70.3	75.3	20	120	23	..
Industrial Countries	835.5a	911.3a	..	..	19	..	..	..	7	37	9	7
Australia	18.3	24.7	1.2	1.87	21	85	75.5	81.2	7	24	8	3
Austria	8.0	8.3	0.4	1.60	18	56	73.9	80.1	6	43	7	8
Belgium	10.1	10.4	0.3	1.71	18	97	74.1	80.6	8	35	10	3
Canada	29.8	38.3	1.0	1.93	21	77	75.0	81.2	6	33	8	5
Denmark	5.2	5.1	0.1	1.70	17	85	73.0	78.7	6	25	7	3
Finland	5.1	5.4	0.4	1.92	19	63	72.7	80.2	4	28	5	11
France	58.2	61.2	0.4	1.74	20	73	73.8	81.3	7	34	9	9
Germany	81.8	76.4	0.0	1.30	16	87	73.5	79.8	6	40	7	5
Greece	10.5	9.9	0.2	1.40	18	65	75.6	80.6	8	64	10	5
Ireland	3.6	3.9	0.3	2.10	25	58	73.4	78.9	6	36	7	2
Israel	5.8	7.8	1.5	2.65	30	91	75.4	79.2	7	39	9	3
Italy	57.2	52.3	0.0	1.27	15	67	75.1	81.4	7	50	8	4
Japan	125.4	121.6	0.2	1.50	16	78	76.8	82.9	4	40	6	11
Luxembourg	0.4	0.4	..	1.72	18	89	72.8	80.3	8	41	9	..
Netherlands	15.6	16.3	0.6	1.61	18	89	75.1	80.9	6	22	8	10
New Zealand	3.6	4.4	1.0	2.10	23	86	73.4	79.4	7	26	9	13
Norway	4.4	4.7	0.4	2.00	19	73	74.1	80.6	6	23	8	3
Portugal	9.8	9.7	0.0	1.55	18	36	72.1	78.9	9	112	11	10
Spain	39.7	37.6	0.1	1.23	17	76	75.3	81.0	8	57	9	5
Sweden	8.8	9.8	0.4	2.10	19	83	76.2	81.9	4	20	5	5
Switzerland	7.3	7.8	0.8	1.67	18	61	75.4	81.7	6	27	7	5
United Kingdom	58.4	61.5	0.3	1.81	19	90	74.5	79.4	6	27	7	8
USA	265.8	331.2	0.9	2.08	22	76	73.4	80.1	8	30	10	8
World	5,804.1	8,294.3	1.5	2.98	32	45	63.7	67.8	..	..	..	..

.. Data not available.

a *Bread for the World Institute estimate.*

x *Data refer to a year or period other than that specified in the column heading, differ from the standard definition or refer to only part of a country.*

TABLE 2

Global Health, Nutrition and Welfare

	Human Development Index (HDI) rank 1996	Refugees by country of asylum (thousands) 1995	Adult literacy rate (%) 1993			Combined gross educational enrollment ratio (%) 1993			% infants with low birth-weight 1990	% 1-year-old children immunized (measles) 1990-1994	Food production per capita (index 1979-1981= 100) 1994	Per capita dietary energy supply (DES)		Daily per capita calorie supply as % of requirements 1988-1990
			Total	Female	Male	Total	Female	Male				Per capita DES (calorie/day) 1990-1992	Annual growth rate 1969-1971 to 1990-1992	
Developing Countries	..	..	68.8	59.8	77.6	55	50.6	59.7	19	78	118	..	..	107
Africa (sub-Saharan)	..	..	..	..	..	..	..	..	16	51	84	..	..	93
Angola	165	10.9	42.5	28.0	56.0	32	29.4	34.2	19	44	63	1,840	−0.7	80
Benin	154	23.5	34.3	23.2	45.9	34	21.8	45.4	..	75	127	2,520	0.7	104
Botswana	71	0.3	68.0	57.8	79.4	71	73.2	69.3	8	71	68	2,320	0.4	97
Burkina Faso	170	29.5	18.0	8.4	27.9	19	14.7	24.0	21x	45	130	2,140	1.0	94
Burundi	166	142.7	33.7	20.9	47.7	31	27.5	34.7	..	43	69	1,950	−0.4	84
Cameroon	127	45.9	60.8	49.0	73.1	48	42.7	53.5	13	31	76	2,040	−0.6	95
Cape Verde	122	..	68.1	59.6	78.8	62	60.3	64.5	..	83	92	..	..	..
Central African Republic	148	33.8	56.0	47.9	64.9	37	27.3	47.7	15	44	100	1,720	−1.5	82
Chad	163	0.1	46.0	32.4	60.1	27	16.3	37.9	..	23	96	1,810	−0.9	73
Comoros	139	..	56.2	49.1	63.2	38	35.1	41.6	..	59	83	..	..	..
Congo	125	15.0	72.1	..	..	56	..	..	16	70	77	2,210	0.3	103
Côte d'Ivoire	147	297.9	37.8	27.4	47.6	39	31.1	47.5	14x	49	85	2,460	0.1	111
Djibouti	164	25.7	44.2	..	..	19	..	..	..	75	..	..	..	..
Equatorial Guinea	131	..	76.4	..	..	60	..	..	..	61	..	..	..	..
Eritrea	..	1.1	..	..	..	..	..	..	..	27	..	..	..	..
Ethiopia	168	393.5	33.6	23.5	43.6	16	12.6	18.3	16	29	..	1,620	−0.3	73
Gabon	120	0.8	60.3	..	..	47	..	..	..	65	77	2,490	0.6	104
Gambia	162	7.2	36.6	23.1	50.7	34	26.9	40.8	..	87	74	2,320	0.3	..
Ghana	129	89.2	62.0	50.5	73.9	45	38.8	50.1	17	49	132	2,090	−0.3	93
Guinea	160	633.0	33.9	20.1	47.8	24	14.8	32.3	21	70	111	2,400	0.5	97
Guinea-Bissau	161	15.3	52.8	40.1	66.1	30	21.1	38.5	20	65	114	..	..	97
Kenya	128	239.5	75.7	66.8	84.7	56	54.6	57.0	16	73	85	1,970	−0.5	89
Lesotho	130	..	69.5	60.0	79.7	55	59.9	50.1	11	74	81	2,260	0.6	93
Liberia	158	120.0	36.4	..	..	17	..	..	..	44	43	1,780	−1.1	98
Madagascar	150	..	45.8	41.8	49.8	34	32.9	34.2	17	54	80	2,160	−0.6	95
Malawi	157	1.0	54.7	39.8	70.8	47	43.7	49.2	20	98	61	1,910	−1.0	88
Mali	171	15.6	28.4	20.8	36.6	16	11.8	19.9	17	46	97	2,230	0.4	96
Mauritania	149	40.4	36.7	25.3	48.6	35	29.5	39.5	11	53	86	2,610	1.4	106
Mauritius	54	..	81.7	77.2	86.3	60	60.7	59.0	9	85	101	2,780	0.9	128
Mozambique	167	0.1	37.9	21.4	55.3	25	20.7	28.8	20	65	73	1,740	−0.5	77
Namibia	116	1.4	40.0	..	..	83	..	..	16	68	77	2,190	0.0	..
Niger	174	22.6	12.8	6.1	19.8	15	10.8	19.0	15	19	81	2,190	0.5	95
Nigeria	137	8.1	54.1	43.8	64.7	52	45.3	57.8	16	41	138	2,100	−0.6	93
Rwanda	152	7.8	58.0	..	..	39	..	..	17	25	64	1,860	−0.4	82
Senegal	153	68.6	31.4	21.5	41.3	31	25.4	36.4	11	49	111	2,310	−0.3	98
Sierra Leone	173	4.7	29.6	16.7	43.3	28	22.4	34.0	17	46	91	1,820	−0.8	83
Somalia	172	0.6	24.9	..	..	7	..	..	16	35	75	1,590	−0.6	81
South Africa	100	91.8	81.0	80.8	81.3	78	79.6	77.1	..	76	74	2,810	0.0	128
Sudan	146	558.2	43.8	32.0	55.7	31	27.3	35.1	15	76	111	2,150	−0.1	87
Swaziland	110	0.5	74.9	73.6	76.3	70	68.3	71.9	..	94	87	2,680	0.7	..
Tanzania	144	829.7	65.5	53.9	77.8	34	33.1	35.1	14	75	75	2,110	0.9	95
Togo	140	11.0	49.2	34.3	64.7	51	37.9	63.7	20	58	97	2,290	0.0	99
Uganda	155	229.3	59.7	47.7	72.1	35	30.4	39.7	..	77	100	2,220	−0.2	93
Zaire	141	1,326.5	75.2	64.9	85.1	39	30.5	46.4	15	33	86	2,090	−0.1	96
Zambia	136	130.6	76.2	68.7	84.2	49	44.9	52.5	13	88	88	2,020	−0.4	87
Zimbabwe	124	0.3	84.0	78.6	89.6	70	65.1	74.0	14	77	78	2,080	−0.2	94
South Asia	..	..	48.8	35.0	61.7	52	43.2	59.6	33	82	..	..	..	99
Afghanistan	169	19.6	29.8	13.5	45.2	18	9.2	26.0	20	40	66	1,660	−1.3	72
Bangladesh	143	51.1	37.0	25.0	48.3	40	34.0	44.8	50	95	91	1,990	−0.3	88
Bhutan	159	..	40.2	..	..	31	..	..	..	81	84	..	..	128
India	135	274.1	50.6	36.0	64.3	55	46.4	62.8	33	86	125	2,330	0.6	101
Nepal	151	124.8	26.3	13.0	39.4	57	42.9	70.6	..	57	115	2,140	0.6	100
Pakistan	134	867.6	36.4	23.0	48.6	37	23.9	49.1	25	65	108	2,340	0.3	99
Sri Lanka	89	0.0	89.6	86.2	93.1	66	67.2	65.6	25	84	86	2,230	−0.1	101
East Asia and the Pacific	..	..	..	..	..	..	..	..	11	89	..	..	..	112
Burma (Myanmar)	133	..	82.4	76.6	88.3	49	47.8	49.4	16	77	111	2,580	1.1	114

	Human Development Index (HDI) rank 1996	Refugees by country of asylum (thousands) 1995	Adult literacy rate (%) 1993			Combined gross educational enrollment ratio (%) 1993			% infants with low birth-weight 1990	% 1-year-old children immunized (measles) 1990-1994	Food production per capita (index 1979-1981=100) 1994	Per capita dietary energy supply (DES)		Daily per capita calorie supply as % of requirements 1988-1990
			Total	Female	Male	Total	Female	Male				Per capita DES (calorie/day) 1990-1992	Annual growth rate 1969-1971 to 1990-1992	
Cambodia	156	0.0	35.0	..	..	30	..	..	..	53	136	2,100	−0.8	96
China	108	288.3	80.0	70.9	88.7	57	54.1	60.1	9	89	..	2,710	1.4	112
Fiji	47	..	90.6	88.1	93.1	79	78.7	79.7	..	96	99	..	..	..
Hong Kong	22	1.5	91.5	87.1	95.8	71	70.6	70.9	8	77	69	3,150	0.8	125
Indonesia	102	0.0	82.9	76.9	89.1	61	58.2	63.7	14	92	133	2,700	1.3	121
Korea, N	83	..	95.0	..	..	75	..	..	..	99	87	2,930	1.0	121
Korea, S	29	..	97.6	96.1	99.1	81	76.7	84.9	9	93	99	3,270	0.7	120
Laos	138	..	54.6	42.1	67.7	50	42.1	58.9	18	73	116	2,210	0.1	111
Malaysia	53	0.2	82.2	76.3	88.2	61	61.5	59.7	10	81	154	2,830	0.7	120
Mongolia	113	..	81.7	75.6	87.8	62	65.0	58.4	10	80	69	2,100	−0.3	97
Papua New Guinea	126	9.5	70.5	60.6	79.7	35	31.1	38.4	23	39	99	2,610	0.9	114
Philippines	95	0.1	94.2	93.9	94.6	77	78.4	76.2	15	87	89	2,290	1.2	104
Singapore	34	0.0	90.3	85.0	95.6	68	66.5	69.3	7	87	45	..	..	136
Solomon Islands	118	..	62.0	..	..	46	..	..	..	64	84	..	..	..
Thailand	52	101.4	93.6	91.4	95.9	54	54.9	54.0	13	86	105	2,380	0.4	103
Vietnam	121	..	92.5	89.5	95.8	51	49.2	53.2	17	96	129	2,200	0.0	103
Latin America and Caribbean	..	127.7	85.9	84.2	87.0	69	68.2	68.9	11	83	..	..	..	114
Argentina	30	12.0	96.0	95.9	96.0	80	81.8	78.6	6	95	99	2,950	−0.5	131
Belize	67	8.7	70.0	..	..	68	..	..	..	90	106	..	..	..
Bolivia	111	0.7	81.5	73.9	89.4	68	62.2	73.1	12	86	108	2,030	0.2	84
Brazil	58	2.0	82.4	82.0	82.6	72	71.3	72.0	11	76	117	2,790	0.6	114
Chile	33	0.3	94.7	94.5	95.0	71	70.4	71.2	7	96	122	2,540	−0.2	102
Colombia	49	5.5	90.6	90.6	90.7	68	70.6	65.7	10	87	104	2,630	1.2	106
Costa Rica	31	24.2	94.5	94.6	94.4	68	66.9	68.1	6	88	102	2,870	0.8	121
Cuba	79	1.8	95.2	94.6	95.7	65	67.2	62.2	9	..	66	3,000	0.6	135
Dominican Republic	87	1.0	81.2	81.2	81.2	64	64.9	62.5	16	87	86	2,270	0.6	102
Ecuador	64	14.5	89.0	87.5	91.4	72	71.1	73.5	11	100	117	2,540	0.8	105
El Salvador	115	0.2	70.4	68.5	72.5	54	54.4	54.3	11	81	71	2,530	1.5	102
Guatemala	112	1.5	54.6	47.6	61.7	45	41.5	48.9	14	66	79	2,280	0.4	103
Guyana	103	..	97.7	97.0	98.4	70	70.1	69.3	..	83	98	2,350	0.1	..
Haiti	145	..	43.4	40.5	46.5	30	28.7	30.6	15	24	68	1,740	−0.6	89
Honduras	114	0.1	71.4	71.2	71.5	61	61.6	59.6	9	94	93	2,310	0.4	98
Jamaica	86	2.0	84.1	88.3	79.9	64	65.9	63.1	11	82	126	2,580	0.1	114
Mexico	48	39.5	89.0	86.4	91.1	65	64.3	66.2	12	94	92	3,190	0.7	131
Nicaragua	117	0.6	65.0	65.9	64.0	61	61.6	60.3	15	74	56	2,290	−0.2	99
Panama	43	0.9	90.0	89.5	90.6	69	70.6	67.8	10	84	89	2,240	−0.1	98
Paraguay	85	0.1	91.5	89.9	93.1	62	61.1	61.9	8	79	108	2,620	−0.1	116
Peru	91	0.7	87.8	81.6	93.9	80	74.6	85.5	11	75	..	1,880	−1.0	87
Suriname	75	..	92.5	..	..	71	..	..	..	69	97	2,510	0.6	..
Trinidad & Tobago	38	..	97.6	96.6	98.6	67	67.3	67.0	10	79	112	2,630	0.3	114
Uruguay	32	0.1	97.0	97.4	96.6	76	81.2	71.0	8	80	119	2,680	−0.5	101
Venezuela	44	11.2	90.6	89.9	91.4	69	71.0	67.6	9	94	107	2,590	0.4	99
Middle East and North Africa	..	..	..	..	..	..	..	..	10	84	..	..	..	124
Algeria	69	206.8	58.8	45.8	71.6	66	61.1	70.9	9	65	122	2,900	2.2	123
Bahrain	39	..	84.1	77.6	88.2	84	85.9	82.8	..	90	..	..	..	..
Cyprus	23	0.1	94.0	..	..	76	..	..	..	83	99	..	..	..
Egypt	106	7.7	49.8	37.0	62.4	69	62.0	74.7	10	90	109	3,340	1.4	132
Iran	66	2,024.5	66.1	56.4	75.5	67	61.3	71.9	9	97	128	2,760	1.4	125
Iraq	109	123.3	55.7	42.3	68.8	55	48.0	61.8	15	98	87	2,270	0.0	128
Jordan	70	0.7	84.8	..	..	66	..	..	7	91	141	2,900	0.8	110
Kuwait	51	30.0	77.4	73.6	80.7	53	52.1	53.0	7	96	..	2,460	−0.3	..
Lebanon	97	2.1	91.7	89.4	94.3	74	74.8	73.0	10	73	176	3,260	1.6	127
Libya	59	3.3	73.7	59.3	86.3	88	87.4	88.7	..	89	33	3,290	1.4	140
Morocco	123	0.4	41.7	28.8	54.7	44	36.8	51.5	9	..	156	3,000	1.0	125
Oman	82	..	35.0	..	..	60	..	..	10	97	..	..	..	..
Qatar	50	..	78.5	78.2	78.6	74	76.0	72.4	..	86	..	..	..	..
Saudi Arabia	63	13.3	61.3	47.6	70.4	55	51.8	57.4	7	92	280	2,730	1.8	121
Syria	92	37.0	68.7	53.0	84.3	65	60.4	70.0	11	84	89	3,220	1.5	126
Tunisia	78	0.1	64.1	51.6	76.4	66	62.5	69.8	8	93	106	3,260	1.7	131
Turkey	84	9.9	81.1	70.9	91.0	62	54.9	68.9	8	76	97	3,510	0.8	127

	Human Development Index (HDI) rank 1996	Refugees by country of asylum (thousands) 1995	Adult literacy rate (%) 1993			Combined gross educational enrollment ratio (%) 1993			% infants with low birth-weight 1990	% 1-year-old children immunized (measles) 1990-1994	Food production per capita (index 1979-1981= 100) 1994	Per capita dietary energy supply (DES)		Daily per capita calorie supply as % of requirements 1988-1990
			Total	Female	Male	Total	Female	Male				Per capita DES (calorie/day) 1990-1992	Annual growth rate 1969-1971 to 1990-1992	
United Arab Emirates	42	0.4	78.2	78.2	78.2	81	84.8	78.2	6	90	..	3,370	0.3	..
Yemen	142	40.3	41.1	26.0	50.0	45	22.5	65.2	19	45	80	2,160	0.9	..
Countries in Transition	..		97.6	98.7	98.9	74	76.5	72.4	..	88	..	..	..	..
Albania	104	..	85.0	..	..	59	..	..	7	81	89	2,630	0.3	107
Armenia	93	218.0	98.8	99.5	99.7	78	82.6	73.4	..	95	..	..	..	..
Azerbaijan	96	233.7	96.3	99.5	99.7	72	70.1	73.0	..	91	..	..	..	..
Belarus	61	..	97.9	99.4	99.7	79	81.1	77.8	..	97	..	..	..	..
Bosnia and Herzegovina	..	..	..	..	..	..	..	..	..	48	..	..	..	..
Bulgaria	62	0.1	93.0	..	..	65	..	..	6	87	59	3,160	-0.5	148
Croatia	..	188.6	..	..	..	..	..	..	..	90	..	..	..	..
Czech Republic	37	2.7	99.0	99.0	99.0	67	67.2	66.2	..	97	..	..	..	..
Estonia	68	..	99.0	99.0	99.0	78	80.9	74.4	..	76	..	..	..	..
Georgia	101	0.1	94.9	99.0	99.0	68	69.6	66.1	..	16	..	..	..	..
Hungary	46	11.4	99.0	99.0	99.0	67	67.5	65.7	9	99	86	3,560	0.3	137
Kazakhstan	72	..	97.5	99.5	99.7	65	66.2	64.4	..	72	..	..	..	..
Kyrgyzstan	99	13.2	97.0	99.5	99.7	70	71.5	67.7	..	88	..	..	..	..
Latvia	55	..	99.0	99.0	99.0	72	74.8	69.5	..	81	..	..	..	..
Lithuania	81	..	98.4	98.4	98.4	72	74.7	68.5	..	93	..	..	..	..
Macedonia	..	9.0	..	..	..	..	..	..	..	86	..	..	..	..
Moldova	98	..	96.4	..	..	76	..	..	..	95	..	..	..	..
Poland	56	0.6	99.0	99.0	99.0	76	77.2	74.6	..	95	85	3,340	-0.2	131
Romania	74	0.2	96.9	96.9	98.9	62	62.1	62.6	7	91	94	3,160	0.2	116
Russian Federation	57	42.3	98.7	98.7	98.7	79	82.1	75.8	..	88	..	..	..	..
Slovakia	41	1.9	99.0	99.0	99.0	71	72.1	70.6	..	97	..	..	..	..
Slovenia	..	22.3	..	..	..	..	..	..	..	90	..	..	..	..
Tajikistan	105	0.4	96.7	..	..	69	..	..	..	97	..	..	..	..
Turkmenistan	90	3.0	97.7	..	..	77	..	..	..	84	..	..	..	..
Ukraine	80	5.2	95.0	..	..	76	..	..	..	94	..	..	..	..
Uzbekistan	94	0.9	97.2	..	..	73	..	..	..	91	..	..	..	..
Yugoslavia	..	650.0	..	..	..	..	..	..	..	85	..	..	..	..
Industrial Countries	..	..	98.3	98.5	98.7	82	84.3	81.8	6	81		..	..	134
Australia	11	35.6	99.0	99.0	99.0	79	80.6	77.7	6	86	92	3,180	0.0	124
Austria	13	37.5	99.0	99.0	99.0	85	83.6	86.9	6	60	105	3,530	0.4	133
Belgium	12	31.7	99.0	99.0	99.0	85	85.3	85.2	6	67	..	..	..	149
Canada	1	144.2	99.0	99.0	99.0	100	100.0	100.0	6	98	107	3,100	0.1	122
Denmark	17	35.6	99.0	99.0	99.0	87	88.3	85.1	6	81	126	3,620	0.6	135
Finland	6	13.3	99.0	99.0	99.0	96	100.0	91.4	4	99	101	3,030	-0.2	113
France	7	170.2	99.0	99.0	99.0	88	90.2	86.1	5	76	94	3,640	0.4	143
Germany	18	569.0	99.0	99.0	99.0	79	77.3	81.1	..	75	100	3,410	0.3	..
Greece	21	4.5	93.8	89.0	97.0	78	78.3	78.0	6	72	112	3,770	0.8	151
Ireland	19	0.4	99.0	99.0	99.0	84	85.5	82.9	4	78	114	3,790	0.5	157
Israel	24	..	95.0	..	..	76	..	..	7	95	88	3,140	0.1	125
Italy	20	80.0	97.4	97.4	97.4	70	70.8	69.4	5	50	100	3,540	0.2	139
Japan	3	0.0	99.0	99.0	99.0	78	77.2	79.3	6	69	93	2,900	0.4	125
Luxembourg	27	0.3	99.0	..	..	57	..	..	..	80	..	..	..	..
Netherlands	4	72.0	99.0	99.0	99.0	89	86.5	91.4	..	95	111	3,170	0.2	114
New Zealand	14	1.2	99.0	99.0	99.0	89	91.0	87.9	6	82	92	3,580	0.4	131
Norway	5	22.5	99.0	99.0	99.0	90	91.0	88.9	4	93	111	3,230	0.3	120
Portugal	35	1.4	86.2	81.0	89.0	79	82.5	75.6	5	94	111	3,620	0.9	136
Spain	10	7.1	98.0	98.0	98.0	87	90.3	83.6	4	90	104	3,680	1.3	141
Sweden	9	43.2	99.0	99.0	99.0	80	81.6	78.8	5	95	84	2,960	0.1	111
Switzerland	15	57.3	99.0	99.0	99.0	75	71.7	77.5	5	83	93	3,380	-0.2	130
United Kingdom	16	20.4	99.0	99.0	99.0	83	83.6	82.1	7	92	103	3,280	0.0	130
USA	2	645.5	99.0	99.0	99.0	96	98.3	93.5	7	84	105	3,700	0.6	138
World	..	13,236.5	76.3	69.6	82.5	60	55.6	63.0	..	..	103	2,720	0.5	..

.. Data not available.
0.0 Value rounded to zero (less than 50,000).
x Data refer to a year or period other than that specified in the column heading.

TABLE 3

Global Economic Indicators

	GNP per capita			Distribution of income or consumption by quintiles 1978-1994						Military expenditure as % of combined education & health expenditure 1990-1991	Total debt (US$ billions) 1994	Debt service as % of exports of goods and services[3] 1992-1994	Food as % of total imports 1994	Food as % of total exports 1994	Food as % of household consumption 1980-1985	Per capita energy consumption (kg. of oil equivalent) 1994
	(US$) 1994	PPP$[1] 1994	GNP per capita real growth rate (%) 1985-1994	Lowest 20%	Second quintile	Third quintile	Fourth quintile	Highest 20%	Ratio of highest 20% to lowest 20%[2]							
Developing Countries	..	..	..	..	..	..	..	..	..	60	1,921.50	17	6.2	5.9	41	..
Africa (sub-Saharan)	..	..	..	..	..	..	..	..	..	43	212.40	14	16.3	8.2	38	272
Angola	f	..	−0.9	..	..	..	..	..	..	208	10.61	32	15.4	0.0	..	..
Benin	370	1,660	−0.8	..	..	..	..	..	..	..	1.62	11	17.6	7.2	37	18
Botswana	2,800	5,320	6.6	..	..	..	..	..	..	22	0.69	4	12.8	4.9	25	380
Burkina Faso	300	770c	−0.2	..	..	..	..	..	..	30	1.13	12	13.7	19.3	..	16
Burundi	150	580c	−1.0	..	..	..	..	..	..	42	1.13	40	19.0	..	..	23
Cameroon	680	1,970	−6.6	..	..	..	..	..	..	48	7.28	36	10.5	12.6	24	83
Cape Verde	910	1,850c	1.8	..	..	..	..	..	..	..	0.17	14	32.4	8.6	..	..
Central African Republic	370	1,060c	−2.8	..	..	..	..	..	..	33	0.89	22	23.7	13.0	..	29
Chad	190	740c	0.9	..	..	..	..	..	..	74	0.82	13	5.5	48.3	..	16
Comoros	510	1,130c	−1.3	..	..	..	..	..	..	..	0.19	10	36.9	70.7	..	..
Congo	640	2,000	−2.7	..	..	..	..	..	..	37	5.28	52	16.9	0.7	37	147
Côte d'Ivoire	510	1,340	−5.2	6.8	11.2	15.8	22.2	44.1	6.5	14	18.45	64	15.5	36.0	39	170
Djibouti	f	..	..	..	..	..	..	..	..	..	0.25	4	27.2	23.4	..	..
Equatorial Guinea	430	..	1.6x	..	..	..	..	..	..	..	0.29	14	12.9	4.4	..	..
Eritrea	b	..	..	..	..	..	..	..	..	..	..	..	..	..	..	..
Ethiopia	130	410	−0.6	..	..	..	..	..	..	190	5.06	38	19.7a	5.1a	49	21
Gabon	3,550	..	−2.3	..	..	..	..	..	..	51	3.97	22	12.5	0.1	..	520
Gambia	360	1,150c	0.5	..	..	..	..	..	..	11	0.42	20	31.5	32.1	..	56
Ghana	430	2,020c	1.4	7.9	12.0	16.1	21.8	42.2	5.3	12	5.39	27	9.2	25.0	50	91
Guinea	510	..	1.2x	3.0	8.3	14.6	23.9	50.2	16.7	37	3.10	31	22.9	3.9	..	65
Guinea-Bissau	240	900c	1.9	2.1	6.5	12.0	20.6	58.9	28.0	..	0.82	106	45.7	41.1	..	37
Kenya	260	1,350	0.0	3.4	6.7	10.7	17.0	62.1	18.3	24	7.27	39	15.1	12.8	38	107
Lesotho	700	1,720c	0.5	2.8	6.5	11.2	19.4	60.1	21.5	48	0.60	5	11.5	3.1	..	..
Liberia	b	..	..	..	..	..	..	..	..	47	2.06	8	35.2	0.9	..	..
Madagascar	230	670	−1.7	5.8	9.9	14.0	20.3	50.0	8.6	37	4.13	71	13.5	34.8	59	37
Malawi	140	600	−2.0	..	..	..	..	..	..	24	2.02	24	34.6	8.9	30	39
Mali	250	520	0.9	..	..	..	..	..	..	53	2.78	31	15.0	28.9	57	22
Mauritania	480	1,570c	0.2	3.6	10.6	16.2	23.0	46.5	12.9	40	2.33	60	49.3	7.8	..	103
Mauritius	3,180	13,130	5.6	..	..	..	..	..	..	4	1.36	7	11.6	26.5	24	387
Mozambique	80	550c	3.5	..	..	..	..	..	..	121	5.49	95	15.6	28.5	..	40
Namibia	2,030	3,950c	3.4	..	..	..	..	..	..	23	..	..	9.0	15.1	..	..
Niger	230	800c	−2.2	7.5	11.8	15.5	21.1	44.1	5.9	11	1.57	45	22.2	19.7	..	37
Nigeria	280	1,430	1.2	4.0	8.9	14.4	23.4	49.3	12.3	33	33.49	38	12.6	2.0	48	162
Rwanda	b	..	−2.2	9.7	13.2	16.5	21.6	39.1	4.0	25	0.95	47	25.1	0.8	29	27
Senegal	610	1,660	−0.5	3.5	7.0	11.6	19.3	58.6	16.7	33	3.68	23	28.7	17.7	49	102
Sierra Leone	150	770	−1.9	..	..	..	..	..	..	23	1.39	93	57.1	11.5	56	73
Somalia	b	..	−1.2x	..	..	..	..	..	..	200	2.62	150	42.5	54.6	..	..
South Africa	3,010	..	−1.4	3.3	5.8	9.8	17.7	63.3	19.2	41	..	..	4.6	7.3	34	2,253
Sudan	b	..	−0.2x	..	..	..	..	..	..	44	17.71	87	22.2	48.9	60	..
Swaziland	1,160	2,880	−1.3	..	..	..	..	..	..	11	0.24	3	8.3	33.4	..	..
Tanzania	b	..	1.1x	6.9	10.9	15.3	21.5	45.4	6.6	77	7.44	79	7.6	8.8	64	34
Togo	320	1,060c	−2.7	..	..	..	..	..	..	39	1.46	25	10.3	7.9	..	46
Uganda	200	940c	3.0	6.8	10.3	14.4	20.4	48.1	7.1	18	3.47	89	3.7	10.3	..	23
Zaire	b	..	−0.8x	..	..	..	..	..	..	71	12.34	46	42.2	1.0	..	..
Zambia	350	1,000	−1.3	3.9	8.0	13.8	23.8	50.4	12.9	63	6.57	49	2.7	0.9	36	140
Zimbabwe	490	2,040	−0.6	4.0	6.3	10.0	17.4	62.3	15.6	66	4.37	33	2.8	10.1	40	432
South Asia	..	..	..	..	..	..	..	..	..	72	161.10	26	..	..	51	221
Afghanistan	b	..	..	..	..	..	..	..	..	..	..	..	24.8	32.3	..	..
Bangladesh	230	1,350	2.1	9.4	13.5	17.2	22.0	37.9	4.0	41	16.57	16	14.1	0.5	59	65
Bhutan	400			..	..	..	..	..	..	..	0.09	9	11.0	12.4	..	..
India	310	1,290	2.9	8.5	12.1	15.8	21.1	42.6	5.0	65	98.99	30	5.0	5.6	52	243
Nepal	200	1,080c	2.2	9.1	12.9	16.7	21.8	39.5	4.3	35	2.32	13	9.2	12.1	57	23
Pakistan	440	2,210	1.6	8.4	12.9	16.9	22.2	39.7	4.7	125	29.58	28	10.5	6.8	37	255
Sri Lanka	640	3,150	2.8	8.9	13.1	16.9	21.7	39.3	4.4	107	7.81	13	7.4	2.5	43	111
East Asia and the Pacific	..	..	..	..	..	..	..	..	..	..	421.30	12	..	..	45	670
Burma (Myanmar)	b	..	..	..	..	..	..	..	..	222	6.50	32	15.1	38.8	..	..
Cambodia	b	..	..	..	..	..	..	..	..	..	1.94	7	9.3	0.1	..	..
China	530	2,510	6.9	6.2	10.5	15.8	23.6	43.9	7.1	114	100.54	10	3.4	6.6	61	647

	GNP per capita			Distribution of income or consumption by quintiles 1978-1994						Military expenditure as % of combined education & health expenditure 1990-1991	Total debt (US$ billions) 1994	Debt service as % of exports of goods and services[3] 1992-1994	Food as % of total imports 1994	Food as % of total exports 1994	Food as % of household consumption 1980-1985	Per capita energy consumption (kg. of oil equivalent) 1994
	(US$) 1994	PPP$[1] 1994	GNP per capita real growth rate (%) 1985-1994	Lowest 20%	Second quintile	Third quintile	Fourth quintile	Highest 20%	Ratio of highest 20% to lowest 20%[2]							
Fiji	2,320	5,590c	2.0	..	..	..	..	..	..	37	0.30	9	11.8	46.0	..	..
Hong Kong	21,650h	23,080h	5.3h	5.4	10.8	15.2	21.6	47.0	8.7	10	..	..	3.2	1.3	12	2,280
Indonesia	880	3,690	6.0	8.7	12.3	16.3	22.1	40.7	4.7	49	96.50	32	5.9	5.6	48	393
Korea, N	f	..	..	..	..	..	..	..	..	..	..	..	14.6	2.2	..	..
Korea, S	8,220	10,540	7.8	..	..	..	..	..	..	60	54.54	8	4.0	0.9	35	3,000
Laos	320	..	2.1	9.6	12.9	16.3	21.0	40.2	4.2	..	2.08	7	4.4	21.8	..	38
Malaysia	3,520	8,610	5.7	4.6	8.3	13.0	20.4	53.7	11.7	38	24.77	8	4.0	8.4	23	1,711
Mongolia	340	2,020c	-3.3	..	..	..	..	..	..	..	0.44	18	23.3	6.0	..	1,079
Papua New Guinea	1,160	2,430c	2.1	..	..	..	..	..	..	41	2.88	33	14.1	5.3	..	236
Philippines	960	2,800	1.8	6.5	10.1	14.4	21.2	47.8	7.4	41	39.30	26	5.8	9.1	51	364
Singapore	23,360	21,430c	6.9	5.1	9.9	14.6	21.4	48.9	9.6	129	..	..	3.1	1.7	19	6,556
Solomon Islands	800	2,040c	1.8	..	..	..	..	..	..	..	0.17	16	13.8	19.4	..	..
Thailand	2,210	6,870	8.2	5.6	8.7	13.0	20.0	52.7	9.4	71	60.99	16	1.6	9.7	30	770
Vietnam	190	..	..	7.8	11.4	15.4	21.4	44.0	5.6	..	25.12	44	4.5	16.2	..	105
Latin America and the Caribbean	..	..	..	..	..	..	..	..	..	25	562.80	28	8.9	15.5	34	962
Argentina	8,060	8,920	1.9	..	..	..	..	..	..	51	77.39	54	4.0	37.1	35	1,399
Belize	2,550	..	5.3	..	..	..	..	..	..	..	0.18	8	12.8	58.4	..	..
Bolivia	770	2,520	1.9	5.6	9.7	14.5	22.0	48.2	8.6	57	4.75	46	13.0	18.2	33	307
Brazil	3,370	5,630	-0.4	2.1	4.9	8.9	16.8	67.5	32.1	23	151.10	41	9.3	14.8	35	691
Chile	3,560	9,060	6.2	3.5	6.6	10.9	18.1	61.0	17.4	68	22.94	21	5.4	12.8	29	943
Colombia	1,620	5,970	1.9	3.6	7.6	12.6	20.4	55.8	15.5	57	19.42	32	6.7	9.6	29	613
Costa Rica	2,380	5,760	2.8	4.0	9.1	14.3	21.9	50.7	12.7	5	3.84	19	6.3	39.8	33	558
Cuba	f	..	..	..	..	..	..	..	..	125	..	..	20.5	76.0	..	..
Dominican Republic	1,320	3,790	2.1	4.2	7.9	12.5	19.7	55.7	13.3	22	4.29	24	14.2	41.1	46	340
Ecuador	1,310	4,380	1.0	5.4	8.9	13.2	19.9	52.6	9.7	26	14.95	42	5.3	22.0	30	517
El Salvador	1,480	2,510	1.6	..	..	..	..	..	..	66	2.19	15	10.9	12.8	33	219
Guatemala	1,190	3,490	0.9	2.1	5.8	10.5	18.6	63.0	30.0	31	3.02	23	11.3	35.2	36	186
Guyana	530	2,000c	0.3	..	..	..	..	..	..	21	2.04	31	7.0	39.0	..	47
Haiti	220	930c	-5.0	..	..	..	..	..	..	30	0.71	21	77.0	16.5	..	..
Honduras	580	1,900	-0.1	3.8	7.4	12.0	19.4	57.4	15.1	92	4.42	41	15.5	25.3	39	169
Jamaica	1,420	2,970	1.7	5.8	10.2	14.9	21.6	47.5	8.2	8	4.32	28	10.2	14.9	36	1,112
Mexico	4,010	7,050	0.6	4.1	7.8	12.5	20.2	55.3	13.5	5	128.30	40	9.2	8.4	35	1,577
Nicaragua	330	1,850	-6.4	4.2	8.0	12.6	20.0	55.2	13.1	97	11.02	172	18.5	44.2	..	241
Panama	2,670	6,080	0.0	2.0	6.3	11.6	20.3	59.8	29.9	34	7.11	9	8.2	46.6	38	566
Paraguay	1,570	3,540	1.0	..	..	..	..	..	..	42	1.98	19	7.0	49.9	30	261
Peru	1,890	3,690	-2.5	4.9	9.2	14.1	21.4	50.4	10.3	39	22.62	51	13.3	4.7	35	351
Suriname	870	3,680c	0.6	..	..	..	..	..	..	27	..	..	12.9	15.9	..	..
Trinidad & Tobago	3,740	8,440c	-2.3	..	..	..	..	..	..	9	2.22	34	16.7	4.8	19	4,549
Uruguay	4,650	6,850	3.0	..	..	..	..	..	..	38	5.10	19	7.5	36.0	31	623
Venezuela	2,760	7,890	0.6	3.6	7.1	11.7	19.3	58.4	16.2	33	36.85	26	11.0	1.7	23	2,331
Middle East and North Africa	..	..	..	..	..	..	..	..	..	..	207.70	15	..	..	39	1,250
Algeria	1,690	5,330c	-2.4	6.9	11.0	15.1	20.9	46.1	6.7	11	29.90	73	26.0	0.6	..	1,030
Bahrain	7,500	12,070c	-0.9	..	..	..	..	..	..	41	..	..	6.8	0.2	..	..
Cyprus	e	..	5.2	..	..	..	..	..	..	17	..	..	7.4	15.3	..	..
Egypt	710	3,610	1.6	8.7	12.5	16.3	21.4	41.1	4.7	52	33.36	26	22.0	7.7	49	608
Iran	f	4,650	-1.0	..	..	..	..	..	..	38	22.71	12	15.7	3.9	37	1,565
Iraq	f	..	..	..	..	..	..	..	..	271	..	..	32.1	0.7	..	..
Jordan	1,390	4,290c	-6.3	5.9	9.8	13.9	20.3	50.1	8.5	138	7.05	31	19.5	10.2	35	997
Kuwait	19,040	24,500c	-1.3	..	..	..	..	..	..	88	..	..	14.4	0.2	..	7,615
Lebanon	f	..	..	..	..	..	..	..	..	..	1.96	27	14.4	16.1	..	..
Libya	d	..	..	..	..	..	..	..	..	71	..	..	18.6	0.2	..	..
Morocco	1,150	3,440	1.1	6.6	10.5	15.0	21.7	46.3	7.0	72	22.51	33	10.9	12.4	38	307
Oman	5,200	9,150c	0.6	..	..	..	..	..	..	293	3.08	11	12.6	1.7	..	2,347
Qatar	14,540	..	-0.8	..	..	..	..	..	..	192	..	..	11.8	0.4	..	..
Saudi Arabia	7,240	..	-1.2	..	..	..	..	..	..	151	..	..	11.9	0.8	..	4,744
Syria	f	..	-2.4x	..	..	..	..	..	..	373	20.56	21	10.3	11.4	..	..
Tunisia	1,800	4,960	1.8	5.9	10.4	15.3	22.1	46.3	7.8	31	9.25	20	7.4	9.6	37	590
Turkey	2,450	4,610	1.5	..	..	..	..	..	..	87	66.33	38	3.4	18.3	40	955
United Arab Emirates	e	..	0.2x	..	..	..	..	..	..	44	..	..	6.3	1.5	..	12,795
Yemen	280	..	..	..	..	..	..	..	..	197	5.96	30	24.6	3.1	..	214

	GNP per capita			Distribution of income or consumption by quintiles 1978-1994						Military expenditure as % of combined education & health expenditure 1990-1991	Total debt (US$ billions) 1994	Debt service as % of exports of goods and services[3] 1992-1994	Food as % of total imports 1994	Food as % of total exports 1994	Food as % of household consumption 1980-1985	Per capita energy consumption (kg. of oil equivalent) 1994
	(US$) 1994	PPP$[1] 1994	GNP per capita real growth rate (%) 1985-1994	Lowest 20%	Second quintile	Third quintile	Fourth quintile	Highest 20%	Ratio of highest 20% to lowest 20%[2]							
Countries in Transition	..	..	..	..	..	..	..	..	..	..	..	..	10.8	4.7	..	..
Albania	360	..	−6.0	..	..	..	..	..	..	51	0.93	6	22.7	1.7	..	422
Armenia	670g	2,170g	−12.9g	..	..	..	..	..	..	..	0.21	2	..	..	..	667
Azerbaijan	500g	1,720g	−12.2g	..	..	..	..	..	..	..	0.11	..	..	..	..	1,414
Belarus	2,160g	5,010g	−1.7g	11.1	15.3	18.5	22.2	32.9	3.0	..	1.27	2	..	..	..	2,692
Bosnia and Herzegovina	b															
Bulgaria	1,160	4,230c	−3.2	8.3	13.0	17.0	22.3	39.3	4.7	29	10.47	53	7.6	10.7	..	2,786
Croatia	2,530	..	..	..	..	..	..	..	..	..	2.30	7	8.4	7.7	..	1,057
Czech Republic	3,210	7,910	−2.1	10.5	13.9	16.9	21.3	37.4	3.6	17	10.69	10	5.5	4.5	..	3,902
Estonia	2,820g	..	−6.4g	6.6	10.7	15.1	21.4	46.3	7.0	..	0.19	1	11.2	12.3	..	3,552
Georgia	bg	1,160g	−18.6g	..	..	..	..	..	..	..	1.23	..	..	..	..	572
Hungary	3,840	6,310	−0.9	9.5	14.0	17.6	22.3	36.6	3.9	18	28.02	45	4.1	17.5	25	2,455
Kazakhstan	1,110g	2,830g	−6.5g	7.5	12.3	16.9	22.9	40.4	5.4	..	2.70	1	..	..	..	3,710
Kyrgyzstan	610g	1,710g	−5.4g	..	..	..	..	..	..	..	0.44	2	..	..	..	715
Latvia	2,290g	5,170g	−6.2g	9.6	13.6	17.5	22.6	36.7	3.8	..	0.36	1	7.3	4.7	..	1,755
Lithuania	1,350g	3,240g	−7.8g	8.1	12.3	16.2	21.3	42.1	5.2	..	0.44	1	6.3	14.2	..	2,194
Macedonia	790	..	..	..	..	..	..	..	..	..	0.92	14	13.5	11.2	..	..
Moldova	870g	..	..	6.9	11.9	16.7	23.1	41.5	6.0	..	0.49	2	17.0	34.6	..	962
Poland	2,470	5,380	0.9	9.3	13.8	17.7	22.6	36.6	3.9	30	42.16	40	6.2	8.9	29	2,563
Romania	1,230	2,920	−6.2	9.2	14.4	18.4	23.2	34.8	3.8	25	5.49	10	6.5	5.6	..	1,750
Russian Federation	2,650g	5,260g	−4.4g	3.7	8.5	13.5	20.4	53.8	14.5	132	94.23	19	19.7	0.9	..	4,038
Slovakia	2,230	6,660	−3.3	11.9	15.8	18.8	22.2	31.4	2.6	..	4.07	8	5.9	4.5	..	..
Slovenia	7,140	..	..	9.5	13.5	17.1	21.9	37.9	4.0	..	2.29	4	6.8	3.5	..	1,506
Tajikistan	350g	1,160g	−11.7g	..	..	..	..	..	..	..	0.59	..	..	..	..	642
Turkmenistan	f	..	−1.5gx	6.7	11.4	16.3	22.8	42.8	6.4	..	0.42	2	..	..	..	3,198
Ukraine	1,570g	3,330g	−5.1g	9.5	14.1	18.1	22.9	35.4	3.7	..	5.43	1	..	..	..	3,292
Uzbekistan	950g	2,390g	−2.4g	..	..	..	..	..	..	..	1.16	..	..	..	..	1,886
Yugoslavia	f	..	..	..	..	..	..	..	..	..	13.56	..	..	..	..	..
Industrial Countries	..	..	..	..	..	..	..	..	..	..	..	..	6.1	6.1	14	..
Australia	17,980	19,000	1.2	4.4	11.1	17.5	24.8	42.2	9.6	24	..	..	2.9	18.2	13	5,173
Austria	24,950	20,230	2.3	..	..	..	..	..	..	9	..	..	3.9	2.6	16	3,276
Belgium	22,920	20,450	2.3	7.9	13.7	18.6	23.8	36.0	4.6	20	..	..	8.0i	8.7i	15	5,091
Canada	19,570	21,320	0.4	5.7	11.8	17.7	24.6	40.2	7.1	15	..	..	4.2	5.4	11	7,795
Denmark	28,110	20,800	1.3	5.4	12.0	18.4	25.6	38.6	7.1	18	..	..	5.4	17.1	13	3,996
Finland	18,850	16,390	−0.3	6.3	12.1	18.4	25.5	37.6	6.0	15	..	..	4.3	2.7	16	5,954
France	23,470	19,820	1.7	5.6	11.8	17.2	23.5	41.9	7.5	29	..	..	7.0	9.8	16	3,839
Germany	25,580	19,890	1.9	7.0	11.8	17.1	23.9	40.3	5.8	29	..	..	7.2	3.7	12	4,097
Greece	7,710	11,400	1.3	..	..	..	..	..	..	71	..	..	11.2	21.3	30	2,235
Ireland	13,630	14,550	5.2	..	..	..	..	..	..	12	..	..	6.3	17.5	22	3,136
Israel	14,410	15,690	2.5	6.0	12.1	17.8	24.5	39.6	6.6	106	..	..	5.0	5.0	21	2,815
Italy	19,270	18,610	1.8	6.8	12.0	16.7	23.5	41.0	6.0	21	..	..	8.8	5.0	19	2,710
Japan	34,630	21,350	3.2	8.7	13.2	17.5	23.1	37.5	4.3	12	..	..	9.2	0.2	17	3,825
Luxembourg	39,850	31,090	1.3	..	..	..	..	..	..	10	..	..	j	j	..	..
Netherlands	21,970	18,080	1.9	8.2	13.1	18.1	23.7	36.9	4.5	22	..	..	9.6	15.0	13	4,558
New Zealand	13,190	16,780	0.5	5.1	10.8	16.2	23.2	44.7	8.8	16	..	..	5.6	37.2	12	4,352
Norway	26,480	21,120	1.4	6.2	12.8	18.9	25.3	36.7	5.9	22	..	..	4.1	0.6	15	5,326
Portugal	9,370	12,400	4.0	..	..	..	..	..	..	32	..	..	8.4	2.5	34	1,828
Spain	13,280	14,040	2.7	8.3	13.7	18.1	23.4	36.6	4.4	18	..	..	7.4	12.6	24	2,414
Sweden	23,630	17,850	0.0	8.0	13.2	17.4	24.5	36.9	4.6	16	..	..	4.4	1.4	13	5,603
Switzerland	37,180	24,390	0.5	5.2	11.7	16.4	22.1	44.6	8.6	14	..	..	4.4	2.1	17	3,603
United Kingdom	18,410	18,170	1.4	4.6	10.0	16.8	24.3	44.3	9.6	40	..	..	6.7	3.7	12	3,754
USA	25,860	25,860	1.3	4.7	11.0	17.4	25.0	41.9	8.9	46	..	..	2.7	6.7	10	7,905
World	..	..	..	..	..	..	..	..	..	37	..	..	6.2	6.0	..	1,434

.. Data not available.
[1] Purchasing power parity; see glossary.
[2] Bread for the World Institute calculation.
[3] Regional data are for 1994.
a Aggregated data for Ethiopia and Eritrea.
b Estimated to be low-income ($725 or less).
c World Bank estimates.
d Estimated to be upper-middle-income ($2,896-$8,955).

e Estimated to be high-income ($8,956 or more).
f Estimated to be lower-middle-income ($726-$2,895).
g Preliminary.
h GDP data.
i Aggregated data for Belgium-Luxembourg.
j See Belgium.
x Figures are for years other than specified.
The number 0 or 0.0 means zero or less than half the unit shown.

TABLE 4

Hunger, Malnutrition and Poverty – Developing Countries

| | Relative inadequacy of food supply: % below minimum required[1] 1990-1992 | % under 5 (1980-1994) suffering from: | | | | % of population with access to health services 1985-1995 | % of population with access to safe water 1990-1995 | | | Population in poverty (%)[2] 1990 | | Annual deforestation (as % of total forest)[3] 1981-1990 |
		Underweight moderate & severe	Underweight severe	Wasting moderate & severe	Stunting moderate & severe		Total	Urban	Rural	Urban	Rural	
Africa (sub-Saharan)	..	**31**	**9**	**7**	**41**	**57**	**45**	**63**	**34**	..	..	..
Angola	19.6	..	..	..	..	30x	32	69	15	..	65	0.69
Benin	4.3	..	..	..	..	18	50	41	53	..	..	1.22
Botswana	7.3	15x	..	..	44	89x	93x	100x	91x	30	64	0.51
Burkina Faso	12.4	30	8	13	29	90	78	..	..	..	90	0.65
Burundi	17.6	38x	10x	6x	48x	80	70x	100x	69x	..	..	−2.49
Cameroon	13.3	14	3	3	24	70	50	57	43	..	..	0.56
Cape Verde	..	..	..	..	..	..	..	..	..	..	..	−7.78
Central African Republic	25.5	..	..	..	..	45	18	18	18	..	..	0.40
Chad	25.0	..	..	..	..	30	24	48	17	..	..	0.72
Comoros	..	..	..	..	..	..	..	..	..	..	..	3.13
Congo	9.2	24	..	5	27	83	38x	92x	2x	..	80	0.15
Côte d'Ivoire	5.0	12	2	9	17	30x	72	59	81	..	..	0.96
Djibouti	..	..	..	..	..	..	..	..	..	..	..	0.00
Equatorial Guinea	..	..	..	..	..	..	..	..	..	..	..	0.37
Eritrea	..	..	..	..	..	..	..	..	7	..	..	..
Ethiopia	28.0	48x	16x	8x	64x	46	25	91	19	..	43	0.18a
Gabon	5.7	..	..	..	..	90x	68x	90x	50x	..	41	0.60
Gambia	7.5	..	..	..	..	93	48	67	..	..	..	0.75
Ghana	12.0	27	8	11	26	60	56	70	49	..	54	1.24
Guinea	5.8	..	..	..	..	80	55	50	56	..	70	1.14
Guinea-Bissau	..	23x	..	..	..	40	53	38	57	..	..	0.73
Kenya	15.1	22	6	6	33	77	53	67	49	..	..	0.39
Lesotho	10.0	16	2	5	26	80	52	14	64	..	..	..
Liberia	23.0	20x	..	3x	37x	39	46	79	13	..	..	0.52
Madagascar	8.0	39	9	5	51	65	29	83	10	..	..	0.76
Malawi	16.4	27	8	5	49	80	47x	91x	42x	..	90	1.12
Mali	9.5	31x	9x	11x	24x	30	37	36	38	..	60	0.79
Mauritania	4.4	48	..	16	57	63	66x	67x	65x	..	80	−0.03
Mauritius	4.0	24	..	16	22	100	99	95	100	..	..	−1.32
Mozambique	29.2	..	..	..	..	39	33	17	40	40	70	0.72
Namibia	9.6	26	6	9	28	62	57	87	42	..	70	0.33
Niger	10.4	36	12	16	32	32	54	46	55	..	..	−0.03
Nigeria	11.1	36	12	9	43	66	40	63	26	..	..	0.68
Rwanda	14.5	29	6	4	48	80	66	75	62	..	..	−1.81
Senegal	7.9	20	5	9	22	40	52	85	28	..	70	0.52
Sierra Leone	19.9	29	..	9x	35	38	34	58	21	..	..	0.60
Somalia	35.1	..	..	..	..	27x	37x	50x	29x	..	..	0.36
South Africa	..	..	..	..	25	..	70	..	..	..	..	0.55
Sudan	10.9	20	..	14	32	70	60	84	41	..	..	0.99
Swaziland	2.5	..	..	..	..	..	..	..	..	..	..	−0.05
Tanzania	11.1	29	7	6	47	80	50	67	46	..	..	1.13
Togo	7.8	24x	6x	5x	30x	61	63	74	58	..	30	1.31
Uganda	8.5	23	5	2	45	49	34	47	32	25	33	0.92
Zaire	11.2	28x	..	5x	43x	26	27	37	23	..	..	0.60
Zambia	13.3	25	6	5	40	75x	50	91	11	..	..	1.00
Zimbabwe	12.4	12x	2x	1x	29x	85	77	99	64	..	60	0.62
South Asia	..	**64**	**24**	**13**	**62**	**77**	**80**	**87**	**78**	..	..	..
Afghanistan	34.2	..	..	..	..	29	12	39	5	..	60	0.03
Bangladesh	8.8	67	25	17	63	45	97	99	97	56	51	2.02
Bhutan	..	38	..	4	56	65	..	..	..	..	90	0.54
India	4.9	69x	27x	..	65x	85	81	85	79	37	39	−1.15
Nepal	7.3	70x	5x	14x	69x	..	46	90	43	19	43	0.90
Pakistan	3.5	40	14	9	50	55	79	96	71	20	31	2.64
Sri Lanka	6.4	38	3x	16	24	93x	53	87	49	15	36	1.00

	Relative inadequacy of food supply: % below minimum required[1] 1990-1992	% under 5 (1980-1994) suffering from:				% of population with access to health services 1985-1995	% of population with access to safe water 1990-1995			Population in poverty (%)[2] 1990		Annual deforestation (as % of total forest)[3] 1981-1990
		Underweight moderate & severe	Underweight severe	Wasting moderate & severe	Stunting moderate & severe		Total	Urban	Rural	Urban	Rural	
East Asia and the Pacific	..	23	..	4	33	89	66	92	56	..	..	..
Burma (Myanmar)	2.3	32x	9x	..	..	60	38	36	39	..	..	1.16
Cambodia	7.1	40	7	8	38	53	36	65	33	..	..	0.97
China	3.5	17	3x	4x	32x	92	67	97	56	..	12	−0.59
Fiji	..	..	..	..	..	..	..	..	..	..	..	−0.17
Hong Kong	0.8	..	..	..	..	99x	100	100	96	..	..	..
Indonesia	2.2	40	..	..	..	80	62	79	54	20	16	0.71
Korea, N	1.6	..	..	..	..	..	..	..	..	..	20	−1.43
Korea, S	0.1	..	..	..	..	100	93	100	76	5	4	0.02
Laos	5.6	37	..	11	40	67	45	57	43	..	85	0.89
Malaysia	1.1	23	1	..	..	..	78	96	66	8	22	1.81
Mongolia	8.4	12x	..	2x	26x	95	80	100	58	..	..	0.00
Papua New Guinea	1.9	35	..	..	..	96	28	84	17	..	..	0.30
Philippines	4.5	34	5	6	37	76	85	93	77	40	54	2.82
Singapore	..	14x	..	4x	11x	100	100x	100x	..	..	..	0.00
Solomon Islands	..	..	..	..	..	..	..	..	..	..	..	0.18
Thailand	6.5	26x	4x	6x	22x	90	86x	98x	87x	7	29	2.68
Vietnam	6.0	42	14	6	51	90	36	53	32	..	60	0.83
Latin America and the Caribbean	..	11	2	3	21	73	80	87	51	..	..	..
Argentina	1.6	..	..	..	..	71	71	77	29	15	20	0.57
Belize	..	..	..	..	..	..	..	..	..	..	..	0.24
Bolivia	11.9	16	4	4	28	67	55	78	22	54	76	1.12
Brazil	1.1	7	1	2	16	..	87	..	..	33	63	0.58
Chile	5.1	3x	..	1x	10x	97	85	94	37	10	10	0.07
Colombia	3.9	10	2	3	17	60	87	98	74	8	41	0.62
Costa Rica	2.2	2	0	2	8	80x	92	85	99	4	3	2.44
Cuba	1.7	..	..	1	..	98	93	96	85	..	35	0.19
Dominican Republic	8.6	10	2	1	19	80	76	82	46	..	..	2.43
Ecuador	4.1	17	0	2	34	88	71	82	55	24	47	1.65
El Salvador	4.1	11	1	1	23	40	55	78	38	42	51	1.85
Guatemala	6.3	34x	8x	1x	58x	34	62	92	43	55	79	1.58
Guyana	5.6	..	..	..	..	..	..	..	..	..	..	0.09
Haiti	32.4	27	3x	5	34	50	28	37	23	80	99	1.91
Honduras	4.6	21	4	2	39	64	65	81	53	54	83	1.94
Jamaica	5.6	9	1	1	5	90	86	..	..	4	18	5.08
Mexico	1.4	14	..	6	22	78	83	91	62	9	32	1.21
Nicaragua	5.9	12	1	2	24	83	58	81	23	58	76	1.69
Panama	4.1	7	1	1	9	80x	83	..	..	27	37	1.70
Paraguay	2.9	4	1	0	17	63	35	50	24	8	48	2.38
Peru	15.9	11	2	1	37	75x	71	88	28	49	73	0.37
Suriname	4.9	..	..	..	..	..	..	..	..	..	..	0.08
Trinidad & Tobago	2.1	7x	0x	4x	5x	100	97	99	91	2	21	1.75
Uruguay	1.5	7	2	..	16	82	75x	85x	5x	5	31	−0.12
Venezuela	4.6	6	..	2	6	..	79	80	75	11	24	1.13
Middle East and North Africa	..	12	..	5	24	85	76	93	58	..	..	..
Algeria	1.6	9	..	6	18	98	79	96	60	..	25	0.88
Bahrain	..	..	..	..	..	..	..	..	..	..	..	..
Cyprus	..	..	..	..	..	..	..	..	..	..	..	..
Egypt	0.9	9	2	3	24	99	80	97	61	34	34	−1.97
Iran	1.2	..	..	..	..	80	84	89	77	..	..	1.38
Iraq	4.8	12	2	3	22	93	44	..	..	..	..	0.00
Jordan	0.5	9	..	2	16	97	89	..	..	..	..	−0.28
Kuwait	4.1	6	..	3	12	100	..	..	..	..	..	..
Lebanon	0.8	..	..	..	..	95	94	96	88	..	15	0.71
Libya	0.5	..	..	..	..	..	97x	100x	80x	..	..	−3.79

	Relative inadequacy of food supply: % below minimum required[1] 1990-1992	% under 5 (1980-1994) suffering from:				% of population with access to health services 1985-1995	% of population with access to safe water 1990-1995			Population in poverty (%)[2] 1990		Annual deforestation (as % of total forest)[3] 1981-1990
		Underweight moderate & severe	Underweight severe	Wasting moderate & severe	Stunting moderate & severe		Total	Urban	Rural	Urban	Rural	
Morocco	1.8	9	2	2	23	70	55	94	18	28	32	0.42
Oman	..	..	..	..	..	96	63	..	..	..	6	..
Qatar	..	..	..	..	..	..	..	..	..	..	..	..
Saudi Arabia	2.4	..	..	..	..	97	95x	100x	74x	..	..	1.85
Syria	0.4	..	..	..	..	90	85	92	78	..	54	−2.85
Tunisia	0.4	10x	2x	3x	18x	90x	99	100	89	16	31	−0.92
Turkey	0.5	10	2	3	21	..	80	91	59	..	14	..
United Arab Emirates	0.6	..	..	..	..	99	95	..	..	..	..	..
Yemen	5.6	30	4	13	44	38	55	89	47	..	..	0.00
Developing Countries	**4.7**	**35**	**12**	**6**	**42**	**80**	**70**	**87**	**60**	..	..	..

.. *Data not available.*

[1] *Applies to underfed population only; see glossary.*

[2] *Poverty data comparable only between rural and urban areas; not comparable between countries.*

[3] *Positive data indicate loss of forest; negative data indicate gain in forest.*

x *Data refer to a year or period other than that specified in the column heading, differ from the standard definition or refer to only part of a country.*

a *Aggregated data for Ethiopia and Eritrea.*

The number 0 means zero or less than half the unit of measure.

TABLE 5

U.S. National Hunger and Poverty Trends

	1970	1980	1982	1984	1985	1986	1987	1988	1989	1990	1991	1992	1993	1994	1995	1996
Total population (millions)	205.1	227.8	232.5	237.0	239.3	241.6	243.9	246.3	248.3	248.7	252.2	255.1	257.9	260.7	262.8	266.1
Total hungry population (millions)	..	..	..	..	20.0	..	..	..	..	..	30.0	..	..	..	..	..
Children under 18 hungry (millions)	..	..	..	..	..	..	..	..	..	..	12.1	..	..	..	..	..
Children under 12 hungry (millions)	..	..	..	..	..	..	..	..	..	..	5.5	..	..	..	4.0	..
Children under 12 at risk of hunger (millions)	..	..	..	..	..	..	..	..	..	..	6.0	..	..	..	9.6	..
Total poverty rate (%)	12.6	13.0	15.0	14.4	14.0	13.6	13.4	13.1	12.8	13.5	14.2	14.8	15.1	14.5	..	..
White poverty rate (%)	9.9	10.2	12.0	11.5	11.4	11.0	10.4	10.1	10.0	10.7	11.3	11.9	12.2	11.7	..	..
Black poverty rate (%)	33.5	32.5	35.6	33.8	31.1	31.1	32.6	31.6	30.7	31.9	32.7	33.4	33.1	30.6	..	..
Hispanic poverty rate (%)	..	25.7	29.9	28.4	29.0	27.3	28.1	26.8	26.2	28.1	28.7	29.6	30.6	30.7	..	..
Elderly poverty rate (%)	24.6	15.7	14.6	12.4	12.6	12.4	12.5	12.0	11.4	12.2	12.4	12.9	12.2	11.7	..	..
Total child poverty rate (%)	15.1	18.3	21.9	21.5	20.7	20.5	20.5	19.7	19.6	20.6	21.1	22.3	22.7	21.8	..	..
White child poverty rate (%)	..	13.9	17.0	16.7	16.2	16.1	15.4	14.6	14.8	15.9	16.1	17.4	17.8	16.9	..	..
Black child poverty rate (%)	..	42.3	47.6	46.6	43.6	43.1	45.6	44.2	43.7	44.8	45.6	46.6	46.1	43.8	..	..
Hispanic child poverty rate (%)	..	33.2	39.5	39.2	40.3	37.7	39.6	37.9	36.2	38.4	39.8	40.0	40.9	41.5	..	..
Poverty rate of people in female-headed households (%)[1]	38.1	36.7	40.6	38.4	37.6	38.3	38.3	37.2	32.2	33.4	39.7	39.0	38.7	34.6	..	..
Percent of federal budget spent on food assistance[2]	0.5	2.4	2.1	2.1	2.0	1.9	1.9	1.9	1.9	1.9	2.0	2.3	2.5	2.47	2.48*	2.45*
Total infant mortality rate (per 1,000 live births)	20.0	12.6	11.5	10.8	10.6	10.4	10.1	10.0	9.7	9.1	8.9	8.5	8.4	..	..	..
White infant mortality rate	17.8	11.0	10.1	9.4	9.3	8.9	8.6	8.5	8.5	7.7	7.3	6.9	6.8	..	..	..
Black infant mortality rate	32.6	21.4	19.6	18.4	18.2	18.0	17.9	17.6	17.6	17.0	17.6	16.8	16.5	..	..	..
Hispanic infant mortality rate	..	..	..	..	..	..	7.9	8.1	8.5	7.8	7.5	6.8	..	..	..	..
Unemployment rate (%)	4.9	7.1	9.7	7.5	7.2	7.0	6.2	5.5	5.3	5.6	6.8	7.5	6.9	6.1	5.6	..
White unemployment rate (%)	4.5	6.3	8.6	6.5	6.2	6.0	5.3	4.7	4.5	4.8	6.1	6.6	6.1	5.3	4.9	..
Black unemployment rate (%)	..	14.3	18.9	15.9	15.1	14.5	13.0	11.7	11.4	11.4	12.5	14.2	13.0	11.5	10.4	..
Hispanic unemployment rate (%)	..	10.1	13.8	10.7	10.5	10.6	8.8	8.2	8.0	8.2	10.0	11.6	10.8	9.9	9.3	..
Household income distribution (per quintile in %)[3]																
All races																
Lowest 20 percent	4.1	4.2	4.0	4.0	3.9	3.8	3.8	3.8	3.8	3.9	3.8	3.8	3.6	3.6	..	..
Second quintile	10.8	10.2	10.0	9.9	9.8	9.7	9.6	9.6	9.5	9.6	9.6	9.4	9.0	8.9	..	..
Third quintile	17.4	16.8	16.5	16.3	16.2	16.2	16.1	16.0	15.8	15.9	15.9	15.8	15.1	15.0	..	..
Fourth quintile	24.5	24.8	24.5	24.6	24.4	24.3	24.3	24.3	24.0	24.0	24.2	24.2	23.5	23.4	..	..
Highest 20 percent	43.3	44.1	45.0	45.2	45.6	46.1	46.2	46.3	46.8	46.6	46.5	46.9	48.9	49.1	..	..
Ratio of highest 20 percent to lowest 20 percent[4]	10.6	10.5	11.3	11.3	11.7	12.1	12.2	12.2	12.3	11.9	12.2	12.3	13.6	13.6	..	..
White																
Lowest 20 percent	4.2	4.4	4.2	4.3	4.1	4.1	4.1	4.1	4.1	4.2	4.1	4.1	3.9	3.8	..	..
Second quintile	11.1	10.5	10.3	10.2	10.1	10.0	10.0	10.0	9.8	10.0	9.9	9.7	9.3	9.2	..	..
Third quintile	17.5	17.0	16.6	16.5	16.4	16.3	16.3	16.2	16.0	16.0	16.0	15.9	15.3	15.1	..	..
Fourth quintile	24.3	24.6	24.4	24.4	24.3	24.2	24.2	24.1	23.8	23.9	24.1	24.1	23.3	23.2	..	..
Highest 20 percent	42.9	43.5	44.4	44.6	45.1	45.4	45.5	45.6	46.3	46.0	45.8	46.2	48.2	48.6	..	..
Ratio of highest 20 percent to lowest 20 percent[4]	10.2	9.9	10.6	10.4	11.0	11.1	11.1	11.1	11.3	11.0	11.2	11.3	12.4	12.8	..	..
Black																
Lowest 20 percent	3.7	3.7	3.6	3.6	3.5	3.1	3.3	3.3	3.2	3.1	3.1	3.1	3.0	3.0	..	..
Second quintile	9.3	8.7	8.6	8.4	8.3	8.0	7.9	7.7	8.0	7.9	7.8	7.8	7.7	7.9	..	..
Third quintile	16.3	15.3	15.3	15.0	15.2	14.9	14.8	14.6	15.0	15.0	15.0	14.7	14.3	14.3	..	..
Fourth quintile	25.2	25.2	25.3	24.7	25.0	25.0	24.4	24.7	24.9	25.1	25.2	24.8	23.7	24.3	..	..
Highest 20 percent	45.5	47.1	47.1	48.4	48.0	49.0	49.7	49.7	48.9	49.0	48.9	49.7	51.3	50.5	..	..
Ratio of highest 20 percent to lowest 20 percent[4]	12.3	12.7	13.1	13.4	13.7	15.8	15.1	15.1	15.3	15.8	15.8	16.0	17.1	16.8	..	..
Hispanic origin																
Lowest 20 percent	..	4.3	4.2	3.9	4.1	3.9	3.7	3.7	3.8	4.0	4.0	4.0	3.9	3.7	..	..
Second quintile	..	10.1	9.6	9.5	9.4	9.5	9.1	9.3	9.5	9.5	9.4	9.4	9.1	8.7	..	..
Third quintile	..	16.4	16.1	16.2	16.1	15.8	15.5	15.6	15.7	15.9	15.8	15.7	15.1	14.8	..	..
Fourth quintile	..	24.8	24.6	24.9	24.8	24.8	24.1	24.2	24.4	24.3	24.3	24.1	23.1	23.3	..	..
Highest 20 percent	..	44.5	45.5	45.5	45.6	46.1	47.6	47.2	46.6	46.3	46.5	46.9	48.7	49.6	..	..
Ratio of highest 20 percent to lowest 20 percent[4]	..	10.3	10.8	11.7	11.1	11.8	12.9	12.8	12.3	11.6	11.6	11.7	12.5	13.4	..	..

.. Data not available.
[1] With no spouse present.
[2] Data refer to fiscal year.
[3] Revised data.
[4] Bread for the World Institute calculation.
* Estimates.

TABLE 6

United States – State Hunger and Poverty Statistics

	Population (millions) July 1995	% of population in poverty 1994	Unemployment rate (%) (seasonally adjusted)[1] May 1996	AFDC and food stamp benefits as % of poverty level (one-parent family of 4 persons) 1995	Infant mortality rate per 1,000 live births[2] 1995	% of children under 12 hungry 1995	% of children under 12 hungry or at risk		% of population all ages hungry 1991
							1991	1995	
Alabama	4.25	16.4	5.6	46	10.1	8.6	35.0	29.5	15.8
Alaska	0.60	10.2	6.8	89	6.8	5.5	17.7	20.3	9.9
Arizona	4.22	15.9	5.1	62	7.3	9.0	25.8	30.4	12.4
Arkansas	2.48	15.3	4.6	50	8.3	10.0	38.5	36.1	14.5
California	31.59	17.9	7.2	79	6.2	11.8	27.8	37.1	13.2
Colorado	3.75	9.0	4.0	63	6.9	6.0	21.0	21.0	8.7
Connecticut	3.27	10.8	4.8	83	..	6.1	16.2	19.4	7.2
Delaware	0.72	8.3	4.8	62	7.3	5.9	21.8	21.8	6.3
District of Columbia	0.55	21.2	8.9	68	16.7	11.3	33.7	40.0	15.6
Florida	14.17	14.9	5.1	59	7.5	11.8	27.5	39.5	12.9
Georgia	7.20	14.0	4.6	57	9.7	7.3	27.1	24.5	14.4
Hawaii	1.19	8.7	6.0	97	6.3	5.4	23.7	19.1	6.5
Idaho	1.16	12.0	5.1	60	6.2	8.2	34.4	30.6	11.7
Illinois	11.83	12.4	5.2	63	8.8	7.9	28.0	26.3	11.3
Indiana	5.80	13.7	4.1	58	9.2	7.2	25.3	28.1	13.2
Iowa	2.84	10.7	3.5	67	7.2	6.4	31.7	23.2	8.0
Kansas	2.57	14.9	4.1	69	7.5	8.1	22.8	29.1	10.3
Kentucky	3.86	18.5	5.1	53	7.9	9.2	29.8	33.7	15.8
Louisiana	4.34	25.7	6.7	49	9.4	12.1	32.1	39.1	15.9
Maine	1.24	9.4	5.5	68	5.5	9.9	24.3	35.0	11.8
Maryland	5.04	10.7	4.9	65	9.1	5.9	16.4	19.9	7.6
Massachusetts	6.07	9.7	4.9	76	5.3	6.5	19.3	22.5	9.2
Michigan	9.55	14.1	4.7	71	8.6	8.4	27.6	29.9	11.8
Minnesota	4.61	11.7	3.4	74	6.2	6.7	21.2	24.4	10.8
Mississippi	2.70	19.9	6.3	42	10.5	10.3	38.7	37.3	19.9
Missouri	5.32	15.6	4.3	58	7.9	9.2	26.9	32.4	12.4
Montana	0.87	11.5	5.6	67	7.0	7.9	31.5	30.3	12.9
Nebraska	1.64	8.8	3.0	63	7.6	6.9	28.6	24.8	8.0
Nevada	1.53	11.1	5.4	62	5.6	6.7	27.9	22.9	9.6
New Hampshire	1.15	7.7	4.0	73	4.7	6.3	12.6	22.8	6.1
New Jersey	7.95	9.2	6.1	67	7.0	7.1	20.3	22.7	8.1
New Mexico	1.69	21.1	6.8	65	7.3	8.7	36.1	31.4	18.8
New York	18.14	17.0	6.4	83	..	9.5	29.7	30.7	12.8
North Carolina	7.20	14.2	4.3	54	9.7	8.3	26.3	29.5	12.2
North Dakota	0.64	10.4	3.1	68	5.6	5.3	27.9	21.2	12.2
Ohio	11.15	14.1	4.9	63	8.4	7.1	24.3	26.5	11.2
Oklahoma	3.28	16.7	4.2	62	8.7	10.6	28.7	38.7	14.2
Oregon	3.14	11.8	5.2	73	6.1	6.9	24.1	25.2	11.3
Pennsylvania	12.07	12.5	5.9	68	7.4	7.6	25.6	28.1	9.2
Rhode Island	0.99	10.3	4.6	78	6.8	6.9	25.6	25.8	8.7
South Carolina	3.67	13.8	5.4	50	8.2	10.0	31.3	35.8	13.7
South Dakota	0.73	14.5	2.8	66	10.0	8.0	28.6	29.9	11.7
Tennessee	5.26	14.6	4.7	48	9.9	10.6	30.7	36.8	13.0
Texas	18.72	19.1	5.9	48	6.6	10.1	28.6	30.6	14.7
Utah	1.95	8.0	3.3	67	5.3	7.0	25.5	24.7	10.8
Vermont	0.58	7.6	4.0	80	6.0	5.2	20.5	21.9	10.6
Virginia	6.62	10.7	4.2	62	7.4	5.8	20.5	20.7	8.3
Washington	5.43	11.7	6.0	77	5.1	7.4	22.7	27.5	8.0
West Virginia	1.83	18.6	7.1	55	7.1	10.2	38.6	37.3	15.0
Wisconsin	5.12	9.0	3.6	73	7.5	7.8	24.7	28.6	8.3
Wyoming	0.48	9.3	4.6	61	9.2	8.9	22.6	28.9	8.3
United States	**262.76**	**14.5**	**5.6**	**65**	**7.4**	**8.9**	**26.8**	**29.0**	**12.0**

.. Data not available.
[1] Preliminary.
[2] Data are provisional and for the 12 months ending with November 1995.

Sources for Tables

Table 1: Global Hunger – Life and Death Indicators

Total population, projected population, projected population growth rate, projected total fertility rate, urban population, life expectancy: United Nations Fund for Population Activities, *The State of World Population 1996* (New York: UNFPA, 1996).

Population below age 15: Population Reference Bureau, *World Population Data Sheet 1996* (Washington: PRB, 1996).

Infant mortality, under-5 mortality, maternal mortality: United Nations Children's Fund (UNICEF), *The State of the World's Children 1996* (New York: Oxford University Press, 1996 – "*SWC*").

Table 2: Global Health, Nutrition and Welfare

Human Development Index rank, adult literacy, gross educational enrollment: United Nations Development Programme, *Human Development Report 1996* (New York: Oxford University Press, 1996 – "*HDR*").

Refugees by country of asylum: United Nations High Commissioner for Refugees, *Populations of Concern to UNHCR,* June 1996.

Low birthweight, percent immunized (measles), daily per capita calorie supply: *SWC.*

Food production per capita: Food and Agriculture Organization of the United Nations, FAOSTAT TS software, 1995.

Per capita dietary energy supply: FAO, *Sixth World Food Survey* (Rome: FAO, 1996).

Table 3: Global Economic Indicators

GNP per capita: The World Bank, *The World Bank Atlas 1996* (Washington: The World Bank, 1995).

Distribution of income or consumption by quintiles: The World Bank, *World Development Report 1996* (New York: Oxford University Press, 1996 – "*WDR*").

Military expenditure as percent of combined education and health expenditure: *HDR.*

Total debt, debt service as percent of exports of goods and services: The World Bank, *World Debt Tables 1996, vol. 1* (Washington: The World Bank, 1996).

Food as percent of total imports, exports: FAO.

Food as percent of household consumption: *SWC.*

Per capita energy consumption: *WDR.*

Table 4: Hunger, Malnutrition and Poverty – Developing Countries

Relative inadequacy of food supply: FAO, *Sixth World Food Survey.*

Underweight, wasting, stunting; access to health services and safe water: *SWC.*

Population in poverty: International Labour Organization, *World Labour Report* (Geneva: ILO, 1995).

Annual deforestation: World Resources Institute, *World Resources 1996-97* (New York: Oxford University Press, 1996).

Table 5: U.S. National Hunger and Poverty Trends

Total population, poverty data, household income distribution: U.S. Bureau of the Census.

Total hungry population, total children hungry: Center on Hunger, Poverty and Nutrition Policy, Tufts University.

Children under 12 hungry, at risk of hunger: Food Research and Action Center (FRAC).

Percent of federal budget spent on food assistance: *Budget of the United States Government, Fiscal Year 1996* (Washington: U.S. Government Printing Office, 1995).

Infant mortality: National Center for Health Statistics, *Monthly Vital Statistics Report: Advance Report of Final Mortality Statistics, 1993,* 44:7 (February 1996).

Unemployment: U.S. Bureau of Labor Statistics.

Table 6: United States – State Hunger and Poverty Statistics

Total population, population in poverty: U.S. Bureau of the Census.

Unemployment: U.S. Bureau of Labor Statistics.

AFDC and food stamp benefits as percent of poverty level: The Annie E. Casey Foundation, *Kids Count Data Book 1996* (Baltimore: The Annie E. Casey Foundation, 1996).

Infant mortality: National Center for Health Statistics, *Monthly Vital Statistics Report: Births, Marriages, Divorces and Deaths,* 44:11 (May 1996).

Children under 12 hungry, at risk of hunger: FRAC.

Population all ages hungry: Center on Hunger, Poverty and Nutrition Policy, Tufts University.

Abbreviations

AFDC   –   Aid to Families with Dependent Children
CRS   –   Catholic Relief Services
EITC   –   Earned Income Tax Credit
FAO   –   Food and Agriculture Organization of the United Nations
FRAC   –   Food Research and Action Center
FY   –   Fiscal Year
GATT   –   General Agreement on Tariffs and Trade
IFPRI   –   International Food Policy Research Institute
ILO   –   International Labor Organization
NAFTA   –   North American Free Trade Agreement
NGO   –   Nongovernmental Organization
NIS   –   Newly Independent States of the former Soviet Union
ODS   –   Office of Development Studies (UNDP)
PCFN   –   Pennsylvania Coalition on Food and Nutrition
PVO   –   Private Voluntary Organization
U.K.   –   United Kingdom
U.N.   –   United Nations
UNDP   –   U.N. Development Programme
UNECLAC   –   U.N. Economic Commission for Latin America and the Caribbean
UNFPA   –   U.N. Fund for Population Activities
UNICEF   –   U.N. Children's Fund
U.S.   –   United States
USAID   –   U.S. Agency for International Development
USDA   –   U.S. Department of Agriculture
VIEW   –   Virginia Initiative for Employment, not Welfare
W-2   –   Wisconsin Works
WHO   –   World Health Organization
WIC   –   Special Supplemental Nutrition Program for Women, Infants and Children

Glossary

Anemia – A condition in which the hemoglobin concentration (the number of red blood cells) is lower than normal due to disease or as a result of a deficiency of one or more essential nutrients such as iron.

Bilateral aid – Financial or material assistance provided to an individual developing country by a single donor country (as distinguished from multilateral aid).

Block grants – Federal government lump-sum payments to the states, which then have wide discretion over the use of these funds.

Cold War – The global state of tension and military rivalry that existed from 1945 to 1990 between the United States and the former Soviet Union and their respective allies.

Combined gross enrollment ratio – A comparison of the enrollment of all schools and colleges with the population of the relevant age groups.

Complex humanitarian emergencies – Crises arising from conflicts within countries, leading to large-scale displacement of people, mass famine, environmental degradation and fragile or failing economic, political and social institutions.

Daily calorie requirement – The average number of calories needed to sustain normal levels of activity and health, taking into account age, sex, body weight and climate: roughly 2,350 calories per person per day.

Debt service – The sum of repayments of principal and payments of interest on debt.

Deforestation – Clearing of forest lands for other land uses, including all forms of agriculture, settlements, other infrastructure and mining.

Developing countries – Countries in which most people have a low economic standard of living. Also known as the "Third World," the "South" and the "less-developed countries."

Dietary energy supply (DES) – The total calories available for human consumption within a country during one year.

Entitlement – In the U.S. government budget, a program for which spending is mandatory, rather than subject to annual appropriations. Distinguished from "discretionary spending programs," which are subject to appropriations.

Ethnicity – Identifying characteristics shared by a group of people such as culture, custom, race, language, religion or other social distinctions.

Exchange rate – The official international value of a country's currency, usually expressed in U.S. dollars.

Famine – A situation of extreme scarcity of food, potentially leading to widespread starvation.

Fertility rate – The average number of children borne by a woman during her lifetime; used as a measure of long-term population changes.

Food security – Assured access for every person, primarily by production or purchase, to enough nutritious food to sustain an active and healthy life with dignity.

Globalization – In economic terms, a process whereby an increased portion of economic activity is carried out across national borders.

Gross domestic product (GDP) – The value of all goods and services produced within a nation during a specified period, usually a year.

Gross national product (GNP) – The value of all goods and services produced by a country's citizens, wherever they are located.

Human development – A measure of well-being devised by the U.N. Development Programme, based on economic growth, educational attainment and health.

Human rights – The basic rights and freedoms of all human beings, including, but not limited to, the right to life and liberty, freedom of thought and expression and equality before the law.

Hunger – A condition in which people lack the basic food intake to provide them with the energy and nutrients for fully productive, active and healthy lives.

Industrial countries – Countries in which most people have a high economic standard of living (though there are often significant poverty populations). Also called the "developed countries" or the "North."

Inequality ratio – The ratio between incomes of the richest and poorest people within a population (i.e., those with incomes at the 90th percentile of income and those with incomes at the 10th percentile).

Infant mortality rate (IMR) – The annual number of deaths of infants under 1 year of age per 1,000 live births.

Inflation – An increase in overall prices, which leads to a decrease in purchasing power.

Infrastructure – The basic facilities, services and installations needed for the functioning of a community or society such as transportation, communications, financial, educational and health care systems.

International financial institutions (IFIs) – Intergovernmental agencies, including the International Monetary Fund, World Bank and regional development banks, which make loans to governments.

International Monetary Fund (IMF) – An international organization that makes loans to countries to help resolve foreign exchange and monetary problems. These loans are conditioned upon the willingness of the borrowing country to adopt IMF-approved economic policies.

Least developed countries – According to the United Nations, low-income countries that are suffering from long-term handicaps to economic growth, in particular low levels of human resource development and/or severe structural weaknesses.

Livelihood security – The ability of a household to meet all of its basic needs – for food, shelter, water, sanitation, health care and education – without making tradeoffs among them.

Low birth-weight infants – Babies born weighing 2,500 grams (5 pounds, 8 ounces) or less who are especially vulnerable to illness and death during the first months of life.

Malnutrition – Failure to achieve nutrient requirements, which can impair physical and/or mental health. Malnutrition may result from consuming too little food or from a shortage or imbalance of key nutrients, e.g., micronutrient deficiencies or excess consumption of refined sugar and fat.

Means-tested – Government benefit programs that base eligibility on strict income and assets limits.

Microenterprises – Very small economic ventures owned and managed by one entrepreneur and employing fewer than five people.

Micronutrients – Vitamins, major minerals and trace elements needed for a healthy, balanced diet. Often contrasted with "macronutrients" – protein and calories. Micronutrient deficiencies are also called "hidden hunger."

Multilateral aid – Financial or material assistance channeled to developing countries via international organizations such as the World Bank, the European Union or U.N. agencies (as distinguished from bilateral aid).

Population at risk – People who are in need of or dependent on outside aid to avoid large-scale malnutrition and deaths as a result of complex humanitarian emergencies. These people include refugees, internally displaced people and others in need.

Poverty line – An official measure of poverty defined by national governments. In the United States, it is based on ability to afford the U.S. Department of Agriculture's "Thrifty Food Plan," which provides a less-than-adequate diet, and other essentials.

Privatization – The transfer of companies and services from government to private ownership and operation.

Protectionism – A trade policy that protects domestic producers by impeding or limiting, as by tariffs or quotas, the importation of foreign goods and services.

Purchasing Power Parity (PPP) – An estimate of the amount of money required to purchase comparable goods in different countries, expressed in U.S. dollars.

Recession – A period during which a country's GDP declines in two or more consecutive three-month periods. The reduction in economic activity is less severe than during a "depression."

Relative food inadequacy – A measure of the gap between actual food supplies and minimum needs for people with inadequate access to food.

Sovereignty – Supreme political authority over a territory, generally residing in a national government.

Starvation – Suffering or death from extreme or prolonged lack of food.

Structural adjustment program (SAP) – Economic policy changes, often imposed upon an indebted country by its lenders as a condition for future loans, intended to stimulate economic growth. These generally involve reducing the role of government in the economy and increasing exports.

Stunting – Failure to grow to normal height caused by chronic undernutrition during the formative years of childhood.

Subsidiarity – The principle that decisions should be made and carried out at the lowest possible level.

Subsistence crops – Crops that farm families grow to feed themselves.

Sustainability – Society's ability to shape its economic and social systems so as to maintain both natural resources and human life.

Sustainable development – The reduction of hunger and poverty in environmentally sound ways. It includes four objectives: meeting basic human needs, expanding economic opportunities, protecting and enhancing the environment, and promoting pluralism and democratic participation.

Underemployment – The situation of not being fully employed year round. Underemployed people include unemployed, discouraged (those who have stopped looking for work) and involuntary part-time workers.

Under-5 mortality rate – The annual number of deaths of children under 5 years of age per 1,000 live births; a high rate correlates closely with hunger and malnutrition.

Undernutrition – As used by nutritionists, a term describing a form of mild, chronic or acute malnutrition characterized by inadequate intake of food energy (measured by calories), usually due to eating too little. Stunting, wasting and underweight are common symptoms of undernutrition.

Underweight – A condition in which a person is seriously below normal weight for her or his age.

Value-added tax (VAT) – A tax on the estimated market value added to a product or material at each stage of its manufacture or distribution, ultimately passed on to the consumer.

Vulnerability to hunger – Individuals, households, communities or nations who have enough to eat most of the time, but whose poverty makes them especially susceptible to hunger due to changes in the economy, climate or political conditions.

Wasting – A condition in which a person is seriously below the normal weight for her or his height due to acute undernutrition or a medical condition.

World Bank – An intergovernmental agency that makes long-term loans to the governments of developing nations.

Notes

Introduction

1. Colbert I. King, "A Boy Who Climbed Into a Garbage Can," *Washington Post*, January 27, 1996.

2. *Washington Post*, January 19, 1996.

3. Theodore C. Sorensen, ed., *Let the Word Go Forth: The Speeches, Statements and Writings of John F. Kennedy* (New York: Delacorte Press, 1988), p. 350.

Chapter 1

1. Unless otherwise noted, statistical information on developing countries and countries in transition in this chapter comes from Food and Agriculture Organization of the United Nations, *The Sixth World Food Survey* (Rome: FAO, 1996). This is the most comprehensive current study of global food and hunger issues. We are also grateful to FAO staff for their help in preparing this chapter.

2. Based on a study by the Center on Hunger, Poverty and Nutrition Policy at Tufts University prepared for the U.S. Congress.

3. Federation of American Societies for Experimental Biology, Life Sciences Research Office, *Third Report on Nutrition Monitoring in the United States*, vol. 1 (Washington: U.S. Government Printing Office, 1995), pp. 123, 125-126.

4. Unless otherwise noted, data on hunger in Canada, Western Europe and Australia are taken from Graham Riches, ed., *First World Hunger: Food Security and Welfare Politics* (London: Macmillan, forthcoming).

5. Scott Kraft, "Spare a Franc? Ranks of French Homeless Soar," *Washington Post*, August 30, 1995.

6. Rick Atkinson, "Germany, Europe's Engine, Revs Up Jobs Losses and Deficit," *Washington Post*, February 19, 1996.

7. Timothy M. Smeeding and Peter Gottschalk, "The International Evidence on Income Distribution in Modern Economies: Where Do We Stand?," *Luxembourg Income Study Working Paper* No. 137 (December 1995).

8. *Washington Post*, June 22 and 28, 1996.

9. UNICEF, *The Progress of Nations 1996* (New York: UNICEF, 1996), p. 45.

10. Sheldon Danziger, Timothy M. Smeeding and Lee Rainwater, "The Western Welfare State in the 1990s: Toward a New Model of Antipoverty Policy for Families with Children," *Luxembourg Income Study Working Paper* No. 128 (August 1995), p. 19; see also Rick Atkinson, "Mass Protest Opposes German Cuts," *Washington Post*, June 16, 1996; Amy Kaslow, "World's Politicians Grope for Ways to Cut Safety Net," *Christian Science Monitor*, October 11, 1995.

11. As in previous FAO world food surveys, analysis of food supplies in *The Sixth World Food Survey* is based on three-year averages to minimize errors due to difficulties related to matching annual trade, production and stock data.

12. Joachim von Braun, "Food Security and Nutrition," *World Food Summit Technical Background Paper* No. 9 (Rome: FAO, 1996); The World Bank, *World Development Report 1996* (New York: Oxford University Press, 1996), pp. 66-71.

13. According to the International Food Policy Research Institute's Initiative, *A 2020 Vision for Food, Agriculture, and the Environment*; see *Feeding the World, Preventing Poverty, and Protecting the Earth: A 2020 Vision* (Washington: IFPRI, 1996).

14. See also FAO, *The State of Food and Agriculture* (Rome: FAO, 1995).

15. Mark W. Rosegrant, Mercedita Agcaoili-Sombilla and Nicostrato D. Perez, "Global Food Projections to 2020: Implications for Investment," *Food, Agriculture and the Environment Discussion Paper* No. 5 (Washington: IFPRI, 1995).

16. Asia-Pacific consists of two subregions – South Asia and Southeast Asia. South Asia consists of seven countries – Afghanistan, Bangladesh, Bhutan, India, Nepal, Pakistan and Sri Lanka. Southeast Asia includes Burma, Cambodia, China, Fiji, Hong Kong, Indonesia, North Korea, South Korea, Laos, Malaysia, Mongolia, Papua New Guinea, the Philippines, Singapore, Taiwan, Thailand and Vietnam.

17. *The Sixth World Food Survey* measures adult undernutrition as being below the minimum acceptable Body Mass Index (BMI)-level (18.5).

18. Amartya Sen, *Food for Freedom: Sir John Crawford Memorial Lecture* (Washington: Consultative Group on International Agricultural Research, 1987).

19. Jashinta D'Costa, "Sri Lanka: Food Security During Conflict," in Marc J. Cohen, ed., *Countries in Crisis: Hunger 1996* (Silver Spring, MD: Bread for the World Institute, 1995), pp. 32-34.

20. U.N. Economic Commission for Latin America and the Caribbean, *Strengthening Development*, (Santiago, Chile: UNECLAC, 1996).

21. "The New World Order and the Health of the Poor," *Critical Perspectives in Health and Social Justice* Series 2, Paper 1, November 1995, p. 1.

22. The World Bank, *Poverty Reduction and The World Bank* (Washington: The World Bank, 1996).

23. United Nations Development Programme, *Human Development Report 1995* (New York: Oxford University Press, 1995), p. 4.

24. Barbara Crossette, "U.N. Survey Finds World Rich-Poor Gap Widening," *New York Times*, July 15, 1996.

25. Patrick E. Tyler, "Lacking Iodine in Their Diets, Millions in China are Retarded," *New York Times*, June 4, 1996; von Braun.

26. UNICEF, *The State of the World's Children 1995* (New York: Oxford University Press, 1995), pp. 12-20; "Small Miracles: World Bank Report Cites Major Gains from Minor Nutrients," *World Bank News*, December 15, 1994, p. 3.

27. Kristin Helmore, "Cities on the Brink Try New Tactics," *Choices*, vol. 5, no. 1, p. 18.

28. United Nations, *World Urbanization Prospects: The 1994 Revision*, (New York: UN, 1995), p. 20; Michael A. Cohen *et al.* eds., *Preparing for the Urban Future: Global Pressures and Local Forces* (Washington: Woodrow Wilson Center Press, 1996), p. 27.

29. Joachim von Braun *et al.*, *Urban Food Insecurity and Malnutrition in Developing Countries* (Washington: International Food Policy Research Institute, 1993); Sarah J. Atkinson, *Food for Cities: Urban Nutrition Policy in Developing Countries* (London: London School of Hygiene and Tropical Medicine, Urban Health Programme, Health Policy Unit, Department of Public Health and Policy, 1992), p. 6.

30. World Resources Institute, *World Resources 1996-97* (New York: Oxford University Press, 1996), p. 35.

31. Marc J. Cohen, "Finding 100 Million of the Poorest Families," Paper Presented at the Microcredit Summit Preparatory Meeting I, Washington, DC, November 18, 1995; Jikum Huang and Howarth Bouis, *Structural Changes in the Demand for Food in Asia* (Washington: IFPRI, 1996); United Nations Population Fund, *The State of World Population 1996* (New York: UNFPA, 1996).

32. Steven Hansch, "An Explosion of Complex Humanitarian Emergencies," in *Countries in Crisis*, p. 12.

33. U.S. Mission to the United Nations, *Global Humanitarian Emergencies* (New York: U.S. Mission to the United Nations, 1996), p. 27.

34. According to the International Food Policy Research Institute's Initiative, *A 2020 Vision for Food, Agriculture, and the Environment*.

35. This section is based on Steven Hansch, *How Many People Die of Starvation in Humanitarian Emergencies?* (Washington: Refugee Policy Group, 1995).

36. Lester R. Brown, "Worldwatch Institute Urges World Bank and FAO to Overhaul Misleading Food Supply Projections," *Vital Sign Brief* 96-2 (Washington: Worldwatch Institute, 1996).

Chapter 2

1. Barbara Vobejda, "Welfare Bills Would Increase Child Poverty, Study Says," *Washington Post*, July 26, 1996.

2. John T. Cook and Laura P. Sherman, *Economic Security Among America's Poor: The Impact of State Welfare Waivers on Asset Accumulation* (Medford, MA: Tufts University Center on Hunger, Poverty and Nutrition Policy, 1996).

3. *The Future of Capitalism: How Today's Economic Forces Shape Tomorrow's World* (New York: William Morrow, 1996).

4. James P. Pinkerton, *What Comes Next? The End of Big Government and the New Paradigm* (New York: Hyperion, 1995), p. 267.

5. *The Economic Transformation of America: 1600 to the Present, 2nd Edition* (New York: Harcourt Brace College Publishers, 1984).

6. Thurow, p. 33.

7. This section is drawn in part from Janet Poppendieck, "The USA: Hunger in the Land of Plenty," in Graham Riches, ed., *First World Hunger* (London: Macmillan, forthcoming), and on Barbara Howell, "Ending Hunger in the United States," *Bread for the World Background Paper* No. 136, May 1996.

8. Greg Vanourek, Scott W. Hamilton and Chester E. Finn Jr., *Is There Life After Big Government? The Potential of Civil Society* (Indianapolis: Hudson Institute, 1996), p. 52.

9. *Overcoming World Hunger: The Challenge Ahead* (Washington: U.S. Government Printing Office, 1980), p. 166; see also p. 167.

Chapter 3

1. Cited in James Carville, *We're Right, They're Wrong: A Handbook for Spirited Progressives* (New York: Random House, 1996), p. 60.

2. Paul P. Streeten, "Against Minimalism," in Louis Putterman and Dietrich Rueschemeyer, eds., *State and Market in Development: Synergy or Rivalry?* (Boulder: Lynne Rienner, 1992), p. 18.

3. Newt Gingrich, *To Renew America* (New York: HarperCollins, 1995), p. 74.

4. *Ibid.*, p. 8; see also James P. Pinkerton, *What Comes Next? The End of Big Government and the New Paradigm* (New York: Hyperion, 1995); Greg Vanourek, Scott W. Hamilton and Chester E. Finn Jr., *Is There Life After Big Government? The Potential of Civil Society* (Indianapolis: Hudson Institute, 1996).

5. Pinkerton, p. 265.

6. Gingrich, p. 25.

7. Carville, pp. 67-75, 150.

8. Pinkerton, p. 156.

9. *Ibid.*, p. 19.

10. *Ibid.*, p. 40; Ralph Reed, *Politically Incorrect* (Dallas: Word Publishing, 1994), p. 10.

11. Pinkerton, p. 230.

12. Amitai Etzioni, *The Spirit of Community: Rights, Responsibilities and the Communitarian Agenda* (New York: Crown Publishers, 1993), pp. 16, 31, 39, 42, 44, 256-259.

13. Robert Rector & William F. Lauber, *America's Failed $5.4 Trillion War on Poverty* (Washington: The Heritage Foundation, 1995). The estimate arbitrarily defines certain programs as "welfare," while excluding others. For example, the estimate includes food stamps and Medicaid, which automatically expand during recessions, but it excludes Unemployment Compensation, which operates in much the same way and serves many of the same people in hard times. Medicaid benefits an increasing number of low-income families, but it also reaches a large number of formerly middle-class nursing home residents and other chronically ill people who have exhausted their resources. Also, the estimate includes virtually all federal education and training programs for low-income people, even though these are precisely the type of programs needed to lift people out of poverty and "end welfare," and might well be categorized as investment in future workers.

14. Pinkerton, p. 156.

15. Center on Hunger, Poverty and Nutrition Policy, *Statement on Key Welfare Reform Issues: The Empirical Evidence* (Medford, MA: Tufts University, 1995).

16. *Let's Get Real About Welfare*, Occasional Paper No. 4 (Silver Spring, MD: Bread for the World Institute, 1995).

17. This section is based in part on *Statement on Key Welfare Reform Issues*; John T. Cook and J. Larry Brown, *Asset Development Among America's Poor: Trends in the Distribution of Wealth and Income* (Medford, MA: Tufts University Center on Hunger, Poverty and Nutrition Policy, 1995); and John T. Cook and Laura P. Sherman, *Economic Security Among America's Poor: The Impact of State Welfare Waivers on Asset Accumulation* (Medford, MA: Tufts University Center on Hunger, Poverty and Nutrition Policy, 1996).

18. Rector and Lauber, pp. 1-3, 24-25, 29-31; Gingrich, pp. 71-80.

19. Rector and Lauber, p. 3.

20. Sharon Parott and Robert Greenstein, *Welfare, Out-of-Wedlock Childbearing and Poverty: What is the Connection?* (Washington: Center on Budget and Policy Priorities, 1995); Lester Thurow, *The Future of Capitalism: How Today's Economic Forces Shape Tomorrow's World* (New York: William Morrow, 1996), p. 31.

21. Parott and Greenstein, p. x; Carville, pp. 23-24, 28-30.

22. Robert D. Novak, "The GOP's Health Failure," *Washington Post*, April 1, 1996.

23. Cited in *The Chronicle of Philanthropy*, May 30, 1996, p. 38.

24. These examples were provided by World Hunger Year.

25. Sandra K. Danziger and Sherrie A. Kossoudji, *When Welfare Ends: Subsistence Strategies of Former GA Recipients, Final Report of the General Assistance Project* (Ann Arbor: University of Michigan School of Social Work, 1995), pp. 5-6.

26. This section is based in part on Cook and Sherman.

27. Information on Virginia's waivers provided by Fairfax County, VA, Department of Family Services; see also Spencer S. Hsu, "N. Virginia Takes Its Turn at Cutting Welfare Rolls," *Washington Post*, Metro Section, April 1, 1996, and "Judge Suspends Welfare Link to Fathers in Va.," *Washington Post*, June 26, 1996.

28. Peter Finn, "In New World of Va. Welfare, Caseworkers are Team Leaders," *Washington Post*, Metro Section, June 6, 1996.

29. Associated Press, "Wisconsin Workfare Law Signed," *Washington Post*, April 26, 1996; Tommy G. Thompson, "Work Not Welfare: Wisconsin's Independence Plan for Welfare Recipients," no date.

30. "'Wisconsin Works': Breaking a Covenant," *Washington Post*, July 4, 1996.

31. State Legislative Leaders Foundation, *State Legislative Leaders: Keys to Effective Legislation for Children and Families* (Centerville, MA: State Legislative Leaders Foundation, 1995).

32. *New York Times*, August 11, 1996.

33. Kevin Merida, "Organizers Trolling for New Voters In Giant U.S. Pool of Working Poor," *Washington Post*, May 3, 1996.

34. Bread for the World Institute, *Transforming the Politics of Hunger* (Washington, DC: Bread for the World Institute, 1993).

Chapter 4

1. Definition of human development, from: UNDP, *Human Development Report 1995* (New York: Oxford University Press 1995), p. 1.

2. Paul Hirst and Gahame Thompson, *Globalization in Question* (London: Blackwell, 1996).

3. Charles P. Kindleberger, *The World in Depression, 1929-1939* (Berkeley: University of California Press, 1986).

4. UNDP, *Human Development Report, 1996* (New York: Oxford University Press, 1996), p. 20.

5. *Ibid.*, p. 2.

6. Two other international institutions have developed more slowly. The proposal at Bretton Woods to set up an International Trade Organization was scaled back to the General Agreement on Tariffs and Trade, which in several "rounds" of negotiations has substantially reduced tariff barriers to trade. GATT is being succeeded by the World Trade Organization, with increased powers and a stronger dispute settlement mechanism. The International Labor Organization actually pre-dates the three Bretton Woods Institutions. It seeks to persuade national governments to adopt common policies for labor standards, as agreed in a series of negotiated conventions. See also Lucilla L. Tan and Don Reeves, "Labor Rights in a Global Economy," *Occasional Paper* No. 6 (Silver Spring, MD: Bread for the World Institute, 1996).

7. See Izumi Ohno, "Beyond the 'East Asian Miracle': An Asian View," *UNDP/ODS Discussion Paper* No. 5 (January 1996).

8. United Nations, *World Economic and Social Survey 1996* (New York: U.N. Department of Economic and Social Information and Policy Analysis, 1996); The World Bank, *World Development Report 1996* (New York: Oxford University Press, 1996).

9. "Mexican Church Leaders Speak Out Against the 'God of Profit,'" *Financial Times*, April 8, 1996.

10. Manuel Agosin and Ricardo Ffrench-Davis: "Managing Capital Inflows in Latin America," *UNDP/ODS Discussion Paper* No. 8 (January 1996).

11. "After Lifetime Employment", *The Economist*, March 16, 1996, p. 20.

12. United Nations, *World Economic and Social Survey 1995 – Current Trends and Policies in the World Economy* (New York: U.N. Department of Economic and Social Information and Policy Analysis, 1995) pp. 2, 35.

13. International Labour Organization, *World Employment 1995, An ILO Report* (Geneva: ILO, 1995) pp. 65-66.

14. Quoted in "Working Through Stress and Anxiety," undated leaflet from Mead Johnson Pharmaceuticals.

15. "An Unhealthy Workweek," *Financial Times*, December 27, 1995.

16. "Lost To Slavery In The Amazon," *Financial Times*, May 8, 1996.

17. "US Set To Link Two Retailers To Sweatshop-Made Goods," *New York Times*, May 20, 1996.

18. See, for example, the responses to Ethan Kapstein, "Workers and the World Economy," *Foreign Affairs*, May/June 1996. The responses appeared in the July/August issue.

19. "A Report Tries To Counteract Job-Loss Fears," *New York Times*, April 23, 1996.

20. "'Feel Bad' Factor Grips the Western World," *Financial Times*, June 11, 1996.

Chapter 5

1. *Public Action to Remedy Hunger: The Fourth Annual Arturo Tanco Memorial Lecture* (New York: The Hunger Project, 1990), p. 6. The argument is elaborated in much greater depth in Jean Drèze and Amartya Sen, *Hunger and Public Action* (Oxford: Clarendon Press, 1989).

2. *Ibid.*, pp. 125-126.

3. Sen, p. 13.

4. The Indian state of Maharashtra provides public works jobs to unemployed workers. In Bangladesh, the national government has a similar program that uses food for wages. Although China has abolished collective agriculture, it continues to carry out many rural public works projects through collective labor.

5. Information courtesy of Professor William Whitaker, University of Maine School of Social Work.

6. Lance Taylor and Ute Pieper, "Reconciling Economic Reform and Sustainable Human Development: Social Consequences of Neo-Liberalism," *UNDP/ODS Discussion Paper* No.2 (January 1996), pp. 72-73.

7. *Ibid.*, p. 28.

8. United Nations Development Programme, *Human Development Report 1996* (New York: Oxford University Press, 1996), pp. 6-7; Benno Ndulu, Nicolas van de Walle and Contributors, *Agenda for Africa's Economic Renewal* (Washington: Overseas Development Council, 1996).

Sources: Ghana

Abugre, Charles. *Behind the Crowded Shelves: An Assessment of Ghana's Structural Adjustment Experiences, 1983-1991.* San Francisco: Institute for Food and Development Policy, 1993.

Armstrong, Robert P. *Ghana Country Assistance Review: A Study in Development Effectiveness.* Washington: The World Bank, 1996.

Arthur, Kofi. "Kume Preko Shakes the North," *Public Agenda.* September 25-28, 1995.

Bellamy, Carol. *The State of the World's Children 1996.* New York: Oxford University Press for UNICEF, 1996.

Ghana – Statistical Annex. Washington: International Monetary Fund, August 1995.

Levin, Carol. *Food Security and Nutrition in Ghana.* Washington: International Food Policy Research Institute, no date.

The Story of Ghana's Economy: Cuttings from the Press, Feb.-Oct. 1995. Accra: Third World Network, 1995.

The World Bank. *World Development Report 1996: From Plan to Market.* New York: Oxford University Press, 1996.

Chapter 6

1. This section is based on James H. Michel, *Development Cooperation: Efforts and Policies of the Members of the Development Assistance Committee, 1995 Report* (Paris: Organisation for Economic Co-operation and Development, 1996); "Financial Flows to Developing Countries in 1995: Sharp Decline in Official Aid; Private Flows Rise," DAC Press Release, June 11, 1996; Judith Randel and Tony German, eds., *The Reality of Aid 1996* (London: EARTHSCAN, 1996); Roger Riddell, "Aid in the 21st Century," *United Nations Development Programme Office of Development Studies Discussion Paper* No. 6 (February 1996). The figures on 1995 aid are preliminary.

2. Bryan T. Johnson and Thomas P. Sheehy, *The Index of Economic Freedom* (Washington: The Heritage Foundation, 1995) and *1996 Index of Economic Freedom* (Washington: The Heritage Foundation, 1996).

3. *Ibid.*, p. vii.

4. Doug Bandow and Ian Vásquez, "Introduction: The Dismal Legacy and False Promise of Multilateral Aid," in Bandow and Vásquez, eds., *Perpetuating Poverty: The World Bank, the IMF and the Developing World* (Washington: Cato Institute, 1994), p. 1.

5. Bread for the World Institute and RESULTS Educational Fund, *Putting Children First: A Report on the Effectiveness of U.S. Agency for International Development Child Survival Programs in Fiscal Year 1991* (Silver Spring, MD: Bread for the World Institute, 1995).

6. "At the Crossroads: The Future of Foreign Aid," *Occasional Paper* No. 5 (Silver Spring, MD: Bread for the World Institute, 1995).

7. Amartya Sen, *Public Action to Remedy Hunger: The Fourth Annual Arturo Tanco Memorial Lecture* (New York: The Hunger Project, 1990), p. 29.

8. Quoted in Judy Mann, "How Foreign Aid Can Put America First," *Washington Post*, October 27, 1995.

9. Jo Marie Griesgraber and Bernhard S. Gunter, "Introduction" in Griesgraber and Gunter, eds., *Promoting Development: Effective Global Institutions for the Twenty-First Century* (London: Pluto Press with the Center of Concern, 1995), p. xii; Helene Cooper, "Sub-Saharan Africa is Seen as Big Loser in GATT's New World Trade Accord," *Wall Street Journal*, August 15, 1994; additional information provided by the U.N. Development Programme.

10. A study in Ghana found that the percentage increase in female enrollment in CRS school lunch programs was 46 percent compared to 15 percent in non-food schools.

11. The definitions of personal safety vary, but equitable access to resources is one of the prerequisites of food security. PVOs such as CRS do advocacy, conflict resolution and reconciliation between differing castes, and ethnic and religious groups, thereby tackling some of the causes behind the discrimination and ostracizing that keeps the poorest people from accessing the means to pursue food security (e.g. access to viable land, inclusion in social structures, etc.).

12. In an income-generating project linked to the CRS food program in the Philippines, participants on average increased their monthly income by 79 percent.

13. U.S. General Accounting Office, "Foreign Assistance: Private Voluntary Organizations' Contributions," NSIAD-96-34, December 1995.

14. For emergency programs, decreased famine deaths are clear evidence of this.

15. *United States: Development Cooperation Review Series No. 8* (Paris: Organisation for Economic Co-operation and Development, 1995), pp. 59-60.

16. "Multinationals Raised '95 Investment in 3d World 13%," *New York Times*, March 13, 1996.

17. Inter-Africa Group, "Capacity Building for African NGOs," draft discussion paper, April 1996.

18. "Report on Asia-Pacific Regional Consultation of NGOs on the World Food Summit," provided by the Asian NGO Coalition for Agrarian Reform and Rural Development (ANGOC), Manila, Philippines.

19. *Why* No. 18, Spring 1995 (joint issue with the Brazilian Institute for Social and Economic Analysis).

20. This section is largely based on Peter Uvin, *The International Organization of Hunger* (London and New York: Kegan Paul International) and the essays in Griesgraber and Gunter. We are also grateful to our Bread for the World Institute colleagues Nancy Alexander and Mizanekristos Yohannes for sharing their insights.

21. For further information, contact the International Food Security Treaty Campaign, (805) 563-2193.

22. *International Criminal Tribunal for the Former Yugoslavia Bulletin* Nos. 2 (22 January 1996) and 3 (22 February 1996); John M. Goshko, "U.N. Moving Toward Creation of Criminal Court," *Washington Post*, April 21, 1996.

23. The World Bank, *World Debt Tables 1996*, vol. 1 (Washington: The World Bank, 1996); see also United Nations, *The Debt Crisis* (video).

24. "Rethinking Bretton Woods: From an Historical Perspective," in Griesgraber and Gunter, pp. 18-20.

Sponsors

Bread for the World Institute seeks to inform, educate, nurture and motivate concerned citizens for action on policies that affect hungry people. Based on policy analysis and consultation with poor people, it develops educational resources and activities, including its annual report on the state of world hunger, policy briefs and study guides, together with workshops, seminars, briefings and an anti-hunger leadership development program. Contributions to the Institute are tax deductible. It works closely with Bread for the World, a Christian citizens' movement of 44,000 members who advocate specific policy changes to help overcome hunger in the United States and overseas.

    1100 Wayne Avenue, Suite 1000
    Silver Spring, MD 20910
    Ph. (301) 608-2400
    Fx. (301) 608-2401
    E-mail: bread@igc.apc.org

Brot für die Welt is an association of German Protestant churches that seeks to overcome poverty and hunger in developing countries, as an expression of their Christian faith and convictions, by funding programs of relief and development. Founded in 1959, Brot has funded more than 15,000 programs in over 100 nations in Africa, Latin America and Asia. The emphasis of the programs that Brot funds has shifted from relief to development and empowerment. Brot's programs of education in Germany are intended to lead to changes – in understanding and lifestyle at the personal level, and to policy changes at the national, European Community and international levels.

    Stafflenbergstrasse 76; Postfach 10 11 42
    D-70010 Stuttgart, Germany
    Ph. 011-49-7 11-2159-0
    Fx. 011-49-7 11-2159-368

Christian Children's Fund, founded in Richmond, VA, in 1938, is one of the world's oldest and most respected nonprofit child sponsorship charities. Christian Children's Fund is dedicated to providing long-term sustainable development assistance to approximately 2.5 million needy children and their families in more than 30 countries around the world, including the United States. Services are provided without regard to religion, gender or race. Christian Children's Fund is America's fourth largest relief and development organization.

    2821 Emerywood Parkway, P.O.Box 26484
    Richmond, VA 23261-6484
    Ph. (804) 756-2700
    Fx. (804) 756-2718

Covenant World Relief is the relief and development arm of The Evangelical Covenant Church. Dr. Timothy C. Ek is vice president of the Covenant and director of Covenant World Relief. The Evangelical Covenant Church has its national headquarters in Chicago, IL. The Covenant's historic commitment to being actively involved in Christ's mission to respond to the spiritual and physical needs of others was the basis for the formation of Covenant World Relief.

    5101 North Francisco Avenue
    Chicago, IL 60625-3699
    Ph. (312) 784-3000
    Fx. (312) 784-4366

The **Evangelical Lutheran Church in America World Hunger Program** is a 22-year-old ministry that confronts hunger and poverty through emergency relief, long-term development, education, advocacy and stewardship of financial resources. Seventy-three percent of the program works internationally and 27 percent within the United States. Lutheran World Relief (New York City) and Lutheran World Federation (Geneva, Switzerland) are key partners in international relief and development. Twelve percent is used for domestic relief and development, 9 percent for education and advocacy work in the United States and 6 percent for fundraising and administration.

    8765 West Higgins Road
    Chicago, IL 60631-4190
    Ph. (800) 638-3522
    Fx. (312) 380-2707

LCMS World Relief (The Lutheran Church – Missouri Synod) provides relief and development funding for domestic and international projects. Based under the Synod's Department of Human Care Ministries, LCMS World Relief provides domestic grants for Lutheran congregations and social ministry organizations as well as other groups with Lutheran involvement which are engaged in ministries of human care. Domestic support is also provided to Lutheran Disaster Response and Lutheran Immigration and Refugee Service. International relief and development assistance is channeled through the Synod's mission stations and partner churches as well as Lutheran World Relief.

    1333 So. Kirkwood Road
    St. Louis, MO 63122-7295
    Ph. (800) 248-1930, ext. 1392
    Fx. (314) 965-0541

Lutheran World Relief (LWR), founded in 1945, acts on behalf of U.S. Lutherans in response to natural disasters, humanitarian crises and chronic poverty in over 40 countries throughout Asia, Africa, Latin America and the Middle East. In partnership with local organizations, LWR supports over 150 community projects to improve food production, health care, environment and employment, with special emphasis on training and gender. LWR monitors legislation on foreign aid and development, and advocates for public policies which address the root causes of hunger and poverty. LWR values the God-given gifts that each person can bring to our common task to promote peace, justice and human dignity.

Lutheran World Relief
390 Park Avenue South
New York, NY 10016
Ph. (212) 532-6350
    800-LWR-LWR2
Fx. (212) 213-6081
E-mail: lwr@lwr.org

LWR/CWS Office on Development Policy
110 Maryland Avenue, N.E.
Building Mailbox #45
Washington, DC 20002-5694
Ph. (202) 543-6336
Fx. (202) 546-6232
E-mail: cwslwr@igc.apc.org

North Star Company Inc. is a custom roll former of metal products. Its predominant market is the residential, commercial and industrial building industry, both domestic and overseas. North Star's business is to serve a number of "publics." The first is the customer; then company members, suppliers, the community in which it operates and shareholders. Serving these publics well, through a Total Quality Relationship program, means it makes a profit, which in turn is used to continue service to these publics. A portion of income is contributed to the support of organizations which are directly involved in issues and ministries of human care.

14912 South Broadway
Gardena, CA 90248
Ph. (310) 515-2200
Fx. (310) 715-8090

For 27 years, the **Presbyterian Hunger Program** has provided a channel for congregations to respond to hunger in the United States and around the world. With a commitment to the ecumenical sharing of human and financial resources, the program provides support for programs of direct food relief, sustainable development and public policy advocacy. A network of 100 Hunger Action Enablers leads the Presbyterian Church (USA) in the study of hunger issues, engagement with communities of need, advocacy for just public policies, and the movement toward simpler corporate and personal lifestyles.

100 Witherspoon Street
Louisville, KY 40202-1396
Ph. (502) 569-5819
Fx. (502) 569-8039

Shield-Ayres Foundation

The **United Methodist Committee on Relief** (UMCOR) was formed in 1940 in response to the suffering of people during World War II. It was a "voice of conscience" expressing the concern of the church for the disrupted and devastated lives churned out by the war. UMCOR has expanded its ministry into more than 80 countries to minister with compassion to "persons in need," through programs and services which provide immediate relief and long-term attention to the root causes of their need. Focusing on refugee, hunger and disaster ministries, the work of UMCOR, a program department of the General Board of Global Ministries of the United Methodist Church, is carried out through direct services and a worldwide network of national and international church agencies that cooperate in the task of alleviating human suffering.

475 Riverside Drive, Room 1374
New York, NY 10115
Ph. (212) 870-3816
    (800) 841-1235
Fx. (212) 870-3624

The **United Nations Development Programme** (UNDP) is the United Nations' largest provider of technical cooperation grants and the main coordinator of U.N. development assistance. It works with governments, U.N. agencies, organizations of civil society and individuals in 175 countries and territories to build national capacities for sustainable human development. Activities focus on poverty eradication, creation of jobs and sustainable livelihoods, advancement of women, protection and regeneration of the environment, and good governance. UNDP's central resources, totaling about $1 billion (U.S.) a year, are derived from the voluntary contributions of governments. UNDP also administers several special purpose funds (U.N. Capital Development Fund, U.N. Development Fund for Women, U.N. Volunteers) and, with the World Bank and the U.N. Environment Programme, the $2 billion Global Environment Facility.

1 United Nations Plaza
New York, NY 10017
Ph. (212) 906-5000
Fx. (212) 906-5001

Cosponsors

The **Academy for Educational Development** (AED), founded in 1961, is an independent, nonprofit service organization committed to addressing human development needs in the United States and throughout the world. Under contracts and grants, the Academy operates programs in collaboration with policy leaders; nongovernmental and community-based organizations; governmental agencies; international multilateral and bilateral funders; and schools, colleges and universities. In partnership with its clients, the Academy seeks to meet today's social, economic and environmental challenges through education and human resource development; to apply state-of-the-art education, training, research, technology, management, behavioral analysis and social marketing techniques to solve problems; and to improve knowledge and skills throughout the world as the most effective means for stimulating growth, reducing poverty, and promoting democratic and humanitarian ideals. AED is registered with the U.S. Agency for International Development as a private voluntary organization. The Academy is exempt from federal income taxes under Section 501 (c)(3) of the Internal Revenue Code. Contributions to the Academy are tax deductible.

> 1875 Connecticut Avenue, N.W.
> Washington, DC 20009-1202
> Ph. (202) 884-8000
> Fx. (202) 884-8430
> E-mail: admindc@aed.org

Baptist World Aid (BWAid) is a division of the Baptist World Alliance, a fellowship of almost 200 Baptist unions and conventions around the world, comprising a membership of over 40 million baptized believers. This represents a community of over 80 million Baptists ministering in more than 200 countries. For over 75 years Baptists have been working in partnership to entrust, empower and enable the indigenous Baptist leadership to carry out programs of emergency relief, sustainable development and fellowship assistance.

> 6733 Curran Street
> McLean, VA 22101-6005
> Ph. (703) 790-8980
> Fx. (703) 893-5160
> E-mail: bwa@baptistnet.org

Canadian Foodgrains Bank is a specialized food programming agency established and operated by 13 church-related relief and development organizations. It collects substantial amounts of foodgrain donations directly from Canadian farmers using an extensive network of grain elevators. The Foodgrains Bank uses donated cash and grain matched by cost-sharing funds from Canadian International Development Agency (CIDA) to procure and ship food assistance to food deficit countries, and to provide related services to partner agencies. Using food assistance to build and reconcile relationships with and within communities and countries such as Cuba, North Korea, Iran, Afghanistan, Rwanda and Guinea is a key interest. Other program involvements include monetization, food security reserves and household food security monitoring. Canadian Foodgrains Bank staff and partners also take a very active interest in food security policy issues. To support this policy dialogue, the Foodgrains Bank has a number of discussion papers related to the relationship between food security and peace, human rights, economic sanctions, gender, humanitarian action and international action.

> Box 747, 400-280 Smith Street
> Winnipeg, MB, Canada R3C 2L4
> Ph. (204) 944-1993
> Fx. (204) 943-2597

CARE is one of the world's largest and most effective private relief and development organizations. Each year, CARE reaches more than 35 million people in over 60 nations in Africa, Asia and Latin America. The organization's work began in 1946, when CARE packages helped Europe recover from World War II. Today, CARE provides famine and disaster victims with emergency assistance, improves health care, helps subsistence farmers and small-business owners produce more goods, addresses population and environmental concerns, and helps to develop economies and societies in a sustainable manner. The scope of CARE's work is broad, but its vision focuses on a single concept – helping people help themselves.

> 151 Ellis Street
> Atlanta, GA 30303
> Ph. (404) 681-2552
> Fx. (404) 577-5977

Catholic Charities USA is the nation's largest network of independent social service organizations. The 1,400 agencies and institutions work to reduce poverty, support families and empower communities. Catholic Charities organizations provide social services ranging from adoption and counseling to emergency food and housing. More than 11 million people of all religious, national, racial, social and economic backgrounds received services in 1994. Catholic Charities USA promotes public policies and strategies that address human needs and social injustices. The national office provides advocacy and management support for agencies. The Disaster Response Office organizes the Catholic community's response to U.S. disasters.

> 1731 King Street, Suite 200
> Alexandria, VA 22314
> Ph. (703) 549-1390
> Fx. (703) 549-1656

Catholic Relief Services-USCC (CRS) is the overseas relief and development agency of the U.S. Catholic community. Founded in 1943, CRS provides almost $300 million in development and relief assistance in 80 nations around the world. Working in partnership with the Catholic Church and other local institutions in each country, CRS works to alleviate poverty, hunger and suffering, and supports reconciliation and peacemaking initiatives. Assistance is given solely on the basis of need. Even while responding to emergencies, CRS supports over 2,000 development projects designed to build local self-sufficiency. CRS works in conjunction with Caritas International and CIDSE, worldwide associations of Catholic relief and development agencies. Together, these groups build the capacity of local nonprofit organizations to provide long-term solutions. In the United States,

CRS seeks to educate and build awareness on issues of world poverty and hunger and serve as an advocate for public policy changes in the interest of the poor overseas.

209 West Fayette Street
Baltimore, MD 21201-3443
Ph. (410) 625-2220
Fx. (410) 685-1635

The **Center on Hunger, Poverty and Nutrition Policy** was established at Tufts University in 1990. Its purpose is to advance public policy choices which reduce hunger and poverty, and enhance the development and productive capacities of American families and children. The Center carries out policy research and analyses, and works with government leaders and the media to promote greater understanding of policy alternatives for the nation.

11 Curtis Avenue
Medford, MA 02155
Ph. (617) 627-3956
Fx. (617) 627-3020

The **Christian Reformed World Relief Committee** (CRWRC) is a ministry of the Christian Reformed Church in North America. CRWRC shows God's love to people in need through *development* – working with families and communities in food production, income earning, health education, literacy learning, spiritual and leadership skills – through *relief* – working with disaster survivors by providing food, medicines, crisis counseling, rebuilding and volunteer assistance – and through *education* – working with people to develop and act on their Christian perspective of poverty, hunger and justice. CRWRC works with communities in North America and in over 30 countries worldwide to create permanent, positive change in Christ's name.

CRWRC U.S.
2850 Kalamazoo Avenue, S.E.
Grand Rapids, MI 49560-0600
Ph. (800) 552-7972
Fx. (616) 246-0806

CRWRC CANADA
3475 Mainway, P.O. Box 5070
Burlington, ON L7R 3Y8
Ph. (800) 730-3490
Fx. (905) 336-8344

Church World Service (CWS) is a global relief, development and refugee-assistance ministry of the 33 Protestant and Orthodox communities that work together through the National Council of Churches. Founded in 1946, CWS works in partnership with local church organizations in more than 70 countries worldwide, supporting sustainable self-help development of people which respects the environment, meets emergency needs, and addresses root causes of poverty and powerlessness. Within the United States, CWS resettles refugees, assists communities in responding to disasters, advocates for justice in U.S. policies which relate to global issues, provides educational resources, and offers opportunities for communities to join a people-to-people network of global and local caring through participation in a CROP WALK.

475 Riverside Drive, Suite 678
New York, NY 10115-0050
Ph. (212) 870-2257
Fx. (212) 870-3523

EuronAid is a European association of nongovernmental organizations (NGOs) which facilitates dialogue with the Commission of the European Union in the areas of food security and food aid. EuronAid cooperates with the Commission in programming and procuring food aid for the NGOs, then arranges and accounts for delivery to Third World NGOs for distribution. In recent years, triangular operations (purchases within Third World nations) have accounted for half of EuronAid's food aid, which meets mainly development purposes. EuronAid assimilates the experiences of NGOs involved in food aid and employs this knowledge in its dialogue with the Commission and the European Parliament to achieve improved management of food aid. EuronAid was created in 1980 by major European NGOs in cooperation with the Commission of the European Union. The association has at present 27 member agencies and services an additional 60 European NGOs on a regular basis.

P.O. Box 12
NL-2501 CA Den Haag
The Netherlands
Ph. 31 70 330 57 57
Fx. 31 70 362 17 39
E-mail: euronaid@euronaid.nl

The **Food Research and Action Center** (FRAC) is a national nonprofit organization working to end hunger and undernutrition in the United States. Since 1970, FRAC has worked to assure all persons in this country access to a nutritionally adequate diet with dignity, primarily through the federal food assistance programs. FRAC has worked both to improve access to and enhance the nutritional quality of the programs.

1875 Connecticut Avenue, N.W., Suite 540
Washington, DC 20009
Ph. (202) 986-2200
Fx. (202) 986-2525
E-mail: HN0050@handsnet.org

The **International Fund for Agricultural Development** (IFAD) is an international financial institution headquartered in Rome, Italy. Established in 1977 as a result of the 1974 World Food Conference, IFAD is a Specialized Agency of the United Nations with an exclusive mandate to provide the rural poor of the developing world with cost-effective ways of overcoming hunger, poverty and malnutrition. IFAD advocates a targeted, community-based approach to reducing rural poverty. The Fund's task is to help poor farmers raise their food production and improve their nutrition by designing and financing projects which increase their incomes. Since 1978, IFAD has committed $4.8 billion for 429 projects in 106 developing countries. The governance and funding of the institution are the result of a unique partnership among developed and developing countries. With the recent additions of South Africa and Moldova, IFAD now has 160 member states.

1775 K Street, N.W., Suite 410
Washington, DC 20006
Ph. (202) 331-9099
Fx. (202) 331-9366

MAZON: A Jewish Response to Hunger has granted more than $11 million since 1986 to nonprofit organizations confronting hunger in the United States and abroad. MAZON (the Hebrew word for "food") awards grants principally to programs working to prevent and alleviate hunger in the United States. Grantees include emergency and direct food assistance programs, food banks, multi-service organizations, anti-hunger advocacy/education and research projects, and international hunger-relief and agricultural development programs in Israel and impoverished countries. Although responsive to organizations serving impoverished Jews, in keeping with the best of Jewish tradition, MAZON responds to all who are in need.

> 12401 Wilshire Boulevard, Suite 303
> Los Angeles, CA 90025-1015
> Ph. (310) 442-0020
> Fx. (310) 442-0030

Mennonite Central Committee (MCC), founded in 1920, is an agency of the Mennonite and Brethren in Christ Churches in North America, and seeks to demonstrate God's love through committed women and men who work among people suffering from poverty, conflict, oppression and natural disaster. MCC serves as a channel for interchange between churches and community groups where it works around the world and North American churches. MCC strives for peace, justice and dignity of all people by sharing experiences, resources and faith. MCC's priorities include disaster relief and refugee assistance, rural and agricultural development, job creation (SELFHELP Crafts), health and education.

> 21 South 12th Street
> Akron, PA 17501-0500
> Ph. (717) 859-1151
> Fx. (717) 859-2171

The mission of the **National Association of WIC Directors** (NAWD) is to provide leadership to the WIC community to promote quality nutrition services, serve all eligible women, infants and children and assure sound and responsive management of the Special Supplemental Nutrition Program for Women, Infants and Children (WIC). The purpose of the association is to link state WIC directors, local WIC directors, nutrition services coordinators and others in a national forum to act collectively on behalf of the program to include the following functions: (A) to promote the improved health, well-being and nutritional status of women, infants and children; (B) to provide a national resource network through which ideas, materials and procedures can be communicated to persons working in the WIC community; (C) to promote good management practices and to assist WIC program directors at the state and local levels; (D) to act as a resource at the request of governmental bodies and individual legislators regarding issues particular to the health and nutrition of women, infants and children and to assist WIC clients; and (E) to do whatever is necessary to promote and sustain the WIC program.

> P.O. Box 53405
> 1627 Connecticut Avenue N.W., Suite 5
> Washington, DC 20009-3405
> Ph. (202) 232-5492
> Fx. (202) 387-5281

PARTNERS in Rural Development is an international voluntary organization that addresses poverty at the village level in developing countries. In partnership with southern NGOs, PARTNERS supports self-help projects; strengthens the capacity of community organizations; promotes policies that alleviate poverty and raises public understanding of development issues. In so doing the partnership increases the access of the rural poor to land, water, energy, technology and training. These productive resources enable poor communities to attain food security and sustainable livelihoods. Since 1960 PARTNERS has managed over 800 projects in 38 countries of Africa, Asia, Central and South America and the Caribbean.

> International Office
> 323 Chapel Street
> Ottawa, ON, Canada K1N 7Z2
> Ph. (613) 237-0180
> Fx. (613) 237-5969
> E-mail: chfott@web.apc.org

RESULTS is an international, grassroots citizens' lobby dedicated to creating the political will to end hunger and poverty, and committed to breaking through the idea that "I don't make a difference." RESULTS identifies the most cost-effective programs which positively impact the lives of the poorest of the poor, and advocates for increased funding and replication of those programs. RESULTS volunteer activists work with their local media and their elected officials to ensure that governments support cost-effective programs proven to combat hunger and poverty, at home and abroad.

> 236 Massachusetts Avenue N.E., Suite 300
> Washington, DC 20002
> Ph. (800) 900-LEAD
> Fx. (202) 546-3228

Save the Children Federation/U.S. works to make lasting, positive change in the lives of disadvantaged children in the United States and 39 countries around the world. International programs in health, education, economic opportunities and humanitarian response place children at the center of activities and focus on women as key decision makers and participants. Key principles are child centeredness, women focus, participation and empowerment, sustainability, scaling up and maximizing impact. Programs in the United States emphasize youth and community service.

> 54 Wilton Road
> Westport, CT 06880
> Ph. (203) 221-4000
> Fx. (203) 454-3914

Second Harvest is the largest charitable hunger relief organization in the United States. Through a nationwide network of nearly 200 food banks, Second Harvest distributes surplus food and grocery products to nearly 50,000 charitable agencies. These food pantries, soup kitchens, homeless shelters and other feeding programs serve nearly 26 million people each year.

> 116 South Michigan Avenue, Suite 4
> Chicago, IL 60603-6001
> Ph. (312) 263-2303
> Fx. (312) 263-5626

Share Our Strength (SOS) is the nation's leading anti-hunger organization that mobilizes industries and individuals to contribute their talents to fight hunger. By supporting food assistance, treating malnutrition and other consequences of hunger, and promoting economic independence among people in need, Share Our Strength meets immediate demands for food while investing in long-term solutions to hunger and poverty. Since its founding in 1984, Share Our Strength has distributed more than $30 million in grants to over 800 anti-hunger organizations in the United States, Canada and around the world. Operation Frontline, a direct service program in more than 10 cities across the United States, trains volunteer culinary professionals to teach cooking, nutrition and food budgeting skills to people at risk of hunger and malnutrition. SOS's fundraising efforts include: Taste of the Nation, an annual series of food and wine tastings held in April in more than 100 cities throughout the United States and Canada; Writers Harvest: The National Reading, an annual event in which hundreds of authors read from their work to support anti-hunger efforts; Dine Across America, an in-restaurant national dining promotion to raise funds for anti-hunger efforts; Charge Against Hunger, a partnership with American Express, which has generated more than $16 million to combat hunger; and Publishing Ventures, which includes original works donated by authors, artists and chefs.

    1511 K Street, N.W., Suite 940
    Washington, DC 20005
    Ph. (202) 393-2925
    Fx. (202) 347-5868

United Church Board for World Ministries (UCBWM) is the instrumentality of the United Church of Christ for the planning and conduct of its program of global missions, development and emergency relief. The UCBWM's fundamental mission commitment is to share life in partnership with global church partners and ecumenical bodies. Through service, advocacy and mission program, the UCBWM sends as well as receives persons in mission; is committed to the healing of God's creation; engages in dialogue, witness and common cause with people of other faiths; and seeks a prophetic vision of a just and peaceful world order so that all might have access to wholeness of life.

    475 Riverside Drive, Fl. 16
    New York, NY 10115
    Ph. (212) 870-2637
    Fx. (212) 932-1236

United Church of Christ Hunger Action program coordinates and stimulates all UCC hunger and hunger-related ministries; increases awareness and understanding of world hunger and related issues; and promotes, interprets and administrates the Hunger Action Fund of the United Church of Christ. The Hunger Action Program is celebrating its 22nd anniversary in 1997.

    700 Prospect Avenue
    Cleveland, OH 44115
    Ph. (216) 736-3290
    Fx. (216) 736-3293

Winrock International's mission is to help alleviate poverty by working with people to build a better world – increasing agricultural productivity and rural employment while protecting the environment. Projects provide technical assistance, human resource development, and policy and institutional improvement. Winrock works in the United States, Asia, Africa, the Middle East, Latin America, the Caribbean, Eastern Europe and the former Soviet Union. Projects are funded by grants, contracts and contributions from public and private sources. Operations are headquartered outside Little Rock, AR, on the mountaintop farm of the late Winthrop Rockefeller. Regional offices are located in Arlington, VA; Manila, the Philippines; and Abidjan, Côte d'Ivoire.

    38 Winrock Drive
    Morrilton, AR 72110-9537
    Ph. (501) 727-5435
    Fx. (501) 727-5242

World Hunger Committee is the official committee responsible for engaging the membership of the Reorganized Church of Jesus Christ of Latter Day Saints (**RLDS**) in a corporate response to world hunger. Since 1979, the World Hunger Committee, appointed by the RLDS First Presidency, has considered grant proposals submitted by such organizations as Outreach International, World Accord, Oxfam America and the Red Cross. Advocacy, education and direct relief are the committee's main areas of interest. The largest portion of the World Hunger funds is used for relief in disaster aid and self-help programs. Church groups in 12 states have also received World Hunger grants to help establish soup kitchens, food pantries and food banks. Because of the gracious response of RLDS church members, projects funded through the World Hunger Committee include: food aid for Somalia, Africa and Haiti; nutrition centers in Haiti, Honduras and the Dominican Republic; rice improvement projects in the Philippines; disaster aid for countries such as India, Bangladesh, Mexico and Haiti; farming projects in India, Nepal, Sri Lanka and Haiti; and the establishment of a food bank in Florida.

    P.O. Box 1059
    Independence, MO 64051-0559
    Ph. (816) 833-1000
    Fx. (816) 521-3097